The Fear of Islam

The Fear of Islam

An Introduction to Islamophobia in the West

Todd H. Green

Fortress Press
Minneapolis

THE FEAR OF ISLAM

An Introduction to Islamophobia in the West

Cover image: Milo E. Baumgartner, Photograher, Zurich, Switzerland.

Cover design: Laurie Ingram

Library of Congress Cataloging-in-Publication Data

Print ISBN: 978-1-4514-6549-5

eBook ISBN: 978-1-4514-6990-5

The paper used in this publication meets the minimum requirements of American National Standard for Information Sciences — Permanence of Paper for Printed Library Materials, ANSI Z329.48-1984.

Manufactured in the U.S.A.

This book was produced using PressBooks.com, and PDF rendering was done by PrinceXML.

Contents

List of Images

1. Jean Auguste Dominique Ingres, *The Turkish Bath* (1862)

2. Jean-Léon Gérôme, *The Slave Market* (1866)

3. Auguste Renoir, *Odalisque* (1870)

4. Iranian hostage crisis protest in Washington, DC (1979)

5. President Reagan meeting with Afghan mujahideen (1983)

6. Park51 Islamic Center protest in New York City (2010)

7. English Defence League protest in Newcastle, England (2010)

8. Scene in Oslo, Norway, after the Breivik bombing (2011)

9. American Freedom Defense Initiative billboard, Larchmont train station in New York (2012); photo by Cynthia Miller-Idriss

List of Abbreviations

ACLU American Civil Liberties Union

ADL Anti-Defamation League (US)

BBC British Broadcasting Corporation

CAIR Council on American-Islamic Relations

CIA Central Intelligence Agency (US)

DHS Department of Homeland Security (US)

DOD Department of Defense (US)

DOJ Department of Justice (US)

ECHR European Court of Human Rights

ETA Euskadi Ta Askatasuna (Basque Homeland and Liberty) (Spain)

EU European Union

FBI Federal Bureau of Investigation

HRW Human Rights Watch

IRA Irish Republican Army

ISIS The Islamic State of Iraq and Syria

MSA Muslim Students Association (US)

NATO North Atlantic Treaty Organization

NPR   National Public Radio (US)

NSA   National Security Agency (US)

NSEERS National Security Entry-Exit Registration System (US)

NYPD   New York Police Department

OIC   Organisation of the Islamic Conference

SIOA   Stop Islamization of America

UN   United Nations

Preface

This book is born of my experience teaching college students about Islamophobia. I teach two courses in particular that allow me continually to cultivate my knowledge of Islamophobia and to explain this subject to an audience with little prior understanding. The first, a study-abroad course called Islam in Europe, enables me to travel with students to a variety of countries in order to analyze firsthand the tensions between Muslim minorities and the non-Muslim majority in Europe. The second, a survey course on Islamophobia, provides a forum for debating some of the more difficult questions surrounding this topic, including what distinguishes Islamophobia from legitimate criticisms of or disagreements with Islamic beliefs and practices. I am fortunate to work at an academic institution that encourages faculty to explore challenging and controversial topics like this inside and outside the classroom. This book would not be possible without the rich teaching opportunities and the supportive learning environment that Luther College provides.

Teaching about Islamophobia is a daunting task, though in recent years many excellent scholarly sources have emerged that make this topic increasingly accessible to students and nonspecialists. Even so, as of this writing, no single-author volume exists that surveys

Islamophobia in its historical and contemporary manifestations in both Europe and the United States. Most scholarly books and articles focus on one side of the Atlantic or the other, or concentrate on a particular slice of Islamophobia, such as media portrayals of Muslims or constructions of the Muslim enemy in the War on Terror. With this book, I aim to provide an introduction to the problem of Islamophobia that covers a wide range of topics and that draws comparisons between Europe and the United States. This is a massive undertaking, but, in light of the growing interest in the study of Islamophobia, a broad introductory book aimed at nonspecialists seems timely and necessary.

To pull off this ambitious endeavor, I needed plenty of help. After all, no author flies solo. An author's ideas materialize only through an engagement with the ideas and perspectives of others. Writing is always a collaborative endeavor, and I am grateful for so many people whose ideas and feedback have strengthened this book. I want to begin by thanking my editor at Fortress Press, Michael Gibson. Michael is an author's dream editor. He knows exactly when to nudge you in a different direction and when to step aside and let you run with an idea. I benefited greatly from his feedback along the way and from his ability to troubleshoot logistical issues that were all but lost on me. Michael is one of a kind!

I am indebted to those whom I interviewed for the final chapter of the book: Keith Ellison, John Esposito, Myriam Francois-Cerrah, Marjorie Dove Kent, Ingrid Mattson, Dalia Mogahed, Eboo Patel, and Tariq Ramadan. Their impact on this book extends well beyond the excerpts from their interviews found in chapter 9. Their perspectives and insights inspired me to revisit and revise portions of the book and to make some connections that I did not see the first time around. I am grateful for their wisdom and witness, and I am honored to have their voices included in this book.

Colleagues near and far agreed to read drafts of chapters and to offer constructive feedback. The final product is much improved because of their suggestions. To each of the following, I offer my sincere thanks: Kimberly Connor, Jeanine Diller, Kathleen Fischer, Lee Jefferson, Marc Pugliese, Bob Shedinger, and Ria Van Ryan. I can add to this list my wife, Tabita Green, who read the entire manuscript and whose aptitude for writing helped her to see things I might have easily missed in the editing process.

I want to thank my research assistant, Emily Holm. Emily provided stellar support by proofreading portions of the manuscript and by tracking down sources and other supplementary material when needed.

My participation in two seminars prompted considerable thought on this topic and on how one tells and engages the story of a religious tradition and community that are not one's own. I am appreciative of the fellows and instructors of the Luce Summer Seminar in Theologies of Religious Pluralism and Comparative Theology, sponsored by the American Academy of Religion, and the Teaching Interfaith Understanding Seminar, sponsored by the Interfaith Youth Core and the Council of Independent Colleges. My conversations with participants in both seminars made a huge difference in my thinking and writing.

The Koebrick Endowment Fund at Luther College provided generous financial support that enabled me to conduct research trips and interviews for the book. The final chapter is greatly enhanced because of this funding.

Finally, I want to thank my wife and daughter, Tabita and Rebecka, for all of their encouragement. It is not easy to have a spouse or parent who writes and speaks on what is an unpopular topic in many circles. My work on the problem of Islamophobia is increasingly public, and, on occasion, this opens the door for folks with more intemperate views to write some really nasty things about me on social media or elsewhere on the Internet. Of course, this comes with the territory, but I am always sensitive to the impact this can have on my family. Fortunately, Tabita and Rebecka are unyielding in their support. They are also my partners in the fight to make an unjust world more just, to make a broken world more whole. I dedicate this book to them.

Todd Green
Luther College
January 2015

Introduction

In the fall of 2010, the Muslim Students Association (MSA) at a university in the United States invited me to give a public lecture on the controversy surrounding a proposed Islamic center in New York City. The controversy attracted lots of media attention that summer, with many prominent politicians speaking out against the center because of its proximity to Ground Zero. Since my own research at the time focused on mosque and minaret conflicts in Europe, I eagerly accepted the invitation and looked forward to sharing my perspectives on how these conflicts in Europe might shed light on what was happening in New York.

I arrived in my hotel room the night before the lecture. The MSA president called to welcome me to campus. He proceeded to tell me that campus security intended to station additional officers at my lecture the following day. The fear was that the topic and the presence of Muslims in the audience might raise tensions among those in the community who were already anxious about Islam. The MSA president wanted to reassure me that security was a high priority. Better safe than sorry, I thought, so I expressed my gratitude and how much I was looking forward to giving the lecture.

The following day, I arrived at the campus auditorium about twenty minutes prior to the lecture. The MSA president approached me and gave me another update. Campus security was now advising him not to stand up in front of the audience to introduce me because it might not be safe for him to identify himself publicly. If someone in the audience wanted to lash out against Muslims after the lecture, he would be the most obvious target. So he asked me if I would introduce myself. I agreed, but at this point I was definitely starting to get a little jittery.

The event went off without a hitch, but, as I was heading home, I could not help but ask myself what just happened. Keep in mind that I am a historian of religion. When I give lectures, I typically do not need extra muscle or security precautions. I am just thrilled if anyone shows up! Of course, *I* was not the reason campus security was on edge. It was the topic. What happened that day was just another example of the extraordinary anxieties that accompany any attempt to have a calm, rational conversation about Islam in the United States and indeed the West.

Many polls confirm just how much apprehension there is concerning Muslims and Islam. In the United States, 53 percent of Americans hold views of Islam described either as "not favorable at all" or "not too favorable."[1] In the Netherlands, 63 percent of Dutch citizens believe Islam is incompatible with modern European life.[2] In France, 74 percent believe Islam is at odds with French society.[3] Just fewer than one in four people in Britain believe Islam is compatible with the British way of life.[4]

1. Gallup Center for Muslim Studies, "In U.S., Religious Prejudice Stronger against Muslims," *Gallup*, January 21, 2010, http://www.gallup.com/poll/125312/religious-prejudice-stronger-against-muslims.aspx.
2. World Economic Forum, *Islam and the West: Annual Report on the State of Dialogue* (Geneva: World Economic Forum, 2008), 42.
3. Stéphanie Le Bars, "La religion musulmane fait l'objet d'un profond rejet de la part des Français," *Le Monde*, January 24, 2013, http://www.lemonde.fr/societe/article/2013/01/24/la-religion-musulmane-fait-l-objet-d-un-profond-rejet-de-la-part-des-francais_1821698_3224.html.

These statistics point to the larger reality with which this book is concerned—Islamophobia. Islamophobia refers to the fear, hatred, and hostility toward Muslims and Islam. This book surveys both the history and the contemporary manifestations of Islamophobia in Europe and the United States. My purpose in writing this book is twofold. First, I aim to provide readers with an accessible introduction to the fears and anxieties toward Islam that dominate so much of the cultural and political landscape in the West. Second, I want to help improve the conversation about Islam and its 1.6 billion practitioners. Frankly, we in the West are doing a poor job when we talk about Muslims and Islam. We must do better. We must learn where our fears come from so that these fears no longer fuel policies and practices that both dehumanize Muslims and perpetuate discrimination and at times violence against Muslims.

The challenge facing anyone writing a book on Islamophobia is that the news headlines seem to speak against any notion that the West has an *unfounded* fear of Islam. In the year prior to this book's publication, cable news networks inundated audiences with coverage of Israel's invasion of Gaza in the wake of the kidnapping and killing of three Israeli teenagers by Muslim militants. Newspapers called attention to Muslims chanting anti-Semitic slogans and attacking synagogues in Europe. Videos circulated of the beheadings of American journalists James Foley and Steven Sotloff by the radical organization ISIS, or the Islamic State of Iraq and Syria. Columnists and commentators called on Muslims to denounce terrorism and to affirm their support for freedom of expression after two Muslim extremists killed twelve people at the offices of *Charlie Hebdo*, a French satirical magazine with a history of ridiculing Islam. Name

4. Tim Shipman, "Fewer Than One in Four People Think Islam Is Compatible with British Life, Faith Minister Warns," *Daily Mail* (UK), January 24, 2013, http://www.dailymail.co.uk/news/article-2267515/Baroness-Warsi-Fewer-people-think-Islam-compatible-British-life.html.

the global conflict of the day, and Muslims seem to be right in the thick of it. But as I hope to demonstrate throughout the book, there is more than meets the eye when it comes to the way many in the West understand conflicts involving Muslims. At the very least, much of the Western discourse about Islam conflates the actions of a minority with the majority of Muslims. This conflation is also one of the building blocks of Islamophobia.

Because the study of Islamophobia is still a relatively new field of research, misunderstandings about the topic abound. For this reason, let me clarify what this book is and is not. This book is not an introduction to Islam but to Western fears of Islam. I am interested in the historical origins of the anxiety over Islam, the forms this anxiety takes today, and the consequences of this anxiety for Muslims. The book will certainly provide information about Islam along the way. But what readers learn about Islam will primarily be in the service of comprehending the nature of anti-Muslim bigotry.

This book is also not an attempt to condemn every person who has suspicions or misgivings about Islam. True, there are some people who deliberately stir up animosity toward Muslims in order to mobilize voters, increase ratings, generate traffic to blogs and websites, sell books, or justify wars. In other words, there are folks who are in the business of manufacturing Islamophobia for personal or professional gain, and they do deserve special condemnation. But they are also in the minority. In my experience, many of the people who harbor suspicions toward Muslims or Islam do not do so for personal gain or with malicious intent. Oftentimes, they are eager to learn more about Islam and those who practice it in order to see if their fears are justified. It is my hope that this book can be of help to those who may be apprehensive of Islam but who recognize that they need to learn more about where their misgivings come from and how they can be addressed.

Finally, this book is not an attempt to dismiss legitimate criticisms of Muslims. I recognize that for those most skeptical of the study of Islamophobia, such an enterprise comes across as a blatant attempt to ignore all of the problems that exist in Muslim communities inside and outside the West. Islamophobia skeptics often ask the same questions to make their point: Aren't many of the people committing violence in the name of religion Muslims? Don't women in many Muslim-majority countries have restricted freedoms and rights? Isn't it true that many Muslims hold anti-Western or anti-American sentiments? And if the answer to all of these questions is yes, then doesn't it seem like a fear of Islam is more than justified?

These questions sound so simple and are often asked rhetorically. The answer to each question is supposed to be an obvious yes. But when we dig beneath the rhetorical questions and wrestle with the underlying issues, we quickly discover that there are more profound questions we must ask, questions that require considerable self-examination from the non-Muslim majority in the West.

To take one example—the issue of violence: Why do a small minority of Muslims commit violence against civilians in the name of Islam? Why are their efforts increasingly aimed at the West, and why now? If the Qur'an or something inherent to Islam supposedly makes them commit this violence, why aren't the majority of Muslims following suit? What do we make of the fact that the overwhelming majority of the victims of Muslim terrorism are other Muslims? And is it possible that the roots of what is called "Islamic terrorism" are found in historical and political conditions that include European colonialism and Western intervention in Middle Eastern countries and governments?

Conversely, why are Muslims constructed as violent whereas Western governments that carry out extensive military actions in Muslim-majority countries are considered peaceful? Why is the killing of innocent Muslims by US drone attacks in Pakistan not an act of terrorism, but the killing of innocent Americans by Muslim extremists is? What does the United States' history of supporting regimes that practice torture, from prerevolutionary Iran to Jorge Videla's Argentina in the late 1970s to Egypt's current military dictatorship, say about its commitment to peace and human dignity? What does the United States' own practice of torture in the War on Terror, a practice supported by a majority of white Christian Americans, say about its dedication to human rights?

When we wrestle with these types of questions, the answers become more complex and easy assumptions about "violent" Muslims versus the "peaceful" West dissipate quickly. However, wrestling with these questions does not prevent us from criticizing or condemning the violence carried out by some Muslim extremist groups. We can analyze the problem of Islamophobia *and* critique Muslim individuals or groups when appropriate.

As an introduction to the problem of Islamophobia in the West, this book traverses considerable historical, political, cultural, and geographical terrain. The book begins this journey with an opening chapter that discusses both the debates over how to define Islamophobia and the most common questions concerning the concept of Islamophobia. The next two chapters cover the history of anti-Muslim prejudice. Chapter 2 surveys European views of Islam and Muslims from the Middle Ages through the Enlightenment. Chapter 3 examines the European colonization of Muslim-majority regions in the nineteenth and early twentieth centuries and includes a discussion of how the colonial enterprise generated Orientalism, a particular way of thinking that has shaped the modern study of Islam.

Chapters 4 and 5 illuminate the key events in the modern West that have heightened fears and anxieties toward Muslims at home and abroad. Chapter 4 discusses the terrorist attacks of September

11, 2001, and the subsequent US War on Terror. The focus is on how US politicians constructed the Muslim enemy to justify the war and to deflect attention from imperial ambitions in the Middle East. Chapter 5 surveys the most significant events on European soil in recent decades that generated fears of the Muslim "enemy within" and exacerbated tensions between Muslim minorities and the non-Muslim majority.

The next two chapters analyze the most influential sources of the negative images of Muslims in the West today. Chapter 6 addresses the rise of individuals and organizations that make a living manufacturing and perpetuating Islamophobia. Chapter 7 examines the negative representations of Muslims and Islam in the mainstream news media, in television programming, and in Hollywood movies.

Chapter 8 shifts our focus to the practical consequences of Islamophobia for Muslims living in the West. It surveys the discrimination, exclusion, and even violence experienced by Muslims due to surveillance programs, detentions, deportations, renditions, hate crimes, and restrictions on the free exercise of religion.

The book concludes on a constructive note for combating Islamophobia. Chapter 9 invites readers into a conversation with eight prominent individuals who are invested in the battle against anti-Muslim bigotry. Readers have the opportunity to gain insights from Keith Ellison, John Esposito, Myriam Francois-Cerrah, Marjorie Dove Kent, Ingrid Mattson, Dalia Mogahed, Eboo Patel, and Tariq Ramadan on how best to respond to the problem of Islamophobia.

It is impossible to do complete justice to any one of the topics covered in these chapters. As with all introductory books, the intent here is to provide a bird's-eye view of the subject in an effort to stimulate critical thought and encourage further exploration. This book marks only the beginning of a conversation about the most widely accepted prejudice in the West today.

1

What Is Islamophobia?

The word *Islamophobia* is not new, despite the fact that one would be hard pressed to find many instances of it prior to the 1990s. It first appeared in its French form, *Islamophobie*, in a book by the painter Etienne Dinet in 1918.[1] In the past few decades, however, the word has become an integral part of political and public discourse. This is due

Islamophobia: hatred, hostility, and fear of Islam and Muslims, and the discriminatory practices that result.

largely to a much-cited study conducted by a British think tank, the Runnymede Trust, in 1997. The study defines Islamophobia as "dread or hatred of Islam" and as "unfounded hostility towards Islam."[2] It also defines Islamophobia in light of the concrete expressions this hostility

---

1. Jocelyne Cesari, "Islamophobia in the West: A Comparison between Europe and the United States," in *Islamophobia: The Challenge of Pluralism in the 21st Century*, ed. John L. Esposito and Ibrahim Kalin (New York: Oxford University Press, 2011), 21.
2. Commission on British Muslims and Islamophobia, *Islamophobia: A Challenge for Us All* (London: Runnymede Trust, 1997), 1, 4.

takes, such as the deliberate exclusion of Muslims from mainstream social and political life. This definition is the one most frequently employed in debates pertaining to anti-Muslim sentiment in the West.

The term has plenty of critics. Some scholars, sympathetic with the need to analyze and combat anti-Muslim prejudice, maintain that the very word *Islamophobia* is a misnomer. They argue that a literal interpretation suggests that the primary object of fear or discrimination is religion (Islam), when in fact the prejudice in question is best understood under a different framework, such as racism or xenophobia. Other critics reject the word because they believe it stifles freedom of speech and the freedom to criticize the beliefs and practices of a particular religious tradition or community.

This chapter will unpack this controversy and develop a working definition of Islamophobia. After an overview of the Runnymede Trust's findings in its 1997 study, I will tackle some of the most common questions and criticisms raised about Islamophobia. I will conclude by putting forth a definition of Islamophobia that is informed largely by the Runnymede definition—the fear, dislike, or hatred of Muslims and Islam—yet nuanced to address some of the more significant concerns from critics.

The Runnymede Report

The Runnymede Trust was established in 1968 during a time of significant social and cultural upheaval in Europe and the United States. Its purpose was to counsel the British government on race relations. In 1996, the Runnymede Trust created the Commission on British Muslims and Islamophobia. The commission's purpose was to analyze the discrimination experienced by many Muslims in Britain and to make policy recommendations to the government that would help combat this discrimination. Its report, *Islamophobia: A Challenge for Us All*, was released one year later. Often referred to as the Runnymede Report, this study has served as the starting point for many subsequent analyses of Islamophobia in Europe and North America.

The timing of the report was not coincidental. Increasing tensions between non-Muslims and Muslims, both in the West and between the West and Muslim-majority regions, fed the conditions that gave rise to the report. The Israeli-Palestinian conflict and the Iranian Revolution of 1979, for example, contributed to negative perceptions of Muslims and Islam in the West. On the domestic front, the Rushdie Affair of 1988–1989 revealed the tensions between non-Muslims and Muslims within Britain. The Rushdie Affair refers to the publication of *The Satanic Verses* (1988), a novel by the British-Indian writer Salman Rushdie. It provoked considerable controversy among some Muslims in Britain and abroad due to its critical depictions of Islam. This episode will be described in more detail in chapter 5, but for now what is important is that the strong reaction by some Muslims to *The Satanic Verses* gave rise to a backlash against Muslims in Britain and to the perception that Islam could not adapt to Western standards of free speech. The authors of the Runnymede Report have this event in mind when reflecting on the rise of anti-Muslim prejudice in Britain and the recognition that "there is a new reality which needs naming."[3]

As stated above, the Runnymede Report defines Islamophobia as "dread or hatred of Islam" that, by implication, translates into "fear or dislike of all or most Muslims."[4] It notes that prejudice against Muslims has reached a scale requiring action to protect the basic rights of Britain's Muslim citizens. By identifying Islamophobia as

3. Ibid., 4.
4. Ibid., 1.

a distinct phenomenon that singles out Muslims for special consideration and protection, the commission recognizes the challenges and even dangers of conveying the message that Muslim beliefs and practices should somehow fall outside the realm of critical inquiry. This is why the report goes to great lengths to differentiate what it deems legitimate criticisms of Islam, rooted in "open" views, from the "closed" views that constitute Islamophobia.

Features of Islamophobia

What follows is a brief discussion of the eight closed views identified by the Runnymede Report as characteristic of Islamophobia. While the commission has Britain in mind, its observations apply more broadly to the West. For this reason, the examples I use to illustrate each closed view will reflect a variety of Western contexts.

1. **Islam as monolithic and static.** The list of closed views begins with the notion that Islam lacks both diversity and internal differences and disagreements. In other words, all Muslims are basically the same, holding uniform worldviews and ideologies. In many ways, this perception drives much of the Islamophobia that one encounters in the West. If Islam is monolithic and unchanging, and if media coverage focuses on violence or terrorism carried out in the name of Islam by a small minority of Muslims, then it is easy to draw the conclusion that what one sees on the news is somehow endemic to Islam and all Muslims. Similarly, if women in a Muslim-majority country such as Saudi Arabia face severe restrictions on their public behavior—for example, the prohibition to drive—many in the West might conclude that all Muslim women face similar restrictions, when in fact Saudi Arabia is the exception and not

the rule. This contrasts with the assumption that other religions or belief systems are diverse and dynamic and do not lend themselves to easy characterizations that apply to all practitioners.

To put the difference starkly, if al-Qaeda launches violent attacks against Western targets, some might conclude that this is due to an inherent quality in Islam and that, by extension, all Muslims are prone to violence because all Muslims are fundamentally the same. By contrast, when Anders Breivik, a self-identified Norwegian Christian, went on a killing rampage in and near Oslo in July 2011, Christianity and Christians as a whole were not implicated in his crimes.

Another example involves the US presidential campaign of then Senator Barack Obama in 2008. Some of Obama's opponents frequently suggested that he was a Muslim. They emphasized the time he spent as a child in Indonesia, his Muslim father, and his Muslim-sounding middle name, Hussein. The motivation to brand Obama as a Muslim rested in the assumption that Islam is monolithic. Since the Muslims most Americans were familiar with were the terrorists they saw or read about in the news, any connection between Obama and Islam might also be construed as a link between Obama and terrorism or extremism. The assumption that Islam is monolithic easily lends itself to the guilt-by-association principle at work in the campaign to label Obama a Muslim and in much of the Islamophobic discourse one finds in the West.

2. **Islam as separate and other.** Another characteristic of Islamophobia is the idea that Islam shares none of the core values found in other religions, particularly Judaism and Christianity,

or in Western culture. Western values such as respect for religious diversity or freedom of religion have no home in Islam.

The debate over the building of minarets in Switzerland illustrates this perception. In 2009, the Swiss People's Party, a radical right party, led a campaign in Switzerland to prohibit the construction of new minarets—that is, towers located on or next to mosques. During a television interview, a reporter asked Ulrich Schlüer, a member of the party and a major figure behind the anti-minaret campaign, if the proposed ban was fair in light of the fact that it targeted minarets but not church steeples. Schlüer responded that the comparison was invalid because the steeple and the minaret represent two religions that hold two very different sets of values: "I think Christianity is an attitude of freedom, of recognizing different meanings, of tolerance. Islam has nothing to do with tolerance."[5] Put another way, Christianity embraces and epitomizes Western secular values such as toleration and freedom, the very values Islam rejects. Since Islam is so different, so "other," its symbols cannot be allowed to occupy public space and promote values that are "foreign" to the Swiss people.

3. **Islam as inferior.** A third closed view is that Islam is not only different from but also inferior to the West. Islam is barbaric, irrational, and sexist, in contrast to the civilized, enlightened, and gender-equal West.

Ayaan Hirsi Ali, a former Muslim and prominent critic of Islam, frequently invokes these types of critiques in her writing and speaking. She contrasts the Enlightenment principles pervading the

---

5. Ulrich Schlüer, interviewed by Julie Hunt, "Anti-Minaret Campaigner Puts Case," October 6, 2009, *swissinfo.ch*, http://www.swissinfo.ch/eng/multimedia/video/Anti-minaret_campaigner_puts_case.html?cid=1012760.

West, such as free inquiry and individual freedom, with Islam. "Islam," she writes, "is incompatible with the principles of liberty that are at the heart of the Enlightenment legacy."[6] She argues that Islam's "obsession with subjugating women is one of the things that makes [it] so reprehensible."[7] She does not believe that Islam has anything to offer the West because it lags behind the West intellectually, culturally, and ethically.

4. **Islam as the enemy.** Islam, according to a fourth closed view, is identified as hostile, violent, and aggressive. Islam is a religion bent on conquest, and, for this reason, there is an inevitable "clash of civilizations" between Islam and the West.

We will return to the clash of civilizations thesis in subsequent chapters, but what is important at this point is to emphasize how Islam is linked inextricably to violence and terrorism in a manner that feeds not only Western foreign policies and wars against Muslim-majority countries but also domestic policies that place restrictions on Muslims living in the West or that single out Muslims as people who are particularly susceptible to terrorist activity. For example, the profiling of Muslim passengers in US airport security lines can certainly be interpreted as based in the assumption that all Muslims are prone to terrorism and thus must be targeted for additional security measures in order to protect non-Muslim Americans.

5. **Islam as manipulative.** Another common Islamophobic characteristic is the assumption that Muslims are objects of suspicion because they are viewed as devious, relying on their

---

6. Ayaan Hirsi Ali, *Nomad: From Islam to America: A Personal Journey through the Clash of Civilizations* (New York: Free Press, 2010), 214.
7. Ayaan Hirsi Ali, *The Caged Virgin: An Emancipation Proclamation for Women and Islam* (New York: Free Press, 2008), 163.

religion to give them some strategic military or political advantage.

An illustration of this view is the hysteria in recent years over "creeping Sharia" in the United States. Beginning in 2010, a wave of legislation swept through state legislatures. The purpose of the legislation was to ban *Sharia*, or Islamic law, from individual states.

Sharia: Islamic law based on the Qur'an and the Sunna (the example of Muhammad) that provides a blueprint for proper conduct in accordance with God's revelations.

Supporters of this legislation argued that Muslims were taking advantage of the free exercise of religion guaranteed by the First Amendment in order to spread their faith and to grow in numbers and influence. The anti-Sharia lobby insisted, however, that Muslims were not sincere in their admiration or respect for the First Amendment but sought protection under the US Constitution only to wait for a strategic time to attain a critical mass and then to impose Sharia law.

6. **Racial discrimination against Muslims justified.** The report notes that racism and Islamophobia in the British context are often mixed together; as a result, anti-Muslim feelings and anti-Asian sentiment are often connected.[8] In other Western contexts, it might be anti-Muslim and anti-Arab sentiments. When Muslims are involved, racist practices and prejudices get a pass.

---

8. Many Muslims in Britain have a South Asian background.

To take an earlier example, profiling in US airports is often defended not only in light of the religious identities of Muslims but also on the basis of their race and the belief that one can easily spot a Muslim based on outward appearance, presumably including skin color. Sam Harris, a prominent atheist philosopher and critic of Islam, plainly states this in regard to airport security lines: "We should profile Muslims, or anyone who looks like he or she could conceivably be Muslim, and we should be honest about it."[9] Racial discrimination and racist exclusionary practices are typically deemed unconstitutional today in the United States, but here is a case in which such discrimination is presented as normal and necessary.

7. **Muslim criticisms of the West invalidated.** In this closed view, the Western critique of Islam is a one-way street. Western politicians, religious leaders, and journalists can freely criticize Islamic beliefs and practices, but they give little or no heed to Muslim perspectives on and criticisms of Western values or practices.

For example, many Western nations have intense debates about freedom of speech, and all set some limits on the scope of such speech. Some European countries have laws that prohibit Holocaust denial. One is not free in countries such as Belgium or Austria to deny or condone the genocide that took place in Nazi Germany. But when Muslims raise critical questions about the problems with speech that deliberately and disrespectfully denigrates the texts, figures, or practitioners of Islam, their views are often rejected outright. In 2005 and 2006, various Muslims inside and outside of Denmark raised such questions in response to satirical cartoons of Muhammad published

---

9. Sam Harris, "In Defense of Profiling," *Sam Harris: The Blog*, April 28, 2012, http://www.samharris.org/blog/item/in-defense-of-profiling.

by a Danish newspaper. Their questions were largely dismissed, with some public figures going so far as to point out that the real problem was the inability of Muslims to understand and accept the Western commitment to freedom of speech.

8. **Anti-Muslim discourse as natural.** The report finally notes that anti-Muslim discourse is so pervasive that even some public figures who ardently fight for tolerance and equal rights for all citizens may express little or no concern for the discrimination faced by Muslims in their midst. Prejudiced statements or views about Muslims are not deemed bigoted; instead, they are normal.

In October 2010, a well-respected journalist with National Public Radio (NPR) in the United States, Juan Williams, openly proclaimed that the sight of Muslims on an airplane made him nervous. NPR took action and fired him, and Fox News subsequently hired him. A major debate ensued over whether NPR overreacted in its decision to dismiss Williams. Had Williams articulated that the sight of Jews or African Americans on an airplane caused him anxiety, NPR's decision to fire him would have attracted broad support. Instead, Williams articulated a sentiment deemed acceptable enough by a wide spectrum of the American public that NPR's decision to oust him, more than his original statement, became the focal point of the controversy.

In surveying these eight features of Islamophobia, the report focuses more on pointing out the closed views than addressing the open views, views that reflect an engagement with Islam in which common ground and legitimate differences are examined, acknowledged, and respected. The report also devotes considerable attention to detailing the consequences of Islamophobia in Britain, including employment discrimination, exclusion from mainstream politics, and prejudice in the media toward Muslims and Islam.

The Runnymede Report has become a point of reference for many political and scholarly discussions since its publication in 1997. Its definition and framing of Islamophobia have also given rise to critical questions and concerns, including whether the concept of Islamophobia helps or hinders our understanding of anti-Muslim prejudice, how Islamophobia relates to more commonly identified forms of prejudice, and the extent to which Islamophobia is a construct that stifles free speech and inhibits one's right to disagree openly with the teachings of Islam. In the remainder of this chapter, I will address these and other common questions and criticisms in an effort to move toward a working definition of Islamophobia.

Does "Islamophobia" Stifle Legitimate Criticisms of Muslims and Islam?

One frequent criticism voiced against the concept of Islamophobia is that it can suppress freedom of speech and inhibit open discussion and debate about religion.[10] Should Islam receive special protection when it comes to critical discussions about religion in democratic societies? Is there a risk that anyone who criticizes Islamic beliefs and practices is automatically labeled an Islamophobe? These are questions that even those who are sympathetic with Muslims and their experiences of bigotry recognize as legitimate.

The most vocal critics reject out of hand the existence of Islamophobia and warn that any flirtations with the concept will lead the West into the fiery pit of cultural relativism and will undermine the freedoms that set "us" apart from the world of Islam. A notable

10. For a straightforward articulation of this concern, see Kenan Malik, "The Islamophobia Myth," *Prospect*, February 2005, http://www.kenanmalik.com/essays/prospect_islamophobia.html.

instance of this criticism is found in a manifesto issued by twelve authors, among them Salman Rushdie and Ayaan Hirsi Ali, written in response to the violence sparked by the publication of controversial cartoons of the Prophet Muhammad in Denmark and across Europe in 2005 and 2006. Titled "Together Facing the New Totalitarianism," the manifesto denies the existence of Islamophobia:

> We reject the "cultural relativism" which implies an acceptance that men and women of Muslim culture are deprived of the right to equality, freedom and secularism in the name of the respect for certain cultures and traditions.
>
> We refuse to renounce our critical spirit out of fear of being accused of "Islamophobia," a wretched concept that confuses criticism of Islam as a religion and stigmatisation of those who believe in it.
>
> We defend the universality of the freedom of expression, so that a critical spirit can exist in every continent, towards each and every maltreatment and dogma.[11]

The authors view freedom of expression and Islamophobia as mutually exclusive concepts, insisting on the need to reject the latter in order to allow the former to flourish.

The fact that many of these authors are sometimes criticized as inciting or sustaining Islamophobia by doing what they renounce in the manifesto—stigmatizing Muslims under the guise of criticizing Islam—is not the main point I want to make. The larger point is that the freedom of speech issue addressed in the manifesto is a concern shared more broadly across the political and religious spectrum. Even the Runnymede Report recognizes this potential problem. This is why it insists that one can disagree with and criticize the beliefs and practices of Muslims without being Islamophobic: "It can be

---

11. Ayaan Hirsi Ali, Chahla Chafiq, Caroline Fourest et al., "Together Facing the New Totalitarianism," *BBC News* (UK), March 1, 2006, http://news.bbc.co.uk/2/hi/europe/4764730.stm.

legitimate to criticize policies and practices of Muslim states and regimes, for example, especially when their governments do not subscribe to internationally recognized human rights, freedoms and democratic procedures, or to criticize and condemn terrorist movements which claim to be motivated by Islamic values."[12] One of the reasons the report distinguishes between open and closed views of Islam is to safeguard freedom of speech and to set it apart from Islamophobic discourse.

How do we address this dilemma? What standards should apply when differentiating Islamophobia from legitimate, critical discourse about Muslim beliefs and practices? Let me suggest three overlapping criteria for making this crucial distinction.[13] First, criticisms of Islam should be based on aspects of the religion that many Muslims recognize as a part of their faith and should avoid guilt by association. For example, disagreeing with the belief that the Qur'an is God's fullest self-disclosure to humanity does not qualify as Islamophobic. It reflects a legitimate difference of opinion over an *actual* belief held by a large number of Muslims, a belief that one would not reasonably expect Buddhists or Christians to embrace. On the other hand, to accuse all Muslims of being inherently prone to violence in light of the deadly campaigns against civilians conducted by extremist groups such as al-Qaeda or the Islamic State of Iraq and Syria (ISIS) violates this criterion. The

> *Qur'an*: Islam's most sacred and authoritative text, revealed to Muhammad by God via the angel Gabriel; the word literally means "recitation."

12. Commission on British Muslims, *Islamophobia*, 4.
13. Variations on the first and third criteria that I put forth here can be found in John E. Richardson, *(Mis)representing Islam: The Racism and Rhetoric of British Broadsheet Newspapers* (Amsterdam: J. Benjamins, 2004), 25.

accusation does not reflect the authentic beliefs and practices embraced by the overwhelming majority of Muslims. In fact, many Muslims might suspect that the critic has ulterior motives for distorting or misrepresenting their beliefs and perhaps is attempting to stigmatize and malign all Muslims for personal or political gain.

Second, criticism should not lapse into hate speech or otherwise endanger the safety of Muslim citizens. For example, in 2012 the American Freedom Defense Initiative posted an ad on a large billboard at a New York train platform that read: "19,250 Deadly Islamic Attacks Since 9/11/01—and Counting. It's Not Islamophobia, It's Islamorealism" (see image 9). Organizations such as the Anti-Defamation League denounced the ad as hate speech and as a deliberate attempt to mislead the public.[14] The billboard's message is dangerous because it has the potential to incite violence against Muslims by branding them as enemies who are complicit in the killing of innocent people.

hijab: a headscarf worn by some Muslim women that covers the head but leaves the face exposed; more broadly, the term refers to modest dress and behavior for both Muslim women and men.

Finally, criticisms of Islam should not be translated into actions undermining the freedom of religion or the equal opportunity for Muslim minorities to practice their religion as other religious communities do. For example, in Europe, it is commonplace for non-Muslims to voice discomfort over Muslim women who wear *hijabs* or *burqas*, perhaps on the grounds that this

---

14. Christopher Mathias, "Islamophobia Billboard at Metro-North Station Causes Outrage One Month after Pro-Palestinian Billboard," *Huffington Post*, August 17, 2012, http://www.huffingtonpost.com/2012/08/17/islamophobic-billboard-at-metronorth-station-pamela-geller-pro-palestinian-ad_n_1797651.html.

restrictive clothing undermines equality of the sexes. Such criticism is not necessarily Islamophobic; it can represent a valid perspective, one shared by some Muslims. But if this discomfort translates into legislation that prohibits Muslim women from freely choosing to wear hijabs or burqas in light of the dictates of their consciences, we have

burqa: a colorful garment worn by some Muslim women that covers most of the body and face but with eyeholes or a grid around the eyes.

ventured into the realm of Islamophobia. The ban on burqas in public spaces in France and Belgium illustrates the violation of this criterion, particularly given that women from other religious communities, such as Catholic nuns, do not face similar restrictions or scrutiny of what they can and cannot wear.

None of these criteria precludes public scrutiny and criticism of Muslim beliefs and practices. Islam does not get a pass from disagreement with or even dislike of specific Islamic beliefs and practices. The criteria do, however, ensure that this freedom to disagree is not used as a cover to practice outright bigotry or discrimination.

Does "Islamophobia" Reinforce What It Seeks to Combat?

The Runnymede Report's insistence on differentiating between "open" and "closed" views of Islam has another danger. If it is considered Islamophobic to believe that all Muslims are terrorists (a closed view), then one strategy to combat this perception is to argue that "real" Islam is peaceful and nonviolent (presumably an open view, or at least an opposing view). Such a response might be well intentioned, but it actually exchanges one static, monolithic view of

Islam and Muslims for another. Since the view of Islam as lacking in diversity tops the Runnymede Report's list of closed views, it would seem that the response noted here actually reinforces the very concept it seeks to combat.

The scholar most critical of this pitfall in the Runnymede Report's binary approach to Islamophobia is Christopher Allen.[15] Allen argues that the report actually lapses into essentialism in its efforts to combat Islamophobia. To essentialize is to attribute innate and enduring qualities to all people associated with a community, religious or otherwise. To claim that all Muslims are violent, for example, is to engage in essentialism. But to describe all Muslims as peaceful is equally essentialist. Allen believes this is the problem with the report's dualistic model of closed versus open views of Islam. The tendency is to compensate for the closed views by creating open views that reduce all Muslims and all of Islam to one underlying essence.

essentialism: the belief that a people, culture, or religious tradition possesses an unchanging set of characteristics or some inherent essence.

Andrew Shryock has a name for countering the Islamophobic image of "bad Muslims" with "good Muslims"—*Islamophilia*. Critics of Islamophobia who are prone to Islamophilia are sometimes desperate to construct the perfect, acceptable Muslim. The model Muslim is one who espouses nonviolence, is highly educated, embraces gender equality, believes firmly in democracy, and participates actively in interfaith dialogue. Shyrock reminds us that this is not only wishful thinking but also a harmful construct that both neglects diversity within Islam and attempts to force Muslims to

15. See Christopher Allen, *Islamophobia* (Burlington, VT: Ashgate, 2010).

conform to a Western ideal that, in turn, can be manipulated by non-Muslims for political purposes.[16]

Simplistic visions of "good Muslims" are not the answer to sinister depictions of "bad Muslims." Islamophilia is not the cure for Islamophobia.

Is Islamophobia Really about Religion?

Some of the reservations about the term *Islamophobia* are rooted in the belief that the word incorrectly suggests that the object of fear is Islam as a religion. The most prominent representative of this view is Fred Halliday. Halliday's words have been cited so frequently that they are worth reprinting here: "'Islam' as a religion *was* the enemy in the past: in the crusades or the *reconquista*. It is not the enemy now: Islam is not threatening to win large segments of western European society to its faith, as Communism did, nor is the polemic, in press, media or political statement, against the Islamic faith. . . . The attack now is against not *Islam* as a faith but *Muslims* as a people."[17] Halliday suggests that a more accurate term to reflect the focus on the people rather than the religion is "anti-Muslimism." Other scholars propose alternate terms such as "Muslimophobia."[18]

It is true that important differences exist between the ways that Muslims were conceived of as the enemy in the Middle Ages and how this takes place today. Certainly, the Christian theological

16. Andrew Shryock, "Islam as an Object of Fear and Affection," in *Islamophobia/Islamophilia: Beyond the Politics of Enemy and Friend*, ed. Andrew Shryock (Bloomington: Indiana University Press, 2010), 1–25. See also Mahmood Mamdani, *Good Muslim, Bad Muslim: America, the Cold War, and the Roots of Terror* (New York: Pantheon Books, 2004).

17. Fred Halliday, "'Islamophobia' Reconsidered," *Ethnic and Racial Studies* 22 (September 1999): 898.

18. See Burak Erdenir, "Islamophobia qua Racial Discrimination: Muslimophobia," in *Muslims in 21st Century Europe: Structural and Cultural Perspectives*, ed. Anna Triandafyllidou (London: Routledge, 2010), 27–44.

justification for opposing Muslims prevalent in the Middle Ages no longer holds in modern Europe, which is not surprising given the secularization and decline in Christianity's influence that has swept the continent. We are not seeing battles in Europe to eradicate Muslim heretics in order to preserve and defend the ultimate truth of Christianity.

Even so, Halliday's analysis falls short on two grounds. First, stereotypes about Islam as a religion *do* feed much of the Islamophobia that is rampant in the West. Islam is often equated in the media and in public discourse with terrorism, misogyny, backwardness, and so forth, and this is often done with Islam as a religion and an ideology in mind. Islam is attacked as a "faith," even if such attacks, at least in Europe, are not primarily driven by the need to defend Christian truth claims.

Second, if one crosses the Atlantic, it is actually not that difficult to find manifestations of Islamophobia in the United States driven by theologies that view Islam as the enemy of the one true religion—Christianity. The prominent evangelist Franklin Graham contrasted Christianity with Islam, which he called "a religion of hatred" and "a religion of war."[19] In 2003, Lieutenant General William Boykin, a decorated military officer and a high-ranking official in the US Defense Department, made headlines for claiming that the War on Terror was a Christian battle against the representatives of Satan. The opinions of Graham and Boykin are certainly controversial and are in no way representative of the great diversity of Christian views of Islam in the United States. But they are reminders that hostile views of Islam, rooted in concerns to defend and preserve the Christian faith if not the Christian nation, are still alive.

19. Bobby Ghosh, "Islamophobia: Does America Have a Muslim Problem?," *Time*, August 30, 2010, http://www.time.com/time/magazine/article/0,9171,2011936,00.html.

Halliday's alternative to Islamophobia, anti-Muslimism, fails to capture the reality that religion is still a significant part of anti-Muslim sentiment. That said, Halliday's insights about Islamophobia are still helpful because they remind us that religion is not the only explanatory factor worth considering.

Is Islamophobia a Form of Racism?

If there is an explanatory factor that rivals religion in the debate over what drives Islamophobia, it is racism. Islamophobia is not racially blind, nor is it simply a manifestation of older forms of racism rooted in biological inferiority. It is an example of what some scholars have labeled "cultural racism." This form of racism incites hatred and hostility based on religious beliefs, cultural traditions, and ethnic backgrounds.[20] Animosity toward Muslims is expressed in terms of cultural and religious inferiority, with

cultural racism: hatred and hostility of others based on religious beliefs, cultural traditions, and ethnicity.

Muslims and Islam labeled as barbaric, violent, uncivilized, and inferior to Western culture and civilization. The presumed insurmountable differences between "Muslim culture" and the West serve as the basis for exclusion and discrimination. The argument of cultural inferiority has gained significant traction in recent decades, in part because many politicians, journalists, and public figures do not

20. See Commission on British Muslims, *Islamophobia*, 12; Liz Fekete, *A Suitable Enemy: Racism, Migration and Islamophobia in Europe* (New York: Pluto, 2009), 194; Mehdi Semati, "Islamophobia, Culture and Race in the Age of Empire," *Cultural Studies* 24 (2012): 256–75; Raymond Taras, *Xenophobia and Islamophobia in Europe* (Edinburgh: Edinburgh University Press, 2012), 14.

see it as racist; they assume that racism must involve overt appeals to skin color or biological inferiority.

Two questions are frequently raised in debates about whether Islamophobia is a form of racism. First, if Islamophobia represents a fear of Islam as a religion, does labeling it racism confuse matters? How can it be both? Some scholars prefer to choose one or the other. But in light of the complexities of cultural racism, it is nearly impossible to choose one over the other. Islamophobia is driven by animosity toward religion *and* race. Race, culture, ethnicity, and religion are often conflated in Western discourse about Islam, and hostility based on religious differences is difficult to extricate from bigotry based on cultural and ethnic differences.

An illustration of Islamophobia as a manifestation of cultural racism can be found in "We Owe Arabs Nothing," an article written by Robert Kilroy-Silk, a former British politician and television talk show host. Published by the *Sunday Express* on January 4, 2004, the article describes Kilroy-Silk's views of Arab countries as anything but "shining examples of civilization." He indiscriminately labels all Arabs as "suicide bombers, limb amputators, [and] women repressors," making obvious references to negative stereotypes of Muslims and Islam.[21] The article generated so much controversy that his BBC program, *Kilroy*, was canceled soon after the article's publication. The article demonstrates how religion and race are easily conflated in Islamophobic rhetoric. Where animosity based on race ends and that based on religion begins is unclear. In this case, as in many others, Islam and Muslims are racialized, but not by abandoning religious elements.

A second question that is often debated concerns the matter of choice. Can you call Islamophobia racism when, unlike race,

21. Quoted in Ali Rattansi, *Racism: A Very Short Introduction* (Oxford: Oxford University Press, 2007), 110.

religious identity is a voluntary choice, not something with which you are born? The assumption here is that one chooses to embrace Islam, one chooses to become (or remain) a Muslim, and therefore one can "unchoose" this identification and consequently avoid discrimination. Victims of racism, on the other hand, are targeted for something over which they have no control or choice.

With this question, once again we encounter notions of race and racism rooted in biological categories that do not fully capture the type of racism under analysis here. Moreover, as the scholars Nasar Meer and Tariq Modood argue, people do not, in fact, choose to be born into a Muslim family, nor do they choose to be born into a society in which to be a Muslim, or to have ethnic roots in a Muslim-majority country, automatically makes one an object of suspicion among the non-Muslim majority population.[22] Many people suffer discrimination and hostility in the West simply because they are *perceived* to be Muslim, either because of outward dress or through family heritage or ethnic lineage. These realities would not disappear even if self-identified Muslims chose to identify with another religious community or dropped a religious identity altogether.

Is Islamophobia Connected to Anti-Semitism?

On the surface, a possible connection between anti-Semitism and Islamophobia, particularly in the European context, may seem a bit of a stretch. After all, anti-Semitism, particularly from the late nineteenth century through World War II, resulted in the systematic and mass

anti-Semitism: prejudice and hatred toward Jews.

22. Nasa Meer and Tariq Modood, "Refutations of Racism in the 'Muslim Question,'" *Patterns of Prejudice* 43 (2009): 345.

extermination of over six million Jews, some two-thirds of the Jewish population living in Europe on the eve of the Holocaust. Whatever challenges Muslims have faced in postwar Europe, they have not encountered this level of brutality and violence, even if one takes into account the ethnic cleansing of Bosnian Muslims in the 1990s. The long shadow of the Holocaust makes it very difficult to bring to light significant analogies between anti-Semitism and Islamophobia.

It is not the Holocaust alone that makes comparisons difficult. The anthropologist Matti Bunzl argues that, leaving aside historic animosities aimed at Jews and Muslims by Europe's Christian majority, anti-Semitism and Islamophobia have served two different functions in modern European history. Anti-Semitism reflected an attempt to secure ethnically pure nation-states by recourse to a racist ideology that targeted and excluded Jews from the national community. German nationalism, for example, relied on anti-Semitism and the supposed racial inferiority of Jews to rally support for a strong German nation. Other European countries also experienced strong waves of anti-Semitism and arguments about the incommensurability of Jewish and national (English, French, Norwegian, and so on) identity. Islamophobia, by contrast, reflects a different project of exclusion, one in which the desire to protect and maintain European civilization and anxieties over what it means to be European manifest themselves through anti-Muslim prejudice. The preservation of European identity, as opposed to national identity, is at the heart of Islamophobia.[23]

These differences should not be underestimated, but there are good reasons why comparing Islamophobia and anti-Semitism is worthwhile. First, Europe has a long history of targeting and excluding minority (that is, non-Christian) religious communities.

23. Matti Bunzl, "Anti-Semitism and Islamophobia," in *Anti-Semitism and Islamophobia: Hatreds Old and New in Europe*, ed. Matti Bunzl (Chicago: Prickly Paradigm, 2007), 1–46.

Jews and Muslims constitute the two most prominent communities in this regard, and while the reasons for this exclusion in modern history may be less rooted in Christian theology than was the case in the premodern era, the development of European identity over against these cultural and religious "Others" has been a long process that paved the way for contemporary anti-Semitism and Islamophobia.[24]

Second, both phenomena in the modern era have involved significant elements of racism, whether biological or cultural. In other words, both Jews and Muslims have been racialized by majority populations and have suffered significant discrimination and hostility as a result. For this reason, some organizations, such as the European Monitoring Centre for Racism and Xenophobia, have conducted studies that view the challenges of anti-Semitism and Islamophobia as part of the same continuum. Even the Runnymede Trust embarked on its effort to understand and analyze Islamophobia in 1997 only after publishing a study on anti-Semitism three years earlier that drew parallels between anti-Semitism as a form of racism and the rise of anti-Muslim prejudice.

Finally, in response to Bunzl's argument, it is not at all clear that there are two different projects at work here, one aimed at building the nation-state and the other at preserving European civilization. Much of the anti-Muslim rhetoric that one finds in Europe today expresses concerns for the preservation of both national and European identity.[25] Far right political parties, in particular, have tapped into fears in various electorates that Muslim immigrants pose a significant threat to what it means to be Swiss or French or Danish. At the same time, issues that transcend national identity, such as whether or not

24. Esther Benbassa, "Xenophobia, Anti-Semitism, and Racism: Europe's Recurring Evils?," in Bunzl, *Anti-Semitism and Islamophobia*, 77–89.
25. One example of this argument can be found in Cora Alexa Døving, "Anti-Semitism and Islamophobia: A Comparison of Imposed Group Identities," *Tidsskrift for Islamforskning—Islam og minoriteter* 2 (2010): 52–76.

to admit Turkey, a large Muslim-majority country, to the European Union (EU), bring out anxieties over what it means to be European.

Jews and Muslims have been the historic outsiders in Western history, whether they have been opposed on religious or secular grounds. Any historical analysis of Islamophobia that disregards the similarities with anti-Semitism will fail to get at the deeper anxiety that has permeated projects to construct Western identity over against cultural and religious "Others."

◆ ◆ ◆ ◆ ◆

Despite the questions and concerns discussed above, no scholar has managed to coin an alternate term for anti-Muslim prejudice that has received a significant following. Whatever the reservations some have against the Runnymede Report's analysis of Islamophobia, most scholars agree that its definition continues to serve as the starting point for most studies and discussions of anti-Muslim prejudice.

For these reasons, I will follow the Runnymede Report in defining Islamophobia as "dread or hatred of Islam" and "fear or dislike of all or most Muslims."[26] However, in light of some of the concerns discussed in this chapter, I wish to clarify my use of this term throughout the book by addressing two key points. First, I will use Islamophobia interchangeably with anti-Muslim and anti-Islam bigotry and hostility because I believe that Muslims do experience exclusion and discrimination based on their real or perceived religious identities. Second, my use of the term will assume that it reflects bigotry rooted in cultural racism in addition to perceived religious differences. Race and religion are inextricably intertwined in Islamophobic discourse and actions, and in most of the examples of Islamophobia that I use in this book, I will make no attempt to argue that they are reflections of

---

26. Commission on British Muslims, *Islamophobia*, 1.

only one or the other. With this in mind, let us turn our attention to the origins of anti-Muslim hostility in the West.

2

———

The Historical Foundations of Islamophobia

What is the relationship between Islamophobia today and the anxieties toward Islam that have characterized much of Western history? How and why have hostilities toward Islam developed in Western history, and why does this matter for any contemporary study of Islamophobia? In this chapter, I survey European constructions of Islam from the Middle Ages through the Enlightenment in order to get at these questions and to connect the dots between present-day Islamophobia and the historical forces that have helped give rise to it.

If the following historical overview demonstrates anything, it is that both discontinuity and continuity characterize the link between premodern and modern hostilities toward Islam. The most obvious discontinuity involves the overt theological interpretations of Islam at work in the Middle Ages, such as the common medieval conviction that Islam was a form of Christian heresy. By the time we reach the modern era, Western critics are much less concerned with demonizing Islam in order to promote and protect a particular version of orthodox Christianity. An important continuity pertains to the political rationale behind presenting Muslims as the ultimate enemies. From the Middle Ages to the twenty-first century, the West has feared Muslims because it has seen them as significant obstacles and threats to the building and preservation of Western empires and nations. Put simply, Western perceptions of Muslims as religious and political rivals drive most of the antagonistic renderings of Islam throughout history, with political rationales increasingly dominating religious ones in the modern period.

The Rise of Islam: Conquests and Reconquests

Muhammad (570–632) is considered by Muslims to be the last and greatest of a series of prophets dating back to Adam and including Abraham, Moses, and Jesus. He received his first revelation from God in a cave near Mecca in 610 and eventually became the leader of Muslims in Mecca, Medina, and all of Arabia.

The earliest negative images of Islam among European Christians developed as the Islamic empire spread and posed a political and military threat to Christian domains. Islam arose in the early seventh century under the leadership of Muhammad. According to Islamic tradition, Muhammad received his first revelation from Allah via the angel Gabriel in a cave outside of Mecca around 610. This event marked the first of many revelations that Muhammad would receive in the course of his lifetime.

These revelations would eventually be recorded in written form in Arabic and become the basis of Islam's most authoritative sacred text: the Qur'an. The Qur'an would affirm Muhammad's status as the last and greatest of a series of prophets dating back to the first human being, Adam, and including prominent figures in Judaism and Christianity such as Abraham, Moses, and Jesus. Muhammad preached, and the Qur'an confirmed, that Allah sent these previous prophets to guide humanity in accordance with the divine will but that many failed to heed their message or otherwise misinterpreted it. Muhammad functioned as Allah's final messenger to help steer humanity back to what is referred to in the Qur'an as "the straight path."[1]

Allah: the Arabic word for God.

Muhammad encountered enough resistance to his message in Mecca that he and his followers were forced to flee to Medina in 622, an event known in Islam as the *hijra*, or migration. Muhammad eventually took control of Mecca, and, by the time of his death in 632, much of the Arabian Peninsula had embraced the teachings of Islam. Muhammad's successors built on his success and expanded the scope and influence of Islam. By the mid-eighth century, Islam encompassed much of Central Asia, Afghanistan, Pakistan, North Africa, and Spain. More importantly for our purposes, within the span of approximately one century, a

hijra: the journey from Mecca to Medina by Muhammad and his followers in 622.

---

1. Qur'an 1:6. All English translations (traditionally referred to in Islam as interpretations) of the Qur'an cited throughout this chapter come from *The Qur'an*, trans. M. A. S. Abdel Haleem (Oxford: Oxford University Press, 2005).

considerable portion of what had once been the Christian Roman Empire had fallen into Muslim hands.

Muslims did not have a monopoly on conquering strategic territories. As Islam enveloped Christian lands, European rulers and church leaders responded with calls for crusades and conquests.[2] Pope Urban II ordered the First Crusade in 1095. This crusade was initially in response to the plea for aid from the Byzantine emperor as he sought to fight off invading Seljuk Turks, but the crusade eventually focused on taking Jerusalem and the Holy Land from Muslim hands. In 1099, Jerusalem fell to Christian armies. These armies slaughtered almost all of the Jews and Muslims in the city and subsequently established the Kingdom of Jerusalem. In the course of the First Crusade, European Christian armies founded three additional states. Holding onto the great prize, Jerusalem, proved to be quite difficult for the Christian conquerors. Much of the kingdom would be conquered less than a century later by the prominent Muslim general and sultan, Saladin.

> **Crusades: military campaigns sponsored by European rulers and church leaders to conquer or retake territory from Muslims in the Holy Land (Israel and Palestine) during the Middle Ages.**

The First Crusade was followed by many others, often prompted by Muslim conquests of territory held by European Christian powers.

---

2. For brief overviews of the Crusades in the context of their impact on Muslim-Christian relations, see Rollin Armour, *Islam, Christianity, and the West: A Troubled History* (Maryknoll, NY: Orbis, 2002), 61–79; Hugh Goddard, *A History of Christian-Muslim Relations* (Chicago: New Amsterdam Books, 2000), 84–92; Jonathan Riley-Smith, *The Crusades, Christianity, and Islam* (New York: Columbia University Press, 2008). See also Jill N. Claster, *Sacred Violence: The European Crusades to the Middle East, 1095–1396* (Toronto: University of Toronto Press, 2009); Thomas Asbridge, *The Crusades: The Authoritative History of the War for the Holy Land* (New York: Ecco, 2011).

Most of these crusades were failures. By the end of the thirteenth century, the last significant European stronghold in the Holy Land, Acre, had fallen into Muslim hands.

If Christian gains in the East during the Crusades were somewhat temporary, more lasting success against Muslim forces was found in the West in a series of victories often referred to in Western history as the Reconquista, or "Reconquest." In the Iberian Peninsula, where Muslims had acquired considerable territory from Christians by the eighth century, one Muslim stronghold after another fell to Christian kingdoms and forces beginning in the late eleventh century. Toledo fell in 1085, and, after slow advances by Christians in the twelfth century, other cities rapidly came under Christian control in the thirteenth century, including Cordoba (1236) and Seville (1248). Eventually, all that was left to Muslim rule was the Kingdom of Granada, which finally fell to Isabella of Castile and Ferdinand of Aragon in 1492.[3]

> **Reconquista: the conquering of Muslim states in the Iberian Peninsula by Christian forces in the Middle Ages.**

The struggles for territory and political power set the stage for Muslim-Christian relations in the Middle Ages, but what impact did these power struggles have on Christians living under Muslim rule and vice versa? Both Muslim and Christian rulers devised ways of dealing with religious minorities. In the case of Muslim rule, the Qur'an did not establish clear parameters for how to govern non-Muslims, though it did prohibit Muslims from coercing the "People of the Book" (*ahl al-kitab*)—that is, Jews and Christians—to convert to

---

3. Joseph F. O'Callaghan, *Reconquest and Crusade in Medieval Spain* (Philadelphia: University of Philadelphia Press, 2003); Ira M. Lapidus, *A History of Islamic Societies* (Cambridge: Cambridge University Press, 2002), 309–18.

People of the Book: a reference in the Qur'an primarily to Jews and Christians, both of whom possessed revealed texts and worshipped the God of Abraham.

dhimmi: protected minorities, particularly Jews and Christians, under Islamic law.

jizya: a special tax paid by dhimmis in return for protection by Muslim rulers.

Islam.[4] Islamic law, or Sharia, would eventually elaborate on the place of protected minorities, known as *dhimmis*. Dhimmis consisted primarily of Jews and Christians. They were required to pay a special tax known as the *jizya*.[5] The tax represented the dhimmis' acknowledgment of their subjugation, but it also guaranteed that their Muslim rulers would protect them and give them considerable legal and religious freedoms. Restrictions, however, were imposed on dhimmis. For example, Muslim men could marry Jewish or Christian women, but Jewish and Christian men were not allowed to marry Muslim women.

Nevertheless, most Muslim rulers granted freedom of worship to dhimmis, even if from one region to the next there were variations in other kinds of religious freedom, such as the ability to build new churches or to display religious symbols such as crosses publicly.

The restrictions placed on non-Muslim minorities may strike modern readers as intolerant, but, in fact, Jews and many dissident Christians in portions of the Byzantine and Persian Empires often

---

4. "There is no compulsion in religion" (Qur'an 2:256).
5. The necessity for "People of the Book" to pay the *jizya* is referenced already in Qur'an 9:29.

enjoyed greater freedoms under Islam than under imperial Christianity. As scholar of Islam Frances Peters notes:

> The conquests destroyed little: what they did suppress were imperial rivalries and sectarian bloodletting among the newly subjected population. The Muslims tolerated Christianity but they disestablished it; henceforth Christian life and liturgy, its endowments, politics, and theology, would be a private not a public affair. By an exquisite irony, Islam reduced the status of Christianity to that which the Christians had earlier thrust upon the Jews, with one difference. The reduction in Christian status was merely judicial; it was unaccompanied by either systematic persecution or blood lust and generally, though not everywhere and at all times, unmarred by vexatious behavior.[6]

In the context of the early history of Muslim–Christian encounters, Islam, not Christianity, often proved more accepting of religious diversity.

Christians in the Iberian Peninsula became subject to Muslim rule already in the eighth century. Muslims in Europe found themselves in a similar position beginning in the eleventh and twelfth centuries as Christians conquered Sicily and then ultimately the Iberian Peninsula. In most cases, Christian rulers created a status for Muslims similar to the standing of dhimmis in Muslim territories, including similar legal and religious freedoms. Muslims typically had the ability to practice their religion, but they could not have power over Christians in everyday life, and, like the dhimmis in Muslim lands, they faced severe restrictions in marrying or engaging in sexual relations with Christians. It was also common to pay a tax similar to the jizya, and in the case of the Norman conquest of Sicily in the eleventh century, Norman rulers actually continued to use the Arabic word for this tax.

---

6. Francis E. Peters, "The Early Muslim Empires: Umayyads, Abbasids, Fatimids," in *Islam: The Religious and Political Life of a World Community*, ed. Marjorie Kelly (New York: Praeger, 1984), 79.

Muslim-Christian Collaboration

This brief overview of the rise of Islam and the battles between Muslims and Christians can give the impression that relations between the two were characterized only by conflict and confrontation. Not always. Collaborative endeavors and beneficial exchanges also took place between Muslims and Christians. Two examples illustrate this point. First, in the larger cities of Muslim Spain, such as Cordoba, Seville, and Toledo, authorities established close working relationships with Christian bishops and other prelates, many of whom became significant figures in the courts of Muslim rulers. Despite their minority status, Christians were not prevented from rising high in the ranks of the government, and instances of Muslims doing the same in Christian kingdoms also exist. Such collaboration and cooperation was not limited to government officials but even took place among the rank and file. For example, in Cordoba, Muslims and Christians shared worship space for a time in the Cathedral of Cordoba.[7]

A second illustration of more positive interactions and influences between the two religions pertains to the rise of Islamic sciences and philosophy. During the Abbasid Caliphate in eighth- and ninth-century Iraq, a theological movement known as Mu'tazilism arose that emphasized the importance of reason and human intellect in acquiring a true knowledge of God and the natural world. This theology created an atmosphere of intellectual inquiry and innovation that lasted for centuries and generated a significant exchange of knowledge between the Islamic and European worlds.

---

7. John Tolan, "*Dhimmis* and Mudejars," in *Europe and the Islamic World: A History*, ed. John Tolan, Gilles Veinstein, and Henry Laurens (Princeton: Princeton University Press, 2013), 51–52.

One of the greatest exchanges was of translations of scientific and philosophical texts from antiquity. Thanks to the efforts of Muslim scholars, the writings of Plato, Aristotle, Galen, and Hippocrates became widely accessible to medieval European scholars for the first time.

The impact of the Islamic world on the development of Europe extended well beyond transmitting and translating ancient texts. European science, mathematics, art, architecture, literature, philosophy, and theology all drew inspiration from Islamic and Arab sources. Abū Bakr Muhammad ibn Zakariyya al-Rāzi authored *Liber continens*, one of the most frequently used and respected medical textbooks in Europe during the Middle Ages. Abū Ali al-Hassan ibn al-Haytham corrected ancient theories of vision that had been developed by the likes of Euclid and Ptolemy, arguing that vision is possible because of the refraction of light through the lenses of the eyes. Abū Abdullah Muhammad ibn Mūsa al-Khwārizmi contributed to the formation of a distinctive mathematical discipline now known as algebra; the word *algebra* is Arabic for "restoration" or "completion" and is found in the title of al-Khwārizmi's widely circulated book *The Compendium on Calculation by Restoration and Balancing*. The Romanesque architecture of churches in southern France adopted forms and techniques from Islamic architecture, such as horseshoe arches and the incorporation of ceramic in the building materials. Fables and stories of Arab origin inspired authors from Geoffrey Chaucer to Miguel de Cervantes.[8] The Muslim philosopher Abū al-Walīd Muhammad ibn Ahmad ibn Rushd, referred to simply as Averroës in European writings, developed a series of commentaries

8. Jim al-Khalili, *The House of Wisdom: How Arabic Science Saved Ancient Knowledge and Gave Us the Renaissance* (New York: Penguin, 2011); Jonathan Lyons, *The House of Wisdom: How the Arabs Transformed Western Civilization* (New York: Bloomsbury, 2009); John Tolan, "On the Shoulders of Giants: Transmission and Exchange of Knowledge," in Tolan, Veinstein, and Laurens, *Europe and the Islamic World*, 87–107.

on Aristotle's works that paved the way for Aristotelian thought to serve as an important source of philosophical and theological reflection. Indeed, the most influential Christian theologian of the Middle Ages, Thomas Aquinas, engaged Averroës's philosophy deeply, even if he was critical of it.

The list of Islamic influences on European thought and culture is quite extensive. This list illustrates that there is no *inherent* conflict between the West and Islam. If anything, the West would not be the West apart from Islamic and Arab contributions. It is also clear that, in the course of the Middle Ages, the violent struggles for power and territory left their mark on how European Christians imagined Muslims. It is within this context that Christian constructions of the Muslim "Other" in the Middle Ages must be understood.

Muslims in the Medieval Christian Imagination

The previous section used the terms *Islam* and *Muslim* without reservation. Yet medieval Christian authors did not use these terms, referring to Muslims by ethnic or quasi-biblical designations: Arabs, Turks, Moors, Ishmaelites, and Hagarenes. The most common designation, Saracens, a word of uncertain etymology, predated the rise of Islam and initially referred to Arabs. By the Middle Ages, Christian authors applied the term to all Muslims, though it was not a designation that Muslims used to describe or define themselves.[9]

> **Saracen: a term commonly used in medieval Europe to refer to Muslims.**

9. John V. Tolan, *Saracens: Islam in the Medieval European Imagination* (New York: Columbia University Press, 2002), xv. The word *Islam* first came into use in French in 1697, in English by 1818. The word *Muslim* was in use by the sixteenth and seventeenth centuries in French

In the earliest encounters between Christians and Muslims, the lack of awareness about Islam is easily explained. Christians simply did not show much curiosity in learning about Islam because most Christian authors initially viewed Muslims as a scourge sent from God to punish Christians for their sins. Dionysus of Tel-Mahre, a ninth-century Syrian patriarch, viewed the Muslim invasions of Syria as God's punishment of the Byzantine church for embracing Dyophysite theology—that is, the belief put forth by the Council of Chalcedon in 451 that Jesus consists of two distinct natures, divine and human, united in one person. There was no shortage of Byzantine theologians to adopt the flip side of the coin and maintain that God was punishing the Monophysites, those who rejected the Chalcedonian position and insisted on the divine and human natures merging into one nature in the person of Jesus. Both sides shared in common the hope that God might lift the scourge if genuine repentance ensued.[10] Few thought it worth the trouble to study the religious beliefs of Muslims in order to find relief from divine chastisement.

One sees the same phenomenon in the earliest encounters between Christians and Muslims in the West. As Muslims conquered vast portions of Spain, Christians viewed their conquerors as a punishment from God for their sins. The problem was with Christians, and therefore the solution, repentance, could only be found within the Christian community. It was only after a significant number of Christians converted to Islam that Christian authors began to view Muslims not simply as God-ordained military adversaries but as religious rivals.[11]

---

and English respectively. See John Tolan, Gilles Veinstein, and Henry Laurens, "General Introduction," Tolan, Veinstein, and Laurens, *Europe and the Islamic World*, 3.
10. Tolen, *Saracens*, 40.
11. Ibid., 71–72.

Christian authors in Spain and in the East quickly came to see Islam as a form of heresy, but it took time for this approach to take root in much of Europe. In the interim, many Latin chroniclers and Western theologians developed the view that the Saracens were pagans who bore a striking resemblance to the Roman idolaters of antiquity against which the earliest generations of Christians struggled. This construction of Islam as paganism was particularly prominent around the time of the First Crusade, serving as one of the major propagandistic tools used by crusaders to justify their efforts to conquer the Holy Land. The struggles of ancient Christians against Roman idolaters were now replicated in the battles waged by Christians against Saracen pagans. Crusaders could find comfort in knowing that the risks they undertook were not in vain but were part of an ongoing battle in Christian history to eradicate those enemies of Christ who worshipped false gods and idols.[12]

A French epic poem from the twelfth century, *The Song of Antioch*, provides us with a clear example of how a Christian author portrayed Saracens as pagans to justify the actions of the First Crusade, particularly the conquest of Antioch.[13] In the poem, the author implicates both the pagans of Rome and the Jews for the crucifixion of Jesus. With Saracens serving as contemporary stand-ins for Roman pagans, they, along with Jews, must be defeated in the name of Christ and for the sake of divine vengeance. The author even appropriates the figure of Muhammad into the Saracen pagan cult. Muhammad takes the form of an idol named Mahomes, suspended in midair by magnets. When the Saracen general, Sansadoines, is defeated, he destroys the idol, demonstrating in the process how powerless Mahomes was to protect the Saracens from defeat. Sansadoines goes on to predict that Christian armies will "break the walls and palisades

12. Ibid., 105–6, 120–21.
13. For a summary of the *Chanson d'Antioche*, see ibid., 120–23.

of Mieque [Mecca], will take Mahomet down from the pedestal where he is placed, [and will take] the two candelabra that sit there."[14] Given that Mecca serves as the cultic center of the Saracens, the city's defeat would mark the demise of paganism.

With the victories of the First Crusade, Christians came into closer contact with Muslims and learned that Muslims were not pagan idolaters but monotheists. Chronicles written during later crusades devoted much less attention to portrayals of Saracens as idolaters. Nonetheless, the image of the Saracen pagan lives on in the European imagination. Festivals of Moors and Christians take place to this day in small towns throughout contemporary Spain. These festivals commemorate Christian victories over the Moors, or Muslims of North African origin, during the Reconquista. Some of these festivals include reenactments in which locals, dressed up as Moors, conquer a citadel and erect a *Mahoma*—an effigy of Muhammad—on the walls. Christian troops then attack the citadel and destroy the Mahoma.[15] The reenactment taps into visions of Saracen idolaters from long ago.

The depiction of Muslims as pagans and idolaters ultimately gave way after the First Crusade to the belief that Islam was a form of Christian heresy. This perception, prominent by the twelfth century, actually found expression already in the first century of Christianity's encounter with Islam in the writings of John of Damascus. John was an eighth-century theologian from Syria who spent part of his career serving in the government of Caliph Abd al-Malik in Damascus before resigning his post and joining the St. Sabbas Monastery near Jerusalem. He is best known for his defense of the use of icons and images in Christian worship over against those who wanted to destroy images out of fear that Christians were worshipping them. The prominent place that the veneration of icons has held historically

14. Quoted in ibid., 122.
15. Ibid., 133.

in Eastern Orthodox Christianity since the eighth century is due in part to John's theological defense of them.

John was much more concerned with iconoclasm, the destruction of icons, than with Islam, but he was still one of the earliest Christian thinkers to develop the view of Islam as a heretical version of Christianity. He was able to articulate this position in part because he possessed a greater knowledge of Islam than those authors who presented Islam either as a divine scourge or as some form of paganism. This greater knowledge is understandable given several factors: the likelihood that he was educated with Muslims as a child, his status as a religious minority who needed to learn about the Muslim majority to negotiate his own religious identity, and the position he held in a Muslim administration.[16]

A primary source for John's views on Islam can be found in a short chapter called "On the Heresy of the Ishmaelites," in his *Fount of Knowledge*. In it, he describes Islam as "the superstition of the *Ishmaelites* which to this day prevails and keeps people in error, being a forerunner of the Antichrist."[17] John notes that these descendants of Ishmael, Abraham's firstborn son through his servant Hagar, are also known as Saracens and, once upon a time, used to be idolaters. Things changed with the rise of a false prophet named Muhammad: "This man, after having chanced upon the Old and New Testaments and likewise, it seems, having conversed with an Arian monk, devised his own heresy. Then, having insinuated himself into the good graces of the people by a show of seeming piety, he gave out that a certain book had been sent down to him from heaven. He had set down some ridiculous compositions in this book of his and he gave it to them as an object of veneration."[18] John links Muhammad to

16. Goddard, *A History of Christian-Muslim Relations*, 38.
17. John of Damascus, *On Heresies*, in *Saint John of Damascus: Writings*, trans. Frederic H. Chase Jr. (New York: Fathers of the Church, 1958), 153.

Arius, a Christian priest from the fourth century. Arius espoused the belief that Jesus was a creature, albeit a perfect creature, and not the eternal Son of God and divine second person of the Trinity. The Council of Nicaea condemned Arius's views in 325, and thereafter most church leaders and theologians deemed Arianism a heresy, even if Arian churches persisted into the sixth century. John believes that Muhammad's views of Jesus bear a striking resemblance to the older Arian position, and he notes how Muslims label Christians "*Hetaeriasts*, or *Associators*, because, they say, we introduce an associate with God by declaring Christ to be the Son of God and God."[19]

The Muslim understanding of Jesus' relationship to God is not the only sticking point for John. He finds fault with the Muslim view that Jesus was not actually crucified and derides the claim that the Qur'an is a divinely revealed book. He also accuses Muslims of engaging in idolatry in their veneration of the Ka'ba, a cubic structure in Mecca and one of Islam's most sacred sites. Finally, he laments the implications for women in Muhammad's teaching, criticizing the Prophet for allowing polygamy, concubinage, and divorce.[20]

Ka'ba: a cubic structure in Mecca and one of Islam's most sacred sites; Muslims face toward the Ka'ba in daily prayers.

John is one of the first significant theologians to possess a fairly accurate knowledge of Islam based on firsthand familiarity with Islam's sacred texts. He correctly recalls important Islamic beliefs, such as the oneness of God, Jesus as the Word of God and a prophet, Jesus'

18. Ibid.
19. Ibid., 155.
20. Ibid., 156–57.

miraculous birth, the denial of Jesus' crucifixion, the Qur'an as God's revelation to humanity, and so forth. A greater knowledge of Islam, however, does not make him a more benevolent interpreter of Islam. John's agenda is not to provide an impartial description of Islam but to assist Christians who, as dhimmis, need help in their efforts to survive the pervasive claims of Islam and to resist the impulse to convert.[21] The more Christians can see Islam as a perversion of the Christian gospel, the better equipped they will be to maintain steadfastness in the faith.

The view that Islam was a Christian heresy would eventually take root in the West as well. It began in ninth-century Spain where Christians, like their coreligionists in John's Syria, had been forced into the role of dhimmis. In this subservient role, they became more familiar with the beliefs and practices of their rulers.

The most prominent example of Christian writers in Spain adopting a hostile and very public view of Islam as a heresy is the martyrs' movement in Cordoba in the 850s. According to a Cordoban priest, Eulogius, another priest named Perfectus responded to Muslim inquires about how Jesus compared to Muhammad by stating that Muhammad was one of the false prophets predicted in the Gospels who was "seduced by demonic illusions, devoted to sacrilegious sorcery . . . [and who] corrupted with his deadly poison the hearts of many idiots and condemned them to eternal perdition."[22] Perfectus succeeded in offending his Muslim interlocutors, but they let him go without punishment. Several days later, he was summoned by a Muslim judge and asked to recant and convert. Perfectus responded by repeating his insults of Muhammad, and, for this, he was sentenced to death.

21. Tolan, *Saracens*, 54–55.
22. Quoted in ibid., 87.

Other Christians, mostly monks, followed Perfectus's example and made public denouncements of Muhammad and Islam in order to bring about martyrdom. Their deaths at the hands of the Muslim authorities solidified the martyrs' movement and found theological support from Eulogius and his friend Paul Alvarus, who saw in Muhammad a manifestation of the Antichrist and the fulfillment of predictions found in Revelation. But the movement was controversial among church leaders in the city who deemed the quest for martyrdom unnecessarily provocative. A church council condemned the movement in 852.[23]

Both John of Damascus and supporters of the Cordoba martyrs were ahead of their time in how they constructed Islam. Particularly in Western Europe, images of Muslims as idolaters prevailed through the First Crusade, but by the twelfth century most Christian authors writing about Islam began adopting the basic presuppositions found centuries earlier in Eastern Christianity and in Spain: Islam was a form of Christian heresy; Muhammad was the quintessential heresiarch. One of the best examples of a prominent, twelfth-century Christian author articulating this approach is Peter the Venerable, abbot of the Cluny monastery in France. Like John, Peter developed his views of Muslims by studying the sacred texts of Islam, though Peter had to commission a Latin translation of the Qur'an in order to gain access to it.[24]

Peter draws a conclusion about Muhammad that is similar to John's, that Muhammad is best understood as following in the line of heretics in the early church: "Vomiting forth almost all of the

23. Ibid., 90.
24. The medieval theologian Robert of Ketton was the one commissioned by Peter to translate the Qur'an into Latin. His translation made the text available to a broader scholarly audience for the first time in the West. See Maxime Rodinson, *Europe and the Mystique of Islam* (Seattle: University of Washington Press, 1987), 13–15; and R. W. Southern, *Western Views of Islam in the Middle Ages* (Cambridge, MA: Harvard University Press, 1962), 37–38.

excrement of the old heresies (which he had drunk up as the devil poured it out), he denies the Trinity with Sabellius, with Nestorius he rejects the divinity of Christ, with Mani he disavows the death of the Lord, though does not deny that he returned to heaven."[25] All of the figures listed by Peter were labeled heretics by early church theologians. A detailed elaboration of their particular teachings is not really necessary to grasp Peter's overall argument. He insisted that many of the basic core beliefs preached by Muhammad originate with the thoughts and writings of those long ago condemned by church leaders. He includes other heretics beyond the ones listed above, including Arius, to drive home the point that Islam's foundation rests not on divine revelation but on heretical perversions of Christian doctrine.

Many other medieval Christian theologians hold views of Islam that echo John's or Peter's. For instance, Thomas Aquinas argued that Muhammad "did . . . corrupt almost all the teachings of the Old and New Testaments by a narrative replete with fables."[26] However, we find little innovation in the approaches of most medieval theologians beyond Peter. Their arguments often replicate some variation of Islam as a heresy that must be refuted and resisted at all costs.

What purposes did these medieval Christian constructions of Islam serve? Christians increasingly saw in Islam a formidable threat to Christianity's claims of superiority and hegemony in Europe and beyond. Faced with the Muslim world's competing theological claims, impressive military accomplishments, expanding empire, and superior intellectual and scientific advancements, medieval Christian authors responded polemically and aggressively. In the context of the Crusades and the Reconquista, theologians depicted Islam initially as idolatry and ultimately as heresy in order to justify violence and

25. Quoted in Tolan, *Saracens*, 158.
26. Quoted in ibid., 242–43.

aggression against Muslims. In those circumstances in which Christians lived under Muslim rule, these same depictions were aimed at providing Christian dhimmis with the ideological tools to resist converting to Islam or, in the case of ninth-century Cordoba, to embrace martyrdom. By the end of the Middle Ages, centuries of military aggression, political hostility, and anti-Muslim discourse had taken their toll. Muslims became the feared "Other" in the European Christian imagination.

The Renaissnace, the Reformation, and the Turkish Threat

Historians often set the Middle Ages apart from the cultural, political, religious, and intellectual changes taking place beginning in the fourteenth and fifteenth centuries with the Renaissance and continuing in the sixteenth century with the Reformation. With the Renaissance, we encounter a strong desire to return "to the sources" (*ad fontes*) of Greek and Roman antiquity and to apply insights from these sources to literature, art, music, politics, and theology. With the Reformation, we come face-to-face with a theological movement that began in 1517 with Martin Luther, a then unknown Augustinian monk in Wittenberg, Germany, and resulted in permanent divisions within Western Christianity that pitted various Protestant communities against the Catholic Church and even against one another.

> **Renaissance: a cultural movement in Europe dating from the fourteenth century that drew inspiration from ancient Greek and Latin sources in the areas of art, literature, religion, and politics.**

Reformation: a theological movement that began under Martin Luther in 1517 that resulted in a permanent break in Western Christianity between Roman Catholicism and Protestantism.

Both the Renaissance and Reformation marked significant changes and innovations in European thought, but in the context of the topic at hand, we find very little that is new. Many thinkers in these movements continued to recycle images and stereotypes of Muslims and Islam that circulated during the Middle Ages. The historian Gilles Veinstein observes that theologians in this period "were not generally better informed, or more nuanced in their criticisms, or more sophisticated in their arguments than their medieval predecessors."[27] What did change was the political backdrop against which anti-Muslim rhetoric took place, and, for this reason, it is worthwhile to survey briefly the changing political circumstances in Europe in relation to Muslims.

The Rise of the Ottoman Empire

The end of the Middle Ages witnessed the emergence of three major Muslim empires: the Mughal Empire in India, the Safavid Empire in Iran, and the Ottoman Empire in Turkey. The Ottoman Empire was the most powerful and long lasting of the three. Eventually stretching over three continents, it came to symbolize the great external and even internal Muslim threat to Christian Europe.

27. Gilles Veinstein, "Antagonistic Figures," *Europe and the Islamic World*, 163.

The Ottoman Empire arose from modest beginnings in the late thirteenth century within a small Turkish principality under the leadership of Osman I. Osman and his sons were able to expand their territory quickly in the course of the fourteenth century. Constantinople, the capital of the Byzantine Empire and the center of Eastern Orthodox Christianity, fell to

The Ottoman Empire was the most powerful Islamic empire of the early modern period and posed the greatest military threat to Christian Europe. The empire gave way to the Republic of Turkey in 1923.

Ottoman forces in 1453. The Ottoman Empire continued its expansion into Europe into the sixteenth century, and, under the reign of Suleyman the Magnificent from 1520 to 1566, the empire reached the zenith of its power. Suleyman led an unsuccessful siege against Vienna in 1529 but nonetheless alarmed many political and religious leaders who worried that the Ottomans could conceivably conquer much of Christian Europe. We now know that the siege on Vienna marked the limits of Ottoman military power in Europe. Over a century later, in 1683, another siege of Vienna would also fail, and many historians mark this as a significant turning point in the Ottoman retreat from Europe. But, before this decline, the Ottoman Empire had managed to encompass territory within Europe that stretched from Hungary in the north to Greece in the south, and much in between.

The preoccupation with the rapid advancement of the Ottoman Empire in this period makes it understandable why medieval references to Muslims as "Saracens" or "Ishmaelites" gave way to the almost ubiquitous designation of "Turks."[28] Christian authors frequently invoked the problem of "the Turkish threat" in order to rally support for crusades or wars against the Ottomans, but, as we shall see, the designation of "Turk" also functioned to denigrate one's opponents in other Christian communities. The term, like its medieval predecessors, had ethnic, political, and religious dimensions.

Reformation Views on Islam

Despite the changing political and religious conditions, very little emerged in Christian writings of the Renaissance and Reformation that reflected innovation in the way that Muslims were understood, nor was much energy expended in learning more about Islam than what was known in the Middle Ages. Renaissance humanists such as Erasmus of Rotterdam and Thomas More certainly paid attention to the Turks, but they did not really study or engage Islamic texts and traditions with any seriousness. Most of their writings on the Turks supported Christians going to war against them, even as both authors were much more cautious when it came to acts of violence against other Christians.[29]

Most Reformation theologians expressed alarm at the Turkish threat, but few demonstrated any extensive knowledge of Islam or concern with the sacred texts of Muslims. John Calvin's engagement with Islam is typical. He possessed a fairly generic knowledge of Islam that followed closely in the footsteps of his medieval predecessors. Calvin knew that the Turks believed in the one creator God, rejected the divinity of Christ, and claimed that Muhammad had received his revelations from God. He was also aware that the Qur'an contained

28. While *Turk* was the most frequently employed designation in the sixteenth century, *Saracen* and other older terms continued to be used. Adam Francisco, *Martin Luther and Islam: A Study in Sixteenth-Century Polemics* (Leiden: Brill, 2007), 54.

29. Tomaz Mastnak, "Europe and the Muslims: The Permanent Crusade?," in *The New Crusades: Constructing the Muslim Enemy*, ed. Emran Qureshi and Michael A. Sells (New York: Columbia University Press, 2003), 215–16.

many of the beautiful names for God that Muslims used in worship and that it allowed for the possibility of taking multiple wives. But Calvin's knowledge of the Qur'an and other Muslim sources was cursory at best, and at no point did he really attempt to rectify this.[30]

In the quest to find prominent reformers, Protestant or Catholic, who took the time to learn more about Islam than most of their contemporaries, two figures stand out. Theodore Bibliander, a Swiss theologian, devoted considerable energy to studying the Qur'an. He went to great lengths to publish an edition of the Qur'an in Basel based on the medieval Latin translation that had been commissioned by Peter the Venerable, despite the significant opposition he encountered from the authorities.

Martin Luther, the most towering figure of the Reformation, was a supporter of Bibliander's efforts in Basel and the best example of a theologian who sought to learn more about Islam. Luther studied the Qur'an, albeit in its Latin version, and gave considerable attention to Islam and Muslims based on some of this study. That said, his greater knowledge did not translate into a more benevolent assessment of Islam. Many of his thoughts reflected the medieval prejudices that went before him, and his writings more often than not served to justify violence and aggression against the Turks, just as many medieval Christian constructions of Islam served to authorize violence against Muslims during the Crusades and the Reconquista. In this regard, Luther did not even differ from Erasmus, More, or Calvin, all of whom employed negative images of Muslims to rally support for a war against the Turks.

Earlier in his reforming career, Luther was actually not an advocate of a war with the Turks. He viewed Turkish advances into Europe as a form of divine punishment for the sins of the church, a view

---

30. Jan Slomp, "Calvin and the Turks," in *Christian-Muslim Encounters*, ed. Yvonne Yazbeck Haddad and Wadi Z. Haddad (Gainesville: University Press of Florida, 1995), 126–42.

reminiscent of what we find in Christian writings on Islam in the eighth century: "To fight against the Turks is to oppose the judgment God visits upon our iniquities through them."[31] Luther was particularly opposed to a crusade against the Turks under papal oversight. But things changed in the course of the 1520s as the Ottomans made greater inroads into Europe. By the time of the siege of Vienna in 1529, Luther had changed his mind, supporting a war against the Turks, what he referred to as the *Türkenkrieg*, as long as it was led by princes and not by the church.

In his treatise *On War Against the Turk* (1528), Luther develops more fully his assessment of Islam in the context of justifying a violent response to the Turks. He offers three observations about Islam based on his reading of the Qur'an. First, he argues that Muslims believe that Muhammad is superior to Christ and that Christ, while without sin, is merely a prophet and not humanity's savior. Muhammad undermines the very heart of the Christian faith, leaving his readers with a "doctrine of works" that places Muslims in the same category as Jews and Catholics in rejecting justification by faith. Such a doctrine is the work of the devil.[32]

Luther's second observation is that the Qur'an teaches the Turk "to destroy not only the Christian faith, but also the whole temporal government."[33] The Turks rule by the sword—that is, by force and coercion. "The Turkish faith, then, has not made its progress by preaching and the working of miracles, but by the sword and by murder."[34] Islam is a religion of violence and brutality that has rejected the grace and peace that comes with the gospel of Christ.

31. Quoted in ibid., 218.
32. Martin Luther, *On War Against the Turk*, in *Luther's Works* 46, ed. Robert C. Schultz (Philadelphia: Fortress Press, 1967), 176–78.
33. Ibid., 178.
34. Ibid., 179.

Finally, Luther laments the disregard for marriage and for women in the Qur'an: "It is customary among the Turks for one man to have ten or twenty wives and to desert or sell any whom he will, so that in Turkey women are held immeasurably cheap and are despised; they are bought and sold like cattle."[35] The Turks find warrant in the Qur'an to give into their lavish sexual desires and thus forego God's command in Genesis for one woman and one man to join together as one flesh. The implication is that Christianity respects women by enabling people to channel their sexual impulses through proper marriage whereas Islam denigrates women by allowing these impulses to have free rein.

Gregory Miller summarizes quite graphically Luther's views on Islam in this treatise and elsewhere: "In Luther's language, the Turks were the devil incarnate: inhumanly violent, treacherous, demonically lascivious. The Turks were displayed as grotesque slaughterers of children, beasts who even ripped unborn babies from their mother's wombs."[36] Luther's study of the Qur'an does not lead him to draw radically new conclusions about Islam. In fact, Luther's characterization of Islam as violent, lascivious, barbaric, and hateful toward women both reflects views that can be found in medieval authors and also points ahead to Islamophobic discourses prevalent in the West today.

Luther, like many other Protestant reformers, invoked negative images of Islam not only to garner support for a war against the Turks but also to attack his opponents. Luther was quite fond of tarring both Islam and Catholicism with the same brush. He often used the language of the "Antichrist" when referring to both Muhammad and the pope, though eventually he concluded that the title was more

---

35. Ibid., 181.
36. Gregory Miller, "Luther on the Turks and Islam," *Lutheran Quarterly* 14 (2000): 84.

deserving of the pope. Still, Muhammad and the pope were two sides of the same coin:

> The pope is not much more godly than Mohammed and resembles him extraordinarily; for he, too, praises the gospel and Holy Scripture with his lips, but he holds that many things in it are too hard, and these are the very things Mohammed and the Turks also consider too hard. . . . Therefore, he [the pope], too, does not rule with the gospel, or word of God, but has made a new law and Koran, namely, his decretals, and these he enforces with the ban just as the Turk enforces his Koran with the sword.[37]

Catholic writers had no qualms about returning the favor by linking the Turkish threat with Luther and other reformers. In the words of one Catholic pamphlet from the sixteenth century: "The Turk tears down churches and destroys monasteries—so does Luther, the Turk turns convents into horse stables and makes cannon out of church bells—so does Luther. The Turk abuses and treats lasciviously all female persons, both secular and spiritual. Luther is just as bad for he entices monks and nuns out of their monasteries into false marriages."[38] An exiled English Catholic, William Rainolds, compared John Calvin to Islam in a similarly harsh manner: "Both seek to destroy the Christian faith, both deny the divinity of Christ, not only is the pseudo-Gospel of Calvin no better than the Qur'an of Muhammad, but in many respects it is wickeder and more repulsive."[39]

In most Catholic and Protestant theological writings of the Reformation, we do not encounter efforts to nuance or move beyond medieval depictions of Islam. With the extension of the Ottoman Empire into Europe and the fracturing of Western Christianity in

---

37. Luther, *On War Against the Turk*, 197.
38. Quoted in Frederick Quinn, *The Sum of All Heresies: The Image of Islam in Western Thought* (Oxford: Oxford University Press, 2008), 46.
39. Quoted in ibid.

the Reformation, older medieval constructs of Islam are redeployed to respond to new circumstances. However, the underlying fear in Christian Europe remains the same—fear of the power and expansion of Islamic territories. It is only with the period known as the Enlightenment that we witness some of these fears subside, even if temporarily, while more significant efforts to depict Islam sympathetically come to the fore.

Islam in the Age of Enlightenment

The Enlightenment was a cultural and intellectual movement that arose toward the end of the seventeenth century and reached its apex in the eighteenth century. The movement stressed the primacy of reason in the human quest to acquire knowledge and discover truth. The Enlightenment's emphasis on reason contributed to a climate in which philosophers and intellectuals increasingly attacked traditional Christianity, in both its Protestant and Catholic varieties, as irrational and superstitious.

> **Enlightenment: a cultural and intellectual movement of the seventeenth and eighteenth centuries in the West that emphasized reason.**

Approaches to Islam during the Enlightenment must be understood not only against the background of these philosophical challenges to Christianity but also in light of the changing political fortunes of the Ottoman Empire. As noted in the previous section, by the seventeenth century the Ottoman Empire was in decline and struggling to maintain its foothold in Europe. In the century following the failed siege of Vienna in 1683, Ottoman power in the southern and central regions of Europe faded.

As the military and political threat of the Ottoman Empire diminished, a space was opened for the study of Islam and even the Middle East that was not rooted in religious hostility.[40] In the seventeenth and eighteenth centuries, a greater interest in the study of Arabic and Islam developed. Some European universities sponsored Arabic studies, and a host of histories, dictionaries, and textbooks about Islam and Arab peoples emerged.[41] The pieces were in place for a more nuanced picture of Islam.

The Enlightenment, however, did not witness the abandonment of older prejudices. In both philosophical and popular writings, unflattering images of Muslims and Islam persisted. In fact, we have plenty of examples of Enlightenment philosophers who reiterated negative stereotypes even as they articulated more positive appraisals. A case in point is the French philosopher Pierre Bayle. In his monumental *Historical and Critical Dictionary* (1697), Bayle incorporated several articles pertaining to Islam, including an article on "Mahometanism," a common designation for Islam in his day. On the one hand, his study of Islam leads him to conclude that Muhammad "forged a revelation from God" in order to justify his and other men's lascivious behavior, to the detriment of women: "The permission Mahomet [Muhammad] granted to men to have many wives, and to whip them when they were not obedient, and to divorce them when they were not obedient, and to divorce them upon any displeasure, was a law very prejudicial to the female sex."[42]

On the other hand, Bayle takes issue with Christian critics who insist that Muhammad was a fanatic who manufactured a moral system that across the board accommodated "to the corruption of

40. Ibid, 55–56.
41. Veinstein, "Breaches in the Conflict," in Tolan, Veinstein, and Laurens, *Europe and the Islamic World*, 242–45.
42. Pierre Bayle, "Mahometanism," in *Historical and Critical Dictionary* II (London: Hunt and Clarke, 1826), 251, 258.

men's hearts."[43] Bayle counters by insisting that Islamic law intensifies and magnifies the demands of the Christian Gospels, deviating in only two areas: polygamy and revenge (allowing an eye for an eye).[44] Moreover, Bayle argues that Islam historically has shown itself to be much more tolerant of other religions than Christianity has. He even suggests that had Western Christians instead of Ottoman Turks ruled in the East, both Eastern Orthodox Christianity and Islam would have disappeared, but, as it stands, Muslim rulers have fully tolerated Christianity.[45]

Another thinker of two minds on Islam is the poster child of the French Enlightenment: Voltaire. In his play *Mahomet the Prophet, or Fanaticism: A Tragedy in Five Acts* (1741), Voltaire presents Muhammad as a deceitful, manipulative, hypocritical "merchant of camels," the author of an "unintelligible book which affronts common sense at every page."[46] Voltaire, unlike Bayle, has no problem labeling Muhammad a fanatic who in the name of religion cruelly set out to conquer the world. Voltaire's basic depiction of Muhammad is not intended as a scholarly treatment in the manner of Bayle. His intention in making Muhammad the subject of this play is to provide a veneer behind which to attack Roman Catholicism and potentially all fanatical forms of Christianity in France and Europe. Voltaire's Catholic critics did not miss this subtlety, and, as a result, Voltaire pulled the play from public performances for almost a decade.[47]

In other writings, Voltaire articulated a more positive appraisal of Islam, deeming it a moderate and tolerant religion when compared

43. Ibid., 254.
44. Ibid., 255.
45. Jonathan Israel, *Enlightenment Contested: Philosophy, Modernity, and the Emancipation of Man 1670–1752* (Oxford: Oxford University Press, 2006), 618.
46. Norman Daniel, *Islam and the West: The Making of an Image* (Oxford: Oneworld, 1993), 310–11.
47. Quinn, *The Sum of All Heresies*, 62.

to Christianity. In this regard, he echoed the sentiments expressed by Bayle before him. But these observations did not inspire him to change his views on Islam's founding figure. Voltaire continued to view Muhammad as an imposter who deceived others and who established his religion by force and violence.[48]

If Bayle and Voltaire were somewhat equivocal in their interpretation of Muhammad and Islam, the French author Henri de Boulainvilliers offered one of the more flattering portrayals of the Prophet in the Enlightenment. In *The Life of Muhammad* (1730), Boulainvilliers devotes more energy than most of his contemporaries to describing the Prophet as a man who epitomizes the Enlightenment's commitment to reason and free thought. Muhammad's religion is true in its essentials. Muhammad's thought "conformed to the light of reason" and helped others seek truth and perform good works.[49] Sharing the concern of many other Enlightenment philosophers that appeals to the miraculous in religion undermine reason, Boulainvilliers appreciates how Muhammad "constantly declared and protested that he had no power other than to persuade those who would calmly listen unto him."[50] Boulainvilliers's Muhammad closely resembles an Enlightenment deist—that is, someone who rejects appeals to revelation and the miraculous in favor of belief in one creator God and the importance of morality. While this portrayal does not accurately reflect how Muslims historically have understood the Prophet, it does remind us of the Enlightenment's most important legacy in light of our topic: the introduction of an alternative, more sympathetic narrative

---

48. Daniel, *Islam and the West*, 311–12; Veinstein, "Breaches in the Conflict," 248; Quinn, *Sum of All Heresies*, 63–64.

49. Israel, *Enlightenment Contested*, 616.

50. Quoted in Clinton Bennett, *In Search of Muhammad* (New York: Cassell, 1998), 95.

concerning Islam, one that challenged, even if modestly, medieval stereotypes.

◆ ◆ ◆ ◆ ◆

Sympathetic portrayals of Islam during the Enlightenment may have problematized the medieval narrative, but they did not dislodge it. Islam lived on in the European imagination as a religion rooted in deceit, violence, and misogyny. Even if the theological arguments driving polemical constructions of Islam lost some of their potency by the end of the Enlightenment, they did linger into the modern era. The fear of the Muslim "Other" as an obstacle and threat to European power and hegemony did not fade but rather intensified in the face of Ottoman decline and Europe's increasing interest in colonial expansion in the nineteenth century.

3

Colonialism, Orientalism, and the Clash of Civilizations

The failed siege at Vienna in 1683 marked a turning point in the fortunes of the Ottoman Empire. The empire, which for centuries achieved considerable success in its quest to expand further into Europe, began to decline. The decline was slow, and the full dissolution of the empire would not come about until the end of World War I, with the Republic of Turkey taking its place. During this same period, Western Europe entered a new phase in its history as several nation-states, including Britain, France, and the Netherlands, established colonies that covered much of the globe, from the Americas to Africa and Asia. The age of European colonialism reached its height in the late nineteenth and early twentieth centuries, and, as a result, large numbers of Muslims found themselves subject to the imperial designs and rule of Western nations. As decolonization set in after the mid-twentieth century, the United States embarked on its own imperial project, seeking to wield greater influence over the Middle East than its Cold War rival, the Soviet Union.

The Western drive to build and maintain empires that has shaped so much of its animosity toward Muslims and Islam is a prominent theme connecting this chapter to the previous one. The West's investment in the colonial enterprise colored the ways that Westerners imagined and understood Muslims and Islam. Scholars and politicians frequently depicted a superior and civilized West over an inferior and uncivilized Muslim world. These representations not only dominated the colonial era but, as we shall see in subsequent chapters, set the stage for much of the Islamophobia that has arisen since 9/11.

European Colonialism

Colonialism was not a modern European invention. If we adopt Ania Loomba's definition of colonialism as "the conquest and control of other people's land and goods," we must accept that colonialism, with its accompanying ideology of imperialism, has been a recurring feature in human history.[1] Indeed, the achievements of the Romans, the Mongols, and even the Ottomans were not lost on European colonial powers. Aided in their quest for power and territory by a variety of ideologies, including a sense of racial superiority, a desire to civilize and humanize barbaric peoples, and an impulse to spread the Christian gospel, European nations set out to establish their own colonies near and far.

> **colonialism: the conquest, occupation, and control of another country or land.**

---

1. Ania Loomba, *Colonialism/Postcolonialism* (New York: Routledge, 2005), 8.

European colonization began in earnest with Christopher Columbus's "discovery" of the Americas in his 1492 expedition.[2] The Spanish and Portuguese developed extensive colonial networks in North and South America in the century that followed. By the seventeenth century, they were joined by the British, the French, and the Dutch, among others.

European powers also began extending their reach in the Eastern Hemisphere by the sixteenth century—the Portuguese captured Goa in India in 1510 and Malacca in Malaysia in 1511. The European conquests in both hemispheres were made possible by innovations in seafaring and greater control of shipping lanes. By the eighteenth and nineteenth centuries, the Industrial Revolution provided a boost to European military technologies and capabilities that greatly facilitated colonial projects.

Colonial endeavors left many Muslim-majority territories largely untouched prior to the nineteenth century, though Muslims in regions such as the Indian subcontinent certainly felt the effects of colonialism already in the sixteenth century. With Napoleon's invasion of Egypt in 1798, we witness the beginning of serious European attempts to conquer Muslim lands in North Africa and the Middle East. Napoleon's efforts failed, in part as a result of British intervention, but the French would succeed in invading and occupying Algeria in 1830. Algeria became the first permanent

2. For succinct overviews of European colonialism, particularly within Muslim-majority regions, see Rollin Armour, *Islam, Christianity and the West* (Maryknoll, NY: Orbis Books, 2002), 122–32; Henry Laurens, "The Age of Empire," in *Europe and the Islamic World: A History*, ed. John Tolan, Gilles Veinstein, and Henry Laurens (Princeton: Princeton University Press, 2013), 322–37; Tamara Sonn, *Islam: A Brief History* (Oxford: Wiley-Blackwell, 2010), 113–46. For more extensive treatments of European colonialism, see Robin Butlin, *Geographies of Empire: European Empires and Colonies c. 1880–1960* (Cambridge: Cambridge University Press, 2009); Thomas Benjamin, ed., *Encyclopedia of European Colonialism since 1450* (Detroit: Macmillan Reference, 2007); Muriel E. Chamberlain, *The Longman Companion to the Formation of the European Empires, 1488–1920* (New York: Longman, 2000); H. L. Wesseling, *The European Colonial Empires: 1815–1919* (New York: Pearson, 2004).

European colony in North Africa, and its conquest marked the beginning of a long, tumultuous, and at times bloody conflict between colonizer and colonized. The French made Tunisia and Morocco into protectorates in 1881 and 1912, respectively, and in 1923 the League of Nations gave the mandate for present-day Syria and Lebanon to France.

France's main competitor in the "scramble" for colonies in the nineteenth and twentieth centuries was Britain. Britain's initial colonial expansion into regions with significant Muslim populations was in South and Southeast Asia, including Singapore (1819), Malacca in Malaysia (1824), and India (1858), "the Jewel in the Crown" of the British Empire. By the early twentieth century, Britain's rule extended over much of the Middle East, including Egypt (1914), Transjordan (1921), Iraq (1921), and Palestine (1923).

Other European nations, while lacking the extensive empires of France or Britain, nonetheless participated in the colonization of Muslim regions as well, including the Netherlands in the Dutch East Indies, or Indonesia (1800), and Italy in Eritrea (1882) and Libya (1911). In many cases, long before these regions came under official colonial oversight, European nations exercised considerable economic and imperial influence through enterprises such as the Dutch and British versions of the East India Company.

By the early twentieth century, much of the Muslim world was subject to European rule, with only a handful of states in the Middle East—Iran, Saudi Arabia, Turkey, and Yemen—escaping European colonial domination as the dust settled from World War I.[3] By the 1930s, Europe, along with its colonies and ex-colonies, constituted almost 85 percent of the earth's land surface.[4] To be sure, European

3. Rashid Khalidi, *Resurrecting Empire: Western Footprints and America's Perilous Path in the Middle East* (Boston: Beacon, 2004), 80–81.
4. Loomba, *Colonialism/Postcolonialism*, 3.

governance of and control over colonies varied considerably. To take one example, the British Empire consisted of a variety of territories with different statuses, ranging from dominions to protectorates to mandates, each with its own degree of political and economic dependence or autonomy. Nevertheless, by World War I, European nations exercised considerable political and economic power over much of the world, including the Muslim world.

Decolonization

The building of European empires was never a smooth, linear process of increasing acquisitions. Colonies both changed hands between European nations and slipped through the fingers of European control altogether in the eighteenth and nineteenth centuries. This was particularly the case in the Americas: the British colonies in North America broke off to form the United States at the end of the eighteenth century, and Spain and Portugal lost their grip on colonies in South America in the nineteenth century.

For much of Africa and Asia, including those regions with significant Muslim populations, independence from European colonial masters was largely a mid-twentieth-century phenomenon. The Netherlands, a European power that did not really compete in the scramble

decolonization: the process by which former colonized nations and peoples became independent from the colonial power.

for colonies in the late nineteenth century, maintained its control of an older colony, the Dutch East Indies, until the Indonesian Republic declared independence in 1945. Italy lost control of Libya and Eritrea as a result of World War II. Libya passed initially into the hands of both the British and French before the country declared independence in 1951. Eritrea fell to British oversight briefly before becoming federated with Ethiopia in 1952.

Algeria achieved independence from France in 1962 after a protracted and bloody war initiated by the National Liberation Front in 1954. Morocco and Tunisia had already attained independence in 1956 under less violent circumstances, and Syria and Lebanon had gained independence from France a decade earlier in 1943.

Britain granted independence to India in 1947 and, in the process, partitioned the subcontinent into the separate Muslim and Hindu states of Pakistan and India, respectively. In Southeast Asia, the Federation of Malaya (later Malaysia), formed in 1948, achieved independence in 1957. In the Middle East, Iraq had acquired the status of an independent kingdom already in 1932. The 1940s and 1950s witnessed a series of nations in the region, including Jordan, Egypt, and the Sudan, achieving independence from the British Empire. One significant exception was Palestine. While Britain's mandate over Palestine expired in 1948, Arabs found themselves in a losing battle for the region with the newly formed state of Israel. This story will be elaborated on later in this chapter.

The decolonization of those regions with significant Muslim populations was largely completed by the 1960s. What were the catalysts for decolonization? For the colonizers, the main reasons for relinquishing colonial control included the difficulty of maintaining colonies in light of the financial burdens they incurred during and after the Second World War and the opposition to maintaining colonies by the two new superpowers, the United States and the Soviet Union.[5] Of course, one must take into account the agency of the colonized as well. Most of the colonies discussed here were sites

5. Butlin, *Geographies of Empire*, 577, 592.

of considerable resistance, and nationalist sentiments and movements increased significantly by the mid-twentieth century. In some cases, opposition took the form of armed resistance, such as the war carried out against the French by Algeria's National Liberation Front. In other cases, resistance manifested itself through peaceful advocacy or diplomatic appeals to the United Nations. Either way, resistance among the colonized, combined with the aforementioned economic and political pressures, made it nearly impossible for European nations to maintain control of their far-flung empires by the end of World War II. Decolonization became inevitable.

But decolonization did not result in complete emancipation. The colonial legacy endured beyond the decolonization process. A new era dawned in which many former European colonies, while achieving formal independence, found themselves still economically and politically dependent on European and Western nations. In 1965, Kwame Nkrumah, a political scientist and the president of Ghana, employed the word *neocolonialism* for this new era: "The essence of neo-colonialism is that the State which is subject to it is, in theory, independent and has all the outward trappings of international sovereignty. In reality its economic and thus its political policy is directed from outside."[6] In most instances, according to Nkrumah, the former colonizing power is the nation-state that continues to wield extraordinary influence over the new nation's economic and political affairs, but this need not be the case. Nkrumah cites the example of South Vietnam,

neocolonialism: the practice of a dominant nation controlling or influencing another country by economic or cultural means as opposed to direct political governance.

subject first to French imperial power but by the 1960s subject instead to US neocolonial control.[7] Nkrumah was already pointing to the new imperial realities of the postwar era in which a nation such as the United States could usurp the role of a dominant colonial power without conquering territory or establishing direct political rule over other nations.

The impact of colonialism and neocolonialism on the relationship between Islam and the West should not be underestimated. Many Muslims in the Middle East and in other Muslim-majority regions blame their political and economic struggles today on past as well as present interference from the West. The anti-Western sentiment that one encounters in these countries cannot be understood apart from the legacy of colonialism, just as any adequate analysis of contemporary Western discourse about Muslims and Islam must take into account the West's past and present colonial enterprises and imperial designs in the Muslim world.

The Israeli-Palestinian Conflict

As many formerly colonized regions were rapidly moving toward formal independence in the decades after World War II, one notable exception was Palestine. With the creation of the state of Israel in 1948 and the war that followed, Palestinians found themselves without a state at a time when Muslims throughout North Africa and the Middle East were starting to see some light at the end of the colonial tunnel. Because many Westerners do not view the establishment of modern Israel as a chapter in the history of Western colonialism, it may seem as if this story does not serve the special attention I am giving it here. But for many Palestinians, not to

6. Kwame Nkrumah, *Neo-Colonialism: The Last Stage of Imperialism* (New York: International Publishers, 1965), ix.
7. Ibid., x.

mention other Arabs, the state of Israel represents the continuation of the Western colonial project. This perception can be contested, but, even so, the story of Israel's formation cannot be adequately narrated without paying attention to the role played by Western nations in Palestine in the early to mid-twentieth century.

The modern story of Israel begins in the late nineteenth century with the rise of Zionism. "Zion" is another word for Jerusalem, and, at the time the movement arose, European Jews were starting to look beyond Europe to the real possibility of a permanent home in Palestine. Palestine was the location of the

Zionism: a Jewish nationalist movement with the goal of creating and maintaining a Jewish state in Palestine.

Promised Land, the land that God promised to Abraham and his descendants according to Jewish tradition. Since the sixth century BCE, other empires, from the Babylonians to the Romans to the Ottomans, had occupied and ruled this land. For almost two millennia, observant Jews, living in the diaspora, prayed for the possibility of returning to this land.

As an organized movement, Zionism did not rely heavily on the religious sentiments historically expressed by Jews. Zionism was primarily a secular nationalist movement, and it came about largely through the work Theodor Herzl, a journalist and playwright from Austria-Hungary.[8] Herzl's interests in a Jewish homeland arose from the increasing anti-Semitism that Jews were encountering in Europe, not to mention the many centuries of anti-Judaism leading up to his time. In 1896, Herzl wrote a book called *The Jewish State* in

8. Avi Shlaim, *The Iron Wall: Israel and the Arab World* (New York: Norton, 2001), 2; Rabbi Michael Lerner, *Embracing Israel/Palestine: A Strategy to Heal and Transform the Middle East* (Berkeley, CA: Tikkun Books, 2012), 58–59.

which he laid forth his argument for a Jewish homeland: "The whole plan is in its essence perfectly simple, as it must necessarily be if it is to come within the comprehension of all. Let the sovereignty be granted us over a portion of the globe large enough to satisfy the rightful requirements of a nation; the rest we shall manage for ourselves."[9] Herzl was open to two possibilities for which "portion of the globe" Jews could make into a homeland: Palestine or Argentina. It would not take long for the former to become the focus of Zionist aspirations.

When Herzl wrote *The Jewish State*, Palestine was still part of the Ottoman Empire. The defeat of the Ottomans in World War I resulted in the partitioning of the former empire among the Allies, which led Britain to receive the mandate to govern Palestine in 1923. However, already in 1917 Britain expressed support for a Jewish homeland in Palestine. In a letter written by Britain's foreign secretary, Arthur Balfour, to Walter Rothschild, a leader in Britain's Jewish community, the British government's support was made public: "His Majesty's Government view with favour the establishment in Palestine of a national home for the Jewish people, and will use their best endeavours to facilitate the achievement of this object, it being clearly understood that nothing shall be done which shall prejudice the civil and religious rights of existing non-Jewish communities in Palestine, or the rights and political status enjoyed by Jews in any other country."[10] This statement, known historically as the Balfour Declaration, laid the foundation for British and Western support for a Jewish homeland in Palestine.

In the following decades, two competing nationalisms, Zionism and Palestinian Arab nationalism, intensified, with no clear

9. Theodor Herzl, "The Jewish State," in *The Israel-Arab Reader: A Documentary History of the Middle East Conflict*, ed. Walter Laquer and Barry Rubin (New York: Penguin, 2001), 7.
10. Arthur Balfour, "British Foreign Minister Arthur Balfour: The Balfour Declaration (November 2, 1917)," in Laquer and Rubin, *The Israel-Arab Reader*, 16.

resolution. The immigration of European Jews to Palestine, which increased for clear reasons during the Holocaust, led to even greater tensions between Jews and Palestinians. With the end of World War II, Britain turned the problem of Palestine over to the United Nations (UN). In November 1947, the UN, whose ranks were dominated by Western nations, many of whom were still involved in colonial projects, developed a plan to partition Palestine into three areas: one Jewish state, one Palestinian state, and an international zone under UN supervision that included Jerusalem. The plan was controversial. While the Jewish settlers constituted approximately one-third of the population, the UN plan granted them some 55 percent of the land.[11] The Palestinians rejected the plan, whereas the Provisional State Council of Israel affirmed it and formally declared the establishment of the state of Israel in 1948. In this effort, Israel received considerable international support from many countries outside the Arab world, including the two new superpowers, the United States and the Soviet Union.

Arab nationalism: a twentieth-century political movement focused on uniting Arab peoples based on their common linguistic, cultural, historical, and religious heritage; the movement was a response to the legacy of Western colonialism.

Immediately following Israel's proclamation, armies from Egypt, Transjordan, Syria, and Iraq joined Palestinian militias in attacking Israel. The Arab-Israeli War lasted until 1949, with Israel the major

11. Yoram Meital, *Peace in Tatters: Israel, Palestine, and the Middle East* (Boulder, CO: Lynne Rienner, 2006), 14; Nicholas Guyatt, *The Absence of Peace: Understanding the Israeli–Palestinian Conflict* (New York: Zed Books, 1998), 3; Sonn, *Islam*, 129–30.

victor. Just over seven hundred thousand Palestinians were displaced from their homes and became refugees.[12] Other wars between Israel and Arab nations followed in the decades to come, most notably the Six-Day War of 1967, as did numerous diplomatic efforts to find a peaceful resolution to the ongoing Israeli–Palestinian conflict.

The Six-Day War in June 1967 between Israel and the Arab states of Egypt, Jordan, and Syria resulted in the Israeli occupation of the Gaza Strip, the Sinai Peninsula, the West Bank, East Jerusalem, and the Golan Heights.

Many in the Arab world view the history of this conflict, beginning with Zionism's emergence and continuing long past the establishment of Israel, through the lens of Western colonial exploitation, with Israel serving as a client state of the West in general and the United States in particular. This perception fuels anti-Western and anti-American sentiment throughout the Middle East. Terrorist groups also exploit this perception to justify violence in the region and beyond.

The Rise of Orientalism

It makes perfect sense that as European nations expanded their empires in the nineteenth century, Europeans developed a greater interest in studying the languages, histories, cultures, and religions of colonized peoples. The term *Orientalism* entered into European

---

12. The United Nations estimated 711,000 Palestinian refugees in light of the war. See United Nations Conciliation Commission for Palestine, *General Progress Report and Supplementary Report of the United Nations Conciliation Commission for Palestine* (New York: General Assembly, 1951).

languages by the nineteenth century to describe the scholarly study of the Middle East, North Africa, and Asia.

Tracing Orientalism's origins, particularly Orientalists' focus on the history and relevant languages of Islam, requires going back even further. Serious attention to the academic study of Islam and particularly Arabic took place already in the late sixteenth century. Regular instruction in Arabic began at the College de France in Paris in 1587. In 1613, the University of Leiden in the Netherlands established a chair in the study of Arabic, with Cambridge and Oxford in England following suit in 1632 and 1634, respectively. With the creation of a special school for the study of Oriental languages in France in 1795, the foundations for Orientalism as an academic discipline were well established.[13]

> **Orientalism: a term originally coined to describe the scholarly study of the Middle East, North Africa, and Asia; in postcolonial thought, the term refers to a discourse of power that enables Western empires to rule and have authority over the Orient.**

The nineteenth and twentieth centuries witnessed a flourishing of European scholarship, literature, and art that focused on the Orient. It is important to stress that some Orientalists held great admiration and respect for the Orient and Islam. Thomas Carlyle, a prominent nineteenth-century British author, presented a famous lecture in 1840 on Muhammad. Contradicting the medieval Christian accounts of Muhammad as an imposter and false prophet, Carlyle insisted that Muhammad was a legitimate prophet and indeed a hero, a

---

13. Albert Hourani, *Islam in European Thought* (Cambridge: Cambridge University Press, 1991), 10–13, 32.

person of great vision who instilled hope in millions upon millions of people and whose impact qualified him to hold a place of honor alongside other transformative figures in history, including Martin Luther, Shakespeare, and Frederick the Great.[14]

Many Orientalists, however, developed images of Muslim and Arab peoples that either perpetuated medieval stereotypes or else reflected more contemporary assumptions, bolstered at times by appeals to science, about the intrinsic cultural and even racial superiority of Europeans over Muslims. An example of the latter type of thinking can be found in the work of Ernest Renan, a French philologist and scholar of religion. In many ways, he represented the growing tendency in much of nineteenth-century Orientalism to move away from Enlightenment universalism, which tended to stress commonalities between all human beings (including Muslims), and toward a worldview that emphasized the fundamental differences between civilizations, with Western civilization seen as inherently superior to Islamic civilization.[15]

Renan's 1883 lecture "Islam and Science" reflects these assumptions, though the achievements of the Enlightenment inform his insights as well. Renan portrays Islam as a monolithic religion possessing a fixed essence and set of cultural traits that make it inferior to European civilization:

> All those who have been in the East, or in Africa, are struck by the way in which the mind of a true believer is fatally limited, by the species of iron circle that surrounds his head, rendering it absolutely closed to knowledge, incapable of either learning anything, or of being open to any new idea. From his religious initiation at the age of ten or twelve years, the Mohammedan child, who occasionally may be, up to that

14. Frederick Quinn, *The Sum of All Heresies: The Image of Islam in Western Thought* (Oxford: Oxford University Press, 2008), 105–6.
15. Maxime Rodinson, *Europe and the Mystique of Islam* (Seattle: University of Washington Press, 1987), 60–71; Zachary Lockman, *Contending Visions of the Middle East: The History and Politics of Orientalism* (Cambridge: Cambridge University Press, 2004), 74–78.

time, of some intelligence, at a blow becomes a fanatic, full of a stupid pride in the possession of what he believes to be the absolute truth, happy as with a privilege, with what makes his inferiority. . . . The [Muslim] has the most profound disdain for instruction, for science, for everything that constitutes the European spirit. This bent of mind inculcated by the Mohammedan faith is so strong, that all differences of race and nationality disappear by the fact of conversion to Islam.[16]

Renan depicts Muslims, with the exception of the occasional Muslim child prior to conversion, as lacking reason and intelligence simply by virtue of adhering to Islam. To be a Muslim is by definition to reject "the European spirit" and all that makes this spirit superior: reason, science, and the drive for knowledge. Fanaticism and irrationality constitute the unchanging essence of Islam and the Arab race. For this reason, Renan has no qualms at the end of his lecture in endorsing European military power to subdue "elements of barbarism" among colonized Muslims in light of his belief that science "gives force for the service of reason."[17]

Premodern stereotypes and concerns also found their way into Orientalism, even if Orientalists repackaged them to reflect the interests of the age. One prominent example concerns the depraved status of women in Islam. French Orientalist art frequently focused on Muslim women and their bodies, often with the subtext that these women were sexually oppressed and exploited by powerful Muslim men. In *The Turkish Bath* (1862), Jean Auguste Dominique Ingres depicts a harem full of naked women in the bath, a place that in the European imagination often functioned as an outlet for eroticism and sexual desire (see image 1 in the gallery).[18] Auguste Renoir's *Odalisque*

16. Quoted in Lockman, *Contending Visions*, 79.
17. Quoted in ibid., 81.
18. Nasser Al-Taee, *Representations of the Orient in Western Music: Violence and Sensuality* (Burlington, VT: Ashgate, 2010), 70; Quinn, *Sum of All Heresies*, 102. For an excellent overview of the harem in the European imagination from the late seventeenth to the early twentieth century, see Ruth Bernard Yeazell, *Harems of the Mind: Passages of Western Art and*

(1870) features a female concubine, fully yet sensually clothed, striking a sexually suggestive pose (see image 3 in the gallery).[19] In both paintings, the oppressive, powerful male who controls these women is absent from the scene, but the status and circumstance of the women still reinforce their sexual subjugation to him.

Jean-Léon Gérôme's *The Slave Market* (1866), by contrast, places menacing Muslim men front and center as a naked female slave undergoes a physical examination by a potential buyer (see image 2 in the gallery). Additional Muslim men surround her and examine her visually while, in the background, veiled Muslim women sit on the ground. Nasser Al-Taee points out that the painting reflects some of the contradictory ways Europeans imagined oppressed Muslim women: "veiled and naked, submissive and dangerous, domesticated and erotic."[20]

Frederick Quinn makes the following observation concerning the depiction of Muslim women in many French Orientalist paintings: "A turn of an arm or of the head or a bit of curving flesh became sexually suggestive, representing the permissive East, a theme never far below the surface in such works. Languid women with fetching smiles, their nipples covered with see-through gauze, sans pubic hair, and reclining in inviting positions on comfortable divans became staples of the Orientalist artistic repertoire."[21] Quinn and other scholars today recognize that many Orientalist depictions of Muslim women reveal more about the European male imagination and its particular erotic and sexual desires than about the complex

---

Literature (New Haven, CT: Yale University Press, 2000). For a perspective that challenges Western stereotypes of harems full of subjugated women, see Reina Lewis, *Rethinking Orientalism: Women, Travel, and the Ottoman Harem* (New York: I. B. Tauris, 2004).

19. Quinn, *Sum of All Heresies*, 102–3.
20. Al-Taee, *Representations of the Orient in Western Music*, 72.
21. Quinn, *Sum of All Heresies*, 102.

circumstances under which women in the Middle East or North Africa lived.

The tendency to construct Muslims as essentialized "Others" over against Europeans, often with the assumption of the latter's inherent cultural and civilizational superiority, ties together much Orientalist scholarship, literature, and art. The European construction of Muslims as the ultimate "Others," of course, was present since the Middle Ages. However, medieval Christians did not necessarily view Islam as an inferior civilization lagging behind the accomplishments of Europe. Rather, as noted in the previous chapter, medieval Europe found inspiration in the achievements of Islamic civilization in areas including philosophy, science, and music.

With nineteenth- and early twentieth-century Orientalism, increasing numbers of scholars, authors, and artists were convinced that Muslims belonged to a once great but now separate and intrinsically inferior civilization, one that not only lacked complexity and diversity but also offered little to benefit Western civilization.[22] The fact that the tendency to essentialize Muslims in this way emerged at a time of significant European colonial expansion suggests that Orientalism was neither a disinterested enterprise nor an objective quest for knowledge of non-Western cultures and religions. Of course, not all Orientalists consciously set out to justify Europe's colonial project, nor did all Orientalists support imperialism. But the political and historical context within which nineteenth-century Orientalism took shape does beg the question: what sort of relationship was there between European colonialism and Orientalism?

22. Lockman, *Contending Visions*, 74–77.

The Postcolonial Critique Of Orientalism

The most significant attempt in the late twentieth century to describe the relationship between colonialism and Orientalism came in the work of Edward Said, a founding figure in postcolonial studies. Born in Jerusalem in 1935, Said moved with his family to Cairo in 1947. He completed secondary school in the United States and went on to study first at Princeton University and then at Harvard University, where he earned a PhD in English literature. In 1963, Columbia University hired him as an instructor, and he remained at the university as a professor of English and comparative literature until his death in 2003.

Edward Said (1935–2003) was a professor of English literature at Columbia University and one of the pioneers of postcolonial studies. His seminal book, *Orientalism* (1978), critiqued the Western study of the Middle East and maintained that Western discourse concerning Arabs and Muslims is linked to imperialism.

In his complex and groundbreaking book *Orientalism* (1978), Said argues that Orientalism is linked to European and Western colonial power. To understand his argument, it is first necessary to grasp what he means by Orientalism. Said defines Orientalism in three interconnected ways. First, Orientalism is an academic discipline pertaining to anyone—historian, philologist, anthropologist, sociologist—who researches, writes, or teaches about the region known as the Orient (primarily the Middle East and North Africa). Second, Orientalism is a mode of thought that posits a sharp dichotomy between "the Orient" and "the Occident," the East and the West. Finally, and most importantly, Orientalism is a discourse of power over the Orient: "Taking the late eighteenth century as a very roughly defined starting point Orientalism can be discussed and analyzed as the corporate institution for dealing with the Orient—dealing with it by making statements about it, authorizing views of it, describing it, by teaching it, settling it, ruling over it: in short, Orientalism as a Western style for dominating, restructuring, and having authority over the Orient."[23]

This third definition connects knowledge *about* the Orient to power *over* the Orient. Said draws on the insights of Michel Foucault, a French philosopher and historian, to develop this connection between knowledge and power.[24] Foucault rejected the Enlightenment's confidence in the capacity of human reason to attain objective knowledge and truth. He did not believe there was any such thing as knowledge for knowledge's sake, nor did he accept that the quest for knowledge is a disinterested enterprise. What we hold to be true is instead a product of a particular discourse. A discourse is a system of meaning that fashions how we perceive, think about, and act in the world. This system possesses its own rules, premises, assumptions, and truth claims. Our knowledge does not operate outside this

> **discourse: a system of meaning that fashions how we perceive, think about, and act in the world.**

framework but in fact is a product of it. It is incorrect to conclude, however, that we must somehow find a way to circumvent this

---

23. Edward W. Said, *Orientalism* (New York: Vintage Books, 1978), 3.
24. For helpful summaries of Foucault's understanding of the relationship between knowledge and power, see Conor McCarthy, *The Cambridge Introduction to Edward Said* (Cambridge: Cambridge University Press, 2010), 70–71; Lockman, *Contending Visions*, 184–87; Loomba, *Colonialism/Postcolonialism*, 37–38.

framework so that we can access some pure reality "out there." A discourse, argued Foucault, is not a distorted perception of reality because, once again, there is no objective reality to perceive. All we have are alternative discourses, each with its own rules, truth claims, and the like, that shape how we understand and articulate "truth." Moreover, Foucault insisted that these discourses do not materialize out of thin air but are intimately and inextricably connected to and produced by power, particularly as this power is manifested in human social relations. Knowledge, as a product of a particular discourse, is therefore bound up with power.

Said understands Orientalism as a discourse in a Foucauldian manner. Orientalism is a particular system of meaning with its own rules, truth claims, and premises, derived from the power that Western nations wielded or aspired to wield over the Orient. Orientalism is part of the power and hegemony exercised by the West over the Orient. This is not to say that Orientalism is a collection of lies, falsehoods, or myths that one can eradicate by doing one's homework on the "real" Orient. Said insists that Orientalism is too formidable to be dispelled in this way: "I myself believe that Orientalism is more particularly valuable as a sign of European-Atlantic power over the Orient than it is as a veridic discourse about the Orient (which is what, in its academic and scholarly form, it claims to be). Nevertheless, what we must respect and try to grasp is the sheer knitted-together strength of Orientalist discourse, its very close ties to the enabling socio-economic and political institutions, and its redoubtable durability."[25]

Said's *Orientalism* is not a book about the Orient per se. It is a book that analyzes Western discourse about the Orient, including Islam and Arab peoples, and how this discourse relates to Western

25. Said, *Orientalism*, 6.

domination over the Orient in light of the colonial projects of the nineteenth and twentieth centuries. Said develops his argument concerning the relationship between Orientalism and colonial power by examining an array of British, French, and American scholarly works, literary texts, travelogues, journals, and political tracts from the height of the colonial era. Among the authors Said analyzes are Sir Richard Burton, Edward William Lane, Gustave Flaubert, and Ernest Renan. Throughout the book, he returns repeatedly to a common theme in Orientalist writings: the assumption that the Orient is fundamentally different from and inferior to the West. If "the Orient is irrational, depraved (fallen), childlike, 'different,'" writes Said, then "the European is rational, virtuous, mature, 'normal.'"[26]

One of the most controversial arguments Said makes in *Orientalism* concerns the extent to which colonial interests permeate not just the writings of select nineteenth- and early twentieth-century authors but almost any text written on the Orient in Europe or the United States. In true Foucauldian fashion, Said believes that humans are so deeply embedded in discourses and the power from which they emanate that they cannot pretend to maintain a dispassionate, disconnected perspective from which to study their object of interest. This applies as much to Orientalism as any other discipline:

> For if it is true that no production of knowledge in the human sciences can ever ignore or disclaim its author's involvement as a human subject in his own circumstances, then it must also be true that for a European or American studying the Orient there can be no disclaiming the main circumstances of *his* actuality: that he comes up against the Orient as a European or American first, as an individual second. And to be a European or American in such a situation is by no means an inert fact. It meant and means being aware, however dimly, that one belongs to a power with definite interests in the Orient.[27]

26. Ibid., 40.
27. Ibid., 11.

No European or American scholar, Said argues, can claim that his or her scholarship on the Orient is untouched by colonial power and interests. This applies even to those Western scholars who express sympathy and admiration for Arabs, Muslims, and Islam.

Said's *Orientalism* generated vigorous debate and controversy after its publication. Among the more prominent criticisms of Said: he is too polemical; he is too focused on literary texts from Britain and France that are not representative of the diversity of Orientalist perspectives; he fails to connect Orientalism concretely to colonial history and its association with the evolution of capitalism; he disregards the many ways that the colonized resisted colonial power, not to mention how they appropriated, altered, and contested Orientalist discourses; he tends to essentialize the West even as he critiques Western essentializations of the Orient.[28]

While it is not my intention to engage in a detailed analysis of each of these critiques, most of them have validity and, in a different context from this book, would be worth discussing and debating at length. However, whatever the shortcomings of Said's *Orientalism*, his larger arguments are on target and raise important questions about how the West has studied and continues to study Islam and Muslims. Many scholars of Islamophobia are indebted to Said for helping them understand just how much anti-Muslim and anti-Islam sentiment has been shaped by discourses rooted in power relations between the West and Muslim-majority regions.

The Clash of Civilizations

Said's study focused primarily on British and French Orientalism from the nineteenth century through World War II. At the very

28. Lockman, *Contending Visions*, 192–201; Loomba, *Colonialism/Postcolonialism*, 46–48 , 193.

end of his book, he devotes a section to Orientalism in the United States since World War II. For Said, a major shift occurred after the war. The French and British empires began to recede, and the United States emerged as the major empire. "A vast web of interests," writes Said, "now links all parts of the former colonial world to the United States."[29] He analyzes the work of American Orientalists in the decades prior to his book's publication. One of his primary targets is Bernard Lewis, a professor of Near East studies at Princeton University. Said's criticisms of Lewis's scholarship inaugurated a feud between the two that lasted until Said's death and that embodied the larger tensions emerging in the field of Middle East studies.

Said's nemesis did not fade from the scene as a result of *Orientalism*. If anything, Lewis became increasingly influential in certain political spheres. His ability to popularize and repackage Orientalist ideas in the last decades of the twentieth century gained him solid credentials in American foreign policy circles in light of the challenges posed by the Arab world to US political and economic interests. By making the case that Islam and the West are involved in a "clash of civilizations," Lewis not only inspired Samuel P. Huntington, a professor of government at Harvard University, to develop the clash of civilizations thesis on a larger scale but also helped American and Western politicians shift their focus to a "new" enemy, Islam, as an old enemy, the Soviet Union, was disintegrating. In fact, the clash of civilizations theory that Lewis and Huntington put forth has become so instrumental in defining Western foreign and domestic policies toward Muslims, particularly since 9/11, that it is necessary to devote some attention to the contours of the theory, including the Orientalist assumptions upon which it is built.

---

29. Said, *Orientalism*, 285.

Bernard Lewis had been invoking the language of "clash of civilizations" for several decades prior to his influential 1990 article, "The Roots of Muslim Rage," but it was in this article that the idea really took off.[30] Lewis begins the article with an almost conciliatory tone. Though he notes the violence that plagues the Muslim world, he is also quick to point out the diversity of Muslim attitudes toward the West. He concedes that there are "significant numbers" of Muslims with whom Westerners "share basic cultural and moral, social and political, beliefs and aspirations."[31] Yes, parts of the Muslim world are going through a phase in which intense hatred is being directed against the West, but this is not a universal sentiment.

clash of civilizations: the belief that global conflict after the Cold War will result from cultural and civilizational differences, including religious ones, and not economic and ideological differences; the phrase is often invoked to reflect the belief that Islam and the West are bound to be in conflict because of irreconcilable cultural and religious values.

It does not take long, however, for such nuances to fall by the wayside. Lewis reflects on the origins of Islam and notes that Muhammad was not only the founder of a religion but also the political ruler of a community. From the beginning, Islam combined religion and the state in an intimate manner. Classical Islamic theology thus moved quickly to divide the world into two realms: the House of Islam, where Islamic law prevails, and the House

30. Bernard Lewis, "The Roots of Muslim Rage," *Atlantic* (September 1990): 47–60.
31. Ibid., 48.

of War, sometimes referred to as the House of Unbelief, the realm where the law of Islam is not recognized. According to Lewis's narrative, all Muslims must strive to incorporate regions from the latter into the former through holy war.

Lewis argues that this aspect of Islamic thought set the stage for the intense rivalry with Christianity that began already in the seventh century and has lasted to this day. Islam held the upper hand in this rivalry until the failed Ottoman siege of Vienna in 1683. Since then, Islam has been bested at almost every turn by Christian and post-Christian civilizations. Islam's change of fortunes vis-à-vis the West provided the basis for the animosity and hatred that Muslims increasingly harbored toward their ancient rival.

After surveying the history of Islam's tumultuous relationship with the West, Lewis turns to the question at hand: why do Muslims have so much hostility toward the West today? Lewis addresses a long inventory of possible causes of anti-Americanism and anti-Westernism: American support for Israel; American backing of unpopular regimes in the Middle East; the West's history of sexism, racism, and imperialism. Over and over again, Lewis rejects these candidates as viable explanations for the "roots of Muslim rage." Such hatred, he argues, cannot be explained by anything "we" in the West have done. The explanation must lie within Islam alone.

Lewis ends his article with a section titled "A Clash of Civilizations." Here he finally explains the real cause of Muslim animosity toward the West: jealousy and humiliation in light of the dominance of Western civilization. Two Western developments in particular, secularism and modernism, have been the specific targets of Muslim anger. This was not always the case. Muslims initially admired these advances in Western civilization and even tried to incorporate them into their own societies. They did this because of "a keen and growing awareness of the weakness, poverty, and backwardness of the Islamic world as compared with the advancing West."[32] But Muslims were never able to achieve any real success with Western-style secularism and modernism. Poverty, tyranny, and military defeat came instead, and this opened the door to Islamic fundamentalists, who convinced many in the Muslim world that a return to the original teachings of Islam was necessary in order to respond to the threat posed by the West. Entrenchment in the antimodern, antisecular Islam of old was the best means according to fundamentalists for helping the Muslim world deal with its extraordinary inferiority complex.

If the trend in Islam is backward not forward and if Islam insists on resisting modernity instead of embracing it, then what remains? Lewis famously concludes: "It should by now be clear that we are facing a mood and a movement far transcending the level of issues and policies and the governments that pursue them. This is no less than a clash of civilizations—the perhaps irrational but surely historic reaction of an ancient rival against our Judeo-Christian heritage, our secular present, and the worldwide expansion of both."[33] According to Lewis, Islam and the West are bound to clash, though not because the West has done anything wrong but because the "irrational" Muslim world is so engulfed in jealousy, rage, and hatred that conflict is inevitable and unavoidable. There is little the West can do except hope that more moderate voices within Islam prevail in the long run.

Many of the classic Orientalist themes are here. Lewis characterizes Islam as monolithic (sometimes referring to all Muslims simply as "the Muslim"), backward, irrational, and emotional (that is, full of rage). The West, by contrast, is dynamic, modern, progressive, and rational, with emotions fully under control. Lewis offers a clear Orientalist framework to help modern Americans and Westerners make sense

32. Ibid., 56, 59.
33. Ibid., 60.

of why "they" hate "us" and to legitimize a feeling of Western superiority and exceptionalism that, in turn, can help reassure the West in its ongoing efforts to maintain its dominance—political, military, and economic—over the Muslim world.

While Lewis is credited with introducing the clash of civilizations framework into political discourse, Huntington is the scholar who developed and popularized the clash of civilizations thesis. In 1993, Huntington's article, "The Clash of Civilizations?," was published by *Foreign Affairs*, an influential journal within the US foreign policy establishment.[34] The importance of Huntington's article cannot be underestimated. The clash of civilizations thesis that he developed in the article, and later in a book by the same name (without the question mark), provided the essential framework in many political circles for understanding and dealing with Muslims and Muslim-majority regions in the post–Cold War era. Driven by ideological differences (American capitalism and democracy versus Soviet communism), the conflict did not involve direct conventional warfare between the two nations, but it did feature proxy wars (discussed further in Chapter 4) and a nuclear arms race. By the time 9/11 came around, the Bush administration and its European allies had an accessible and

The Cold War (1947–1991) was a global conflict between the United States and the Soviet Union that emerged after the end of World War II and lasted until the collapse of the Soviet Union.

34. Samuel P. Huntington, "The Clash of Civilizations?," *Foreign Affairs* 72 (1993): 22–49. For a fuller exposition of the ideas in this article, see Samuel P. Huntington, *The Clash of Civilizations and the Remaking of World Order* (New York: Simon and Schuster, 1996).

straightforward theory to explain the attacks on the United States and to justify the War on Terror.

Huntington argues that we are entering a new phase in global politics regarding the nature of conflict. In the past, conflict took place initially between princes, later between nation-states, and eventually between ideologies such as communism and liberal democracy. With the end of the Cold War, a new source of conflict is emerging: "It is my hypothesis that the fundamental source of conflict in this new world will not be primarily ideological or primarily economic. The great divisions among humankind and the dominating source of conflict will be cultural. Nation states will remain the most powerful actors in world affairs, but the principal conflicts of global politics will occur between nations and groups of different civilizations. The clash of civilizations will dominate global politics. The fault lines between civilizations will be the battle lines of the future."[35]

Huntington defines civilizations as distinct cultures possessing "common objective elements," including religion, customs, institutions, language, and history.[36] He acknowledges that while the boundaries demarcating civilizations can and do change, civilizational identity is nonetheless the fundamental source of identity for people throughout the world, and its importance in the future will only increase as a result of the interaction between the seven or eight major civilizations: Western, Latin American, Islamic, Slavic-Orthodox, Hindu, Confucian, Japanese, and "possibly African civilization."[37]

Of these civilizations, Huntington believes the greatest source of conflict will be between Western and Islamic civilizations. This

35. Huntington, "Clash of Civilizations?," 22.
36. Ibid., 24.
37. Ibid., 25.

conflict, to be sure, is an old one, dating back to the initial Muslim conquest of Spain, continuing through the period of European expansion into the Middle East and North Africa, and playing out more recently in the rise of Islamic fundamentalism and Arab nationalism. This clash of civilizations between Islam and the West is likely to continue, argues Huntington, mostly because Islam is prone to violence and bloodshed. Huntington points out that, almost everywhere you look, Muslims are entrenched in violent conflict with other peoples, from the Orthodox Serbs in the Balkans to Jews in Israel to Buddhists in Burma. Put simply, "Islam has bloody borders."[38]

Conflict between Islam and the West is not likely to subside as the West finds itself "at an extraordinary peak of power in relation to other civilizations."[39] The West is in a position of strength, using its military power and economic resources to protect and promote Western interests throughout the world, including the Muslim world. Huntington notes that the alliance formed between Confucian and Islamic civilizations will likely continue to challenge Western power and interests. For the West to maintain its military and economic hegemony over much of the world, it will need to build alliances with as many civilizations as possible, though this does not include Confucian and Islamic peoples. In the latter case, the West needs "to limit the expansion of the military strength of" Confucian and Islamic states and "to exploit differences and conflicts between them."[40] The West should not seek out conflict, but it must be realistic and understand that, for the foreseeable future, a clash of civilizations between Islamic–Confucian states and the West is inevitable.

38. Ibid., 35.
39. Ibid., 39.
40. Ibid., 49.

Like Lewis, Huntington invokes a number of classic Orientalist themes. He assumes that the West constitutes a distinct and superior civilization. He defines non-Western peoples mostly in religious or ethnic terms (Confucian instead of Chinese, Islamic instead of Egyptian, and so on). He promotes the imperial interests of the West at the expense of Arab and Muslim regions. And he characterizes Islam as violent and inherently prone to aggression. On this last point, his observation that "Islam has bloody borders" is a not-so-subtle suggestion that Muslims are responsible for all of the conflicts in which they find themselves, including clashes with Western powers.

Both Lewis and Huntington have been challenged in many circles, particularly academic ones, for their promotion of the clash of civilizations thesis. Not surprisingly, perhaps the most vocal critic of this thesis is Edward Said. His criticisms are fairly representative of the concerns many other scholars have raised with Lewis's and Huntington's work, so it is worth concluding this discussion with Said's response to both of them.[41]

Said perceives the arguments of both authors to be two sides of the same Orientalist coin:

> Elsewhere I have described [Lewis's] methods—the lazy generalizations, the reckless distortions of history, the wholesale demotion of civilizations to categories like irrational and enraged, and so on. Few people today with any sense would want to volunteer such sweeping characterizations as the ones advanced by Lewis about over a billion Muslims, scattered through at least five continents, dozens of different languages and traditions and histories. . . . But what I do want to stress is, first, how Huntington has picked up from Lewis the notion that civilizations are monolithic and homogenous and, second, how—again

41. Edward W. Said, "The Clash of Definitions," in *The New Crusades: Constructing the Muslim Enemy*, ed. Emran Qureshi and Michael Sells (New York: Columbia University Press, 2003), 68–87.

from Lewis—he assumes the unchanging character of the duality between "us" and "them."[42]

Both Lewis and Huntington rely heavily on essentializing in order to construct a superior Western civilization over against inferior Muslims, and, in the process, they draw tidy and fairly rigid borders to separate the West from the Muslim world. They differ only in that Lewis offers reasons for defining Islam as an inferior civilization, such as their inability to modernize or to separate religion and the state. Huntington, for his part, does not bother with addressing the reasons, though he, like Lewis, believes that the most important thing about Islamic civilization is its anti-Westernism.

Said argues that Lewis and Huntington are not writing neutral descriptions of the relationship between Islam and the West. They are partisans, advocates of Western civilization and the institutions that promote Western interests. Said quite bluntly insists that Huntington's thesis "argues from the standpoint of Pentagon planners and defense industry executives who may have temporarily lost their occupations after the end of the cold war but have now discovered a new vocation for themselves."[43] The clash of civilizations thesis serves the interest of Western imperialism in classic Orientalist fashion. This worries Said because the thesis provides civilian lawmakers and military generals with an overly simplistic map of the world that, in turn, will inform how they understand and act in the world. The result is not the resolution of conflict but rather its perpetuation.

The world is not as simple as Lewis and Huntington want it to be. They desperately want to hold onto a world in which the difference between "us" and "them" is clear. What they ignore, argues Said, is that civilizational identity is not fixed but fluid. All civilizations

42. Ibid., 71.
43. Ibid., 70.

and cultures, including so-called Western civilization, have intense, often contentious internal debates about how to define themselves. Civilizations are also shaped and transformed by all sorts of migrations and movements between peoples of different cultures. Finally, it is hard to imagine a culture today that, in the past or the present, has walled itself off from other cultures. In fact, every culture has been and continues to be involved in transformative exchanges, contacts, and conversations with other cultures.

At its heart, Said's critique challenges the motivations of those, including Lewis and Huntington, who rely on a clash of civilizations paradigm to make sense of the world in general and the relationship between Islam and the West in particular. Such a paradigm feeds on conflict and division, thereby "increasing the rifts between people in order to prolong our dominance."[44] What we need is not conflict but community, not a clash but a coming together of people across cultural barriers to face the dangers that threaten the entire human race.

◆ ◆ ◆ ◆ ◆

The rise of Orientalism in the colonial era and the perpetuation of Orientalist ideas in the post–Cold War era have contributed to the Islamophobia that proliferates in the West today. But how strong is the relationship between Orientalism and contemporary Islamophobia? Is Orientalism just an older word for what today would be labeled Islamophobia?

On the one hand, Orientalism provided the building blocks for what became Islamophobia. Some of the characteristics of Islamophobia discussed by the Runnymede Report have been inherited from Orientalism, particularly the notions that Islam is monolithic, that it is separate from and inferior to the West, and

44. Ibid., 86.

that its adherents constitute a racial category (against whom racism is justified). Moreover, the relationship between Islamophobia and political power in recent decades, discussed in the next chapter, has antecedents in the link between Orientalism and colonial power dating back to the nineteenth century.

Orientalism and Islamophobia, however, are not identical concepts. We must keep in mind that some Orientalist scholars held deep admiration and respect for the languages, histories, and religious convictions of Muslim peoples. An Orientalist is not by definition someone who fears or detests Islam, though plenty of Orientalists did harbor such feelings. Moreover, many Orientalists were academics who studied Islam professionally. Orientalist thought was not confined to the academy. Artists, government officials, and travelers to the East also contributed to Orientalism. But it is difficult to understand Orientalism apart from its connection to the academic world. Islamophobia, by contrast, is not something that emanates first and foremost from the scholarly study of Islam or Arab peoples.

Orientalism and Islamophobia are therefore best understood as overlapping phenomena, both historically and conceptually. But in the post–Cold War era, and particularly after the terrible events of 9/11, the concept of Islamophobia—the fear, dislike, or hatred of Muslims—most adequately captures the prejudices against Muslims and Islam in the West.

4

9/11, the War on Terror, and the Rise of
Political Islamophobia

On September 11, 2001, at 8:46 a.m., American Airlines Flight 11 crashed into the North Tower of the World Trade Center in New York City. News had barely broken of this tragedy when United Airlines Flight 175 pierced the South Tower just seventeen minutes later. In the course of the next hour, two more planes crashed: American Airlines Flight 77 into the Pentagon in Washington, D.C., and United Airlines Flight 93 in a field near Shanksville, Pennsylvania. It soon became clear that these events were the result of coordinated hijackings by Muslim terrorists with the purpose of targeting major American symbols and inflicting mass casualties. Only one of the four planes, United Airlines 93, failed to reach its intended target, presumably either the US Capitol Building or the White House. The immediate deaths resulting from the attacks numbered close to three thousand. Most of the casualties were American, but victims representing over ninety nations also perished.

Al-Qaeda (Arabic for "the base") is a militant Islamist organization founded by Osama bin Laden and Ayman al-Zawahiri, among others, during the waning years of the Soviet-Afghan War (1979–1989). Its initial purpose was to provide funds and warriors to aid the Afghan jihad against the Soviets. After the Soviet withdrawal from Afghanistan, al-Qaeda began to wage violent jihad against US targets, beginning with the bombings of US embassies in Kenya and Tanzania in 1998 and extending to the attacks on the World Trade Center and the Pentagon on September 11, 2001.

In the days, weeks, and months that followed, names such as Osama bin Laden, organizations such as al-Qaeda, and words such as *jihad* entered the everyday vocabulary of Westerners. Americans were facing the dawn of a new era. With few exceptions, such as the Japanese attack on Pearl Harbor in 1941, the United States had largely been immune to external acts of aggression on its own soil. After 9/11, Americans had to come to terms with the fact that their nation was the target of a belligerent and violent campaign by a small minority of Muslim extremists who had no qualms about killing mass numbers of civilians to further their political aims.

The US response to 9/11 was the War on Terror, a global effort to eradicate al-Qaeda, other Muslim terrorist cells, and the political regimes that supported them. While the most visible manifestation of this effort involved military action in Afghanistan and Iraq,

jihad: literally "struggle," the term can refer either to outward action to defend Islam or to internal struggles against sinful inclinations.

the War on Terror has been and continues to be multifaceted, involving intelligence, diplomatic, legal, and political dimensions on both foreign and domestic fronts.[1]

To make the case for war, US political elites constructed and perpetuated an Islamophobic narrative that featured the larger-than-life Muslim enemy as the most significant threat to US values and freedoms. The narrative in question invoked three common Islamophobic stereotypes: Islam as violent, antidemocratic, and misogynist. While US allies also contributed to the narrative, in this chapter I will analyze the narrative as articulated in the American context, particularly during the Bush administration, since this administration made the initial case for war and functioned as the de facto leader in the war. I will demonstrate that the narrative functioned as a means to mobilize and broaden popular support for the war in order to maintain and expand US and Western military, political, and economic hegemony in the Middle East.

---

1. Richard Jackson, Lee Jarvis, Jeroen Gunning, and Marie Breen Smyth, *Terrorism: A Critical Introduction* (New York: Palgrave Macmillan, 2011), 251–56.

From the "Red Scare" to the "Green Menace"

The global dominance of European empires in the nineteenth and early twentieth centuries gave way after World War II to two new superpowers: the United States and the Soviet Union. Allies during the war, the two nations became bitter rivals during the global conflict known as the Cold War (1947–1991). Ideological differences, such as the US commitment to capitalism and democracy and the Soviet embrace of communism, fueled this confrontation. While direct conventional warfare between the two superpowers was not a feature of the Cold War, the confrontation did involve proxy wars, such as the Korean War and Vietnam War, as well as a global nuclear arms race.

The Cold War led to a decades-long obsession in US political circles and the general public with the Soviet threat. The most prominent example of this fixation was the "Red Scare" of the 1950s in which Senator Joseph McCarthy led the way in accusing government employees and public figures of harboring communist sympathies or serving as communist spies. Fear of the Soviet Union's global power and influence continued long after McCarthy's endeavors faded.

When the United States first emerged as a global superpower, its relationship with the Middle East was peaceful. Prior to World War II, the United States adopted a fairly isolationist policy toward the Eastern Hemisphere and did not become significantly involved in the region until after the Cold War began.[2] Moreover, prior to the Cold War, many Middle Eastern countries held a very positive view of the United States, believing it to be a largely benevolent nation lacking any imperialistic designs. Many in the Middle East looked to

---

2. Rashid Khalidi, *Sowing Crisis: The Cold War and the American Dominance in the Middle East* (Boston: Beacon, 2009), 7–8.

the United States as a symbol of hope and a model for democracy and freedom.[3]

But in the context of the Cold War, isolationism was no longer an option. The United States now saw the Middle East as a strategic arena for its Cold War confrontation with the Soviet Union. In fact, both superpowers believed that the region was essential for two reasons. First, the world's most vital travel and trade routes—by land, sea, and air—cut through the region, connecting East to West. Second, the Middle East contained expansive oil and energy reserves.[4] Without access to and dominance over these travel routes and energy resources, neither nation could maintain its superpower status, much less the upper hand in the Cold War rivalry.

Because both superpowers recognized the importance of the Middle East for furthering their Cold War objectives, they vied with one another to form alliances with regimes throughout the region. The Soviet Union generally sought alliances with Arab nationalist governments, such as in Egypt, whereas the United States preferred to throw its support behind absolute monarchies in countries such as Saudi Arabia and Iran. Moreover, in accordance with the Eisenhower Doctrine of 1957, the US

Arab socialism: a twentieth-century political movement focused on state-sponsored economic development; it made inroads in Egypt under General Nasser (r. 1956–1970) and in Iraq and Syria under the Ba'ath Party from the 1960s to the 1980s.

3. Rashid Khalidi, *Resurrecting Empire: Western Footprints and America's Perilous Path in the Middle East* (Boston: Beacon, 2004), 31.
4. Khalidi, *Sowing Crisis*, 110–12.

government opted for a more interventionist policy, promising financial and military aid to Middle Eastern countries threatened by international communism.[5]

Secular Arab nationalism, socialism, and communism were making inroads in the Middle East by the 1950s, all to the benefit of the Soviet Union. The United States increasingly sought ways to counteract these developments. In part as a result of its relationship with Saudi Arabia, American politicians decided that Islam could be a powerful ideological weapon in the battle to curb Soviet influence in the Middle East. This decision, coinciding with the Eisenhower Doctrine, marked the beginning of a period in which the United States occasionally backed various forms of political Islam, also known as Islamism. This strategy not only led the United States to forge alliances with conservative Islamist movements but also inadvertently contributed to 9/11 when some militant Islamists later turned against their former ally and benefactor.

Islamism, along with US support for it, is therefore quite important to the story of 9/11. Islamism arose in the twentieth century as Muslim reformers and organizations sought to create and implement a comprehensive social, economic, and political order rooted in Islam and in opposition to Western secularism. Already in 1928, the Muslim Brotherhood emerged in Egypt as the first major Islamist organization, but it was not until the 1970s that political Islam became a major force in the Middle East.

When many Westerners today think of Islamism, they have images of a violence-prone form of Islamic fundamentalism. It is true that some versions of Islamism have adopted violent tactics. Hamas in Palestine and Hezbollah in Lebanon are Islamist organizations that sometimes resort to violence to achieve their political objectives. Al-Qaeda is another, though members of Hamas and Hezbollah have

5. Ibid., 17–18.

distanced themselves from al-Qaeda's tactics and political strategy. But plenty of other Islamist organizations, including the Muslim Brotherhood in Egypt and the Justice and Development Party in Turkey, have endeavored to pursue a more peaceful course, even if violence has played a role at times in these movements.[6]

What explains the resurgence of political Islam in the 1970s? Two factors are worth highlighting. The first is the defeat of a coalition of Arab militaries from Egypt, Syria, and Jordan in the Six-Day War against Israel in 1967. The defeat resulted in the loss of Sinai, the West Bank, Gaza, and East Jerusalem to Israel. It also generated widespread frustration in the Middle East with the leadership of Arab nations and the inability of existing political regimes, including those grounded in secular nationalism, to exert power against Israel and Western interests. The second is the major economic crisis that swept through the Middle East in the 1970s and that capitalist economic systems seemed powerless to handle. The perception emerged that existing regimes were failing because they relied too much on Western political and economic models.[7] Calls for a return to Islam and the establishment of Islamic states grew louder.

Before the late 1970s, the United States backed the Saudi endeavor to spread Islamist ideas throughout the Middle East. Through the Central Intelligence Agency (CIA), the United States also supported the efforts of the Muslim Brotherhood in Egypt to undermine the regime of General Abdel Nasser. Islamism was therefore not anathema to US foreign policy in the Middle East but rather an integral part of its Cold War strategy. However, two events at the end of the 1970s complicated the United States' relationship to

---

6. Juan Cole, *Engaging the Muslim World* (New York: Palgrave Macmillan, 2009), 44; Mary R. Habeck, *Knowing the Enemy: Jihadist Ideology and the War on Terror* (New Haven, CT: Yale University Press, 2006), 4.

7. John L. Esposito, *The Future of Islam* (New York: Oxford University Press, 2010), 60–61; Deepa Kumar, *Islamophobia and the Politics of Empire* (Chicago: Haymarket Books, 2012), 96–104.

political Islam: the Iranian Revolution (1979) and the Soviet-Afghan War (1979–1989). The former became grounds for the United States to construct the evil Islamist enemy, the latter an opportunity to portray Islamists as heroes and true friends of America. Taken together, the two events signaled the move toward a more ambivalent relationship between the United States and Islamism in the waning years of the Cold War.

The Iranian Revolution refers to the overthrow of Mohammad Reza Shah Pahlavi, who was supported by Western powers, by Islamic revolutionaries in 1979 under the leadership of Ayatollah Ruhollah Khomeini."

The Iranian Revolution was an outgrowth of widespread frustrations over the reign of Mohammad Reza Shah Pahlavi.[8] The Shah had been in power since 1941. Beginning in the 1960s, the Shah worked to westernize Iran and, with strong US support, initiated a series of economic, social, and legal reforms.

Shah: the historic title for a king or ruler in Iran.

However, the reforms failed to benefit many ordinary Iranians, and the Shah began to face significant criticism, including from religious leaders. The Shah cracked down on dissent, arresting, torturing, exiling, and sometimes executing his opponents.

8. For succinct discussions of the causes and consequences of the Iranian Revolution, see William L. Cleveland, *A History of the Modern Middle East* (Cambridge, MA: Westview, 2004), 423–33; Fred Halliday, *Islam and the Myth of Confrontation: Religion and Politics in the Middle East* (New York: I. B. Tauris, 2003), 42–75. For more extended treatments, see David R. Farber, *Taken Hostage: The Iran Hostage Crisis and America's First Encounter with Radical Islam* (Princeton: Princeton University Press, 2005); and Charles Kurzman, *The Unthinkable Revolution in Iran* (Cambridge, MA: Harvard University Press, 2004).

One of the Shah's exiled adversaries and a prominent cleric, Ayatollah Ruhollah Khomeini, had been criticizing the Shah's regime for decades. But with increasing resentment against the Shah in the late 1970s, Khomeini emerged as the leader of a revolution that culminated in 1979 with the Shah going into exile and Khomeini taking power. With the revolution, the United States not only lost one of its staunchest allies in the Middle East, it also found itself facing an anti-American, Islamist government with a leader who referred to America as the "Great Satan."

Later that same year, Iranian students and demonstrators overran the US embassy in Tehran and took sixty-six Americans hostage. The Iranian hostage crisis lasted 444 days (see image 4). In his State of the Union address in 1980, President Jimmy Carter referred to the hostages as "innocent victims of terrorism and anarchy."[9] As a result of the revolution and the hostage crisis, political Islam increasingly became the object of great suspicion if not outright hostility in US political circles. Islamism was becoming the enemy, the "Green Menace" (because green is the color symbolizing Islam) that would eventually replace the Soviet threat.[10]

But political Islam as an ideological weapon of the Cold War still had some life, as evident in the Soviet-Afghan War. The Soviet Union deployed troops to Afghanistan in December 1979 in order to support the communist regime that came to power the previous year. Afghanistan's tribal society, fragmented along religious and ethnic lines, found unity in its overwhelming opposition to the Soviet occupation. Armed resistance drew inspiration from the concept of jihad, in this case understood as a war to liberate Islam and

9. Jimmy Carter, "State of the Union Address 1980," *Jimmy Carter Presidential Library and Museum*, January 23, 1980, http://www.jimmycarterlibrary.gov/documents/speeches/su80jec.phtml.
10. Kumar, *Politics of Empire*, 70–71; Fawaz Gerges, *America and Political Islam: Clash of Cultures or Clash of Interests?* (Cambridge: Cambridge University Press, 1999), 43.

mujahideen: Islamist resistance fighters who battled the Soviets during the Soviet-Afghan War (1979–1989).

Afghanistan. Islamist resistance fighters known as *mujahideen* (literally "those who fight jihad") battled the Soviets for a decade. Radical Islamists from outside Afghanistan, including Arabs, poured into the country and joined the Afghan mujahideen in their struggle against the formidable superpower.

The Soviet-Afghan War (1979–1989) began with the Soviet invasion of Afghanistan in 1979 in an attempt to support a struggling communist regime. The United States, largely through the CIA, helped the Afghan freedom fighters defeat the Soviet Union by providing them with weapons, training, and money.

The United States had a vested interest in the conflict and devoted considerable resources, including weapons, training, and money, to Afghanistan in support of the mujahideen. President Ronald Reagan, like Carter before him, viewed the mujahideen as important Cold War allies and lavished praise on their courage, referring to them as "our brothers" and as "the moral equivalents of America's Founding Fathers"[11] (see image 5). This US support paid off, and in 1989 the Soviets withdrew from Afghanistan. Two years later, the Soviet Union collapsed.

11. Quoted in Kumar, *Politics of Empire*, 33. Quoted in Zahid Shahab Ahmed, "Political Islam, the Jamaat-e-Islami, and Pakistan's Role in the Afghan-Soviet War, 1979–1989," in *Religion and the Cold War: A Global Perspective*, ed. Philip Muehlenbeck (Nashville: Vanderbilt University Press, 2012), 289.

The mujahideen are significant not only because they illustrate yet another instance of the United States' willingness to encourage Islamism when it suited its larger political goals but also because the foundations of al-Qaeda emerged from the mujahideen resistance to the Soviets.[12] A young businessman from Saudi Arabia, Osama bin Laden, began assisting the mujahideen in the 1980s. Bin Laden became increasingly involved in the war over the course of the decade, raising funds and recruiting additional fighters. His involvement in the war led him, along with an Egyptian physician named Ayman al-Zawahiri, to create the radical Islamist organization al-Qaeda ("the Base" in Arabic) as a means to organize and finance the Afghan resistance.

After the war, bin Laden and al-Qaeda increasingly turned

Osama bin Laden (1957–2011) was a wealthy Saudi businessman who provided training camps and financial assistance to Arab fighters during the Soviet-Afghan War (1979–1989). The terrorist organization al-Qaeda emerged from bin Laden's work in Afghanistan and eventually turned its attention to the other superpower, the United States. Bin Laden gave approval to his subordinates to plan and carry out the 9/11 attacks, after which he went into hiding for a decade before US special forces killed him in Pakistan.

12. For succinct overviews of US support for the mujahideen and the rise of Osama bin Laden and al-Qaeda, see John L. Esposito, *Unholy War: Terror in the Name of Islam* (New York: Oxford University Press, 2002), 9–13; Esposito, *Future of Islam*, 66–79. For more extended treatments,

their attention to a global jihad, and the United States, a former ally, became the major target in this holy war. Bin Laden lamented the increasing American presence in the Middle East, including the stationing of US troops in Saudi Arabia during the Persian Gulf War (1990–1991). In 1996, bin Laden issued a declaration of jihad encouraging Muslims to expel the American occupiers from Saudi Arabia and to engage in a war against the Judeo-Christian alliance of the West.[13] With bin Laden's attention now firmly on the United States, al-Qaeda attacked American targets. In 1998, al-Qaeda bombed the US embassies in Nairobi, Kenya, and Dar es Salaam, Tanzania. In 2000, al-Qaeda attacked the USS *Cole*, a US Navy destroyer, in a suicide bombing in Yemen. The subsequent attacks on the World Trade Center and Pentagon represented the continuation of al-Qaeda's strategy to target the United States in its ongoing global jihad.

What we see in both the Soviet-Afghan War and the rise of al-Qaeda is the emergence of a radical version of Islamism that developed a violent jihadist ideology in an effort to resist and defeat the two great superpowers of the Cold War. The United States may have supported this ideology during the Soviet-Afghan War because it was a convenient tool in undermining its Cold War nemesis, but, eventually, some of the mujahideen turned from ally to enemy. By the time of 9/11, the Muslim terrorist, with some assistance from the United States' Cold War tactics, had replaced the Soviet communist as public enemy number one.

see Steve Coll, *Ghost Wars: The Secret History of the CIA, Afghanistan, and Bin Laden, from the Soviet Invasion to September 10, 2001* (New York: Penguin, 2004); and Fawaz A. Gerges, *The Rise and Fall of Al-Qaeda* (New York: Oxford University Press, 2011).

13. For the full text of Osama bin Laden's "Declaration of War against the Americans Occupying the Land of the Two Holy Places" (1996), see "Bin Laden's Fatwa," *PBS NewsHour*, http://www.pbs.org/newshour/updates/military/july-dec96/fatwa_1996.html.

Explaining 9/11

The complex realities of US foreign policy in the Middle East since World War II, including the United States' relationship to political Islam, its support for authoritarian regimes, its military presence, its strong alliance with Israel, and its heavy dependence on the region's oil reserves, certainly deserve attention in any effort to explain the circumstances that led to 9/11. President George W. Bush and the principal members of his administration, however, spent little time analyzing such factors. Instead, they relied on a ready-made, easily accessible explanation for the terrorist attacks: the clash of civilizations.

This mindset emerged already in President Bush's address to the nation on September 20, 2001. In the speech, Bush assumed that Americans were asking one fundamental question: Why do they hate us? The question echoes Bernard Lewis's concerns, discussed in chapter 3, about the "roots of Muslim rage." Bush offered no critical analysis of how US policies and involvement in the Middle East have contributed to the grievances held by many in the region against the United States, not to mention why a small minority of Muslims may have acted on those grievances. Instead, he posited a clear divide between a benevolent and superior "us" and a malevolent and backward "them": "They hate our freedoms: our freedom of religion, our freedom of speech, our freedom to vote and assemble and disagree with each other."[14] Bush invoked the kind of circular reasoning employed by Lewis on "Muslim rage." Muslim terrorists hate us because, well, they are full of hatred (and, thankfully, "we" are not). The clash between "us" and "them" is therefore inevitable.

---

14. George W. Bush, "Address to a Joint Session of Congress and the American People," The White House, September 20, 2001, http://georgewbush-whitehouse.archives.gov/news/releases/2001/09/20010920-8.html.

Bush took pains in the address to point out that he was not referring to all or even most Muslims but rather to a radical minority within Islam so intoxicated with hatred that they have twisted their religion into a tool for terror. However, in doing so, he constructed a binary of "good Muslim" and "bad Muslim" that eventually paved the way for a political Islamophobia in which any Muslim who is not with "us" becomes "our" enemy.

In the months and years following 9/11, the clash of civilizations explanation became the explicit framework within which the Bush administration made sense of and responded to the threat of terrorism. As the second term of Bush's presidency was coming to an end, this framework was still being employed by the administration. In a speech to the American Israel Public Affairs Committee in 2007, Vice President Dick Cheney lamented: "Civilized, decent societies will never fully understand the kind of mindset that drives men to strap on bombs or fly airplanes into buildings, all for the purpose of killing unsuspecting men, women and children who they have never met and who have done them no wrong. But this is the very kind of blind, prideful hatred we're up against."[15]

The frequent recourse to civilizational clashes between radical Muslims and the West is not surprising when one considers the individuals and ideologies influencing the Bush administration. In the aftermath of 9/11, prominent advisors to and members of the administration, many of whom were neoconservatives favoring an aggressive, interventionist foreign policy in the Middle East, looked to a certain cadre of like-minded academics and experts to provide explanations and to weigh in on strategies to deal with the terrorist attacks. One of these academics was Lewis, who, according to Bob

---

15. Quoted in Gerry J. Gilmore, "Cheney: Early Iraq Pullout Would Imperil U.S., Anti-Terror War," U.S. Department of Defense, March 12, 2007, http://www.defense.gov/News/NewsArticle.aspx?ID=3347.

Woodward of the *Washington Post*, was "a Cheney favorite."[16] Lewis was also a longtime friend of Paul Wolfowitz, deputy secretary of defense, and Richard Perle, chairman of the influential Defense Policy Board, both of whom were major architects of the Iraq War. Perle considered Lewis a mentor, and both Wolfowitz and Perle relied on Lewis's insights in developing strategies for the response to 9/11, including the war in Iraq.[17]

Lewis was not in a position to dictate specific policies behind the War on Terror, but his perspectives on radical Islam and Middle Eastern politics held considerable sway in the Bush administration. At a World Affairs Council luncheon in 2006, Cheney raved about Lewis's impact on US foreign policy: "In 1990, [Lewis] wrote 'The Roots of Muslim Rage,' which anticipated the terrorism of that decade. And in this new century, his wisdom is sought daily by policymakers, diplomats, fellow academics, and the news media."[18] Cheney personally appealed to Lewis for advice on a regular basis, and, on more than one occasion in the immediate aftermath of 9/11, Cheney had one-on-one meetings with Lewis.[19]

Lewis's influence within the Bush administration appears substantial. Moreover, the clash of civilizations thesis articulated by Lewis and Huntington and endorsed by important neoconservative advisors became the ideological foundation for the War on Terror. Unfortunately, dependence on this framework also contributed to the administration's failure to address the underlying causes of the 9/11 attacks and the threat of Muslim extremist organizations more

---

16. Bob Woodward, *State of Denial: Bush at War, Part III* (New York: Simon and Schuster, 2006), 83.
17. Stephen Sheehi, *Islamophobia: The Ideological Campaign against Muslims* (Atlanta: Clarity, 2011), 54–55.
18. Dick Cheney, "The Vice President's Remarks at the World Affairs Council of Philadelphia Luncheon Honoring Professor Bernard Lewis," The White House, May 1, 2006, http://georgewbush-whitehouse.archives.gov/news/releases/2006/05/20060501-3.html.
19. Sheehi, *Islamophobia*, 56.

broadly. The clash of civilizations explanation reduced the conflict between radical Muslim terrorism and the West to something inherent within Islam (and thus something that can *only* be fixed within Islam). On this understanding, the irrational anger and hatred of Muslims toward the West leads some Muslims to use the teachings of Islam to justify their terrorist activities against innocent people. Neither the Bush administration nor the larger political establishment devoted much effort to reflecting critically on the history of Western involvement in the Muslim world, nor did they seriously consider whether the particular economic and political grievances toward the West articulated by many Muslims, not just the small minority of terrorists, might require a significant rethinking of foreign policy to minimize the chance of future attacks.[20]

Let me be clear. I am not suggesting that critical reflection by the US government on this history and these grievances would remove the blame of 9/11 from al-Qaeda, nor do I condone in any way al-Qaeda's ideology or tactics. I am suggesting that no effective plan to diminish the long-term threat of terrorism emerged in the months and years following 9/11 because the US government refused to take seriously how its own policies in the Middle East contributed to the conditions that gave rise to 9/11.

The extent of the US government's failure can be seen in the work of the 9/11 Commission, a bipartisan committee responsible for investigating the reasons behind the 9/11 attacks and for making recommendations for defending the United States against future attacks. In its 2004 final report, the commission explains the roots of Islamist terrorism, including al-Qaeda, as part of a stream within Islam that goes back decades and that "is motivated by religion and does not distinguish politics from religion." The commission is clear

---

20. John L. Esposito and Dalia Mogahed, *Who Speaks for Islam? What a Billion Muslims Really Think* (New York: Gallup, 2007), 91–94; Esposito, *Future of Islam*, 71.

that the problem lies within Islam alone and even insists that the problem is not terrorism but "*Islamist* terrorism." The commission acknowledges that Islamist terrorism is fueled "by grievances stressed by Bin Laden and widely felt throughout the Muslim world," including policies perceived as anti-Muslim and anti-Arab, the presence of the US military in the Middle East, and US support for Israel.[21] However, the commission does not concede that any of these larger grievances have legitimacy. The problem is not with "us" but with "them":

> Because the Muslim world has fallen behind the West politically, economically, and militarily for the past three centuries, and because few tolerant or secular Muslim democracies provide alternative models for the future, Bin Laden's message finds receptive ears. It has attracted active support from thousands of disaffected young Muslims and resonates powerfully with a far larger number who do not actively support his methods. . . .
>
> Tolerance, the rule of law, political and economic openness, the extension of greater opportunities to women—these cures must come from within Muslim societies themselves. The United States must support such developments.[22]

The commission simply reinforces what the Bush administration had already indicated, that the disease of terrorism, not to mention the economic and political conditions feeding it, can only be explained by recourse to Islam. Islam alone is what gives rise to the disease, so Islam alone must be the source of its cure. Since the United States lacks the means to "cure" Islamist terrorism, all that it can do is fight it with unprecedented force.

21. National Commission on Terrorist Attacks upon the United States, *The 9/11 Commission Report: Final Report of the National Commission on Terrorist Attacks Upon the United States* (New York: Norton, 2004), 362.
22. Ibid., 363–63.

Constructing the Muslim Enemy in the War on Terror

The Bush administration's ultimate response to 9/11 was the War on Terror. On September 14, 2001, the US Congress authorized the president to use whatever force necessary against any nation, organization, or person involved in the 9/11 terrorist attacks. The authorization clearly indicated that the justification for such force involved the right of the United States to defend itself and to protect its citizens.[23] Self-defense became the first major justification for the War on Terror.

The first phase of the war targeted the Taliban, the ruling Islamic government in Afghanistan. After the Taliban failed to turn over al-Qaeda leaders, including bin Laden, coalition forces, led by the United States and Britain, began airstrikes on the Taliban in October 2001. The Taliban formally surrendered two months later, and a new government was installed, though military action between coalition forces and both the Taliban and al-Qaeda persisted in various regions of the country.

The Taliban is a Muslim militant movement that was formed in the 1990s by former mujahideen from the Soviet-Afghan War. The Taliban ruled Afghanistan from 1996 until 2001, when the US-led invasion attacked and defeated the regime for its support of al-Qaeda and Osama bin Laden.

The second and more controversial phase of the war involved invading Iraq in order to remove Saddam Hussein from power. A force led by the United

23. Authorization for Use of Military Force, S.J. Res. 23, 107th Congress, September 18, 2001, http://news.findlaw.com/hdocs/docs/terrorism/sjres23.enr.html.

States began an assault on Baghdad on March 20, 2003. A few weeks later, Baghdad fell and Hussein's reign came to an end. Coalition forces occupied Iraq for almost a decade, during which a civil war broke out and a new government was established.

For the initial war in Afghanistan, the United States received broad international support, including from the North Atlantic Treaty Organization and the UN Security Council. This support recognized the clear connection between the Taliban and al-Qaeda, and the war was broadly viewed as necessary for the United States to defend itself from future attacks.

Making the case and garnering domestic and international support for expanding the war to Iraq was more challenging. The Bush administration insisted that Iraq possessed weapons of mass destruction and that Hussein was harboring al-Qaeda members. As evidence was not forthcoming to corroborate these charges, and as criticisms of the Bush administration's motives for war grew, the administration increasingly relied on an Islamophobic narrative to mobilize support at home and abroad. The narrative consisted of three broader justifications for war, each undergirded by an anti-Islam, anti-Muslim bias: to defend the United States against Muslim terrorism (because Islam is violent), to introduce democracy in Muslim countries (because Islam is antidemocratic), and to liberate Muslim women (because Islam is misogynist). Let us examine each of these in turn.

Fighting Terrorism

The first justification was actually an extension of the self-defense rationale for war put forth in the original congressional authorization for military force. What was different was the increasing connection made in war rhetoric between Islam and terrorism. The function of this connection was to magnify the threat posed by Muslims and Muslim-majority countries to US security, thereby justifying a broadening of the War on Terror to include preventative war against any nation or regime, particularly in the Middle East, that *could* pose a security threat, and to expand democracy and US military presence in the region. This policy became known as the Bush Doctrine.

President Bush and others in his administration often projected publicly the position that the United States was not at war with Islam and that Islam should not be associated with violence and terrorism. Barely one week after 9/11, Bush gave a speech at the Islamic Center in Washington, DC, in which he stated this position clearly: "The face of terror is not the true faith of Islam. That's not what Islam is all about. Islam is about peace."[24]

Yet so much of the rhetoric from the Bush administration and other political elites after 9/11 linked, explicitly and implicitly, Islam with violence. Within a week of the attacks, Bush used the extraordinarily problematic language of "crusade" to describe the upcoming War on Terror, though he quickly backed off, likely because of Muslim complaints that such language implied a holy war against all Muslims, reminiscent of the Crusades of the Middle Ages.[25] Bush also invoked phrases such as "Islamic radicalism," "Islamic extremists," and "Islamo-fascism" to describe the threat faced by the United States.[26] Each instance in which the word *Islamic* was placed in front of words suggesting extremism and terrorism reinforced the

24. George W. Bush, "Remarks by the President at the Islamic Center of Washington, D.C.," The White House, September 17, 2001, http://georgewbush-whitehouse.archives.gov/news/releases/2001/09/20010917-11.html.

25. George W. Bush, "Remarks by the President upon Arrival," The White House, September 16, 2001, http://georgewbush-whitehouse.archives.gov/news/releases/2001/09/20010916-2.html.

26. For example, see George W. Bush, "President Discusses War on Terror at National Endowment for Democracy," The White House, October 6, 2005, http://georgewbush-whitehouse.archives.gov/news/releases/2005/10/20051006-3.html.

connection between Islam and violence and conveyed the sense at home and abroad that this was a war against Islam.

In fact, many critics, Muslim and non-Muslim alike, pleaded with the administration not to characterize the behavior of al-Qaeda and other terrorists as Islamic because this descriptor suggests an organic connection to the religion of Islam. A Department of Homeland Security memo from 2008, prompted by concerns from American Muslim leaders, reiterated the problems of employing terminology that indicted all of Islam and all Muslims in radicalism and terrorism.[27] These pleas eventually found receptive ears. By the end of Bush's second term and into the Obama administration, the language used to describe terrorism became more cautious.

Even with the emergence of more restrained language, the connection between Islam and terrorism has continued to permeate political discourse. In 2008, former New York City mayor Rudolph Giuliani chastised leaders in the Democratic Party for avoiding the phrase "Islamic terrorism" at their national convention.[28] In the aftermath of terrorist bombings at the Boston Marathon in April 2013, Representative Peter King of New York insisted: "We're at war with Islamic terrorism. It's coming from people within the Muslim community by the terrorists coming from that community."[29] Across the Atlantic, Tony Blair, Britain's former prime minister and the United States' staunchest ally in the War on Terror, responded to the news of a British soldier's murder near London by two Muslim extremists in May 2013 by complaining that "there is a problem

27. Department of Homeland Security, "Terminology to Define the Terrorists: Recommendations from American Muslims," January 2008, http://www.dhs.gov/terminology-define-terrorists-recommendations-american-muslims.
28. Quoted in "Giuliani's Speech at the Republican National Convention," *New York Times*, September 3, 2008, http://elections.nytimes.com/2008/president/conventions/videos/transcripts/20080903_GIULIANI_SPEECH.html.
29. Quoted in Daniel Politi, "Rep. Peter King: Stop Being Politically Correct, Let's Focus on Muslim Communities," *Slate*, April 20, 2013, http://www.slate.com/blogs/the_slatest/2013/04/20/rep_peter_king_let_s_focus_on_muslim_communities.html.

within Islam—from the adherents of an ideology that is a strain within Islam."[30]

This discourse has been aided by the many images in the media of Muslims committing acts of violence or terrorism. The list of events is quite long and, on the surface, appears to reinforce the link between Islam and violence: the Iranian hostage crisis in 1979 to 1981, the first bombing of the World Trade Center in 1993, the 1998 embassy bombings in Kenya and Tanzania, the USS *Cole* bombing in 2000, the 9/11 attacks in 2001, the Madrid and London train bombings in 2004 and 2005, the shootings in Fort Hood, Texas, in 2009, and the beheading of Western journalists by ISIS in 2014. Moreover, when one moves beyond individual episodes and takes into account the ongoing violent conflicts involving Muslims in the Middle East, it seems that Muslims are guilty as charged.

A closer examination of the link between Islam and violence, however, reveals some of the problematic assumptions behind the political rhetoric. First, while violence in the name of religion has certainly been a part of Islamic history, Islam does not have a monopoly on violence. If we take the historically dominant religion in the West, Christianity, the legacy of violence is equally apparent: the Crusades, the Reconquista, the Inquisition, the European and colonial American witch trials and executions, the Thirty Years' War, Catholic-Protestant conflicts in Northern Ireland, the Atlantic slave trade, European colonialism, and so forth. Each of these episodes, and many more beyond them, involved the invocation of Christian teachings to justify violence against or subjugation of others. Judaism, Hinduism, Buddhism, and other major religions have their own

---

30. Tony Blair, "The Ideology behind Lee Rigby's Murder Is Profound and Dangerous. Why Don't We Admit It?: Tony Blair Launches a Brave Assault on Muslim Extremism after Woolwich Attack," *Daily Mail* (UK), June 1, 2013, http://www.dailymail.co.uk/debate/article-2334560/The-ideology-Lee-Rigbys-murder-profound-dangerous-Why-dont-admit--Tony-Blair-launches-brave-assault-Muslim-extremism-Woolwich-attack.html.

histories of violence. Islam is therefore not exceptional in this regard. However, when politicians single out Islam as having an inherent and unique problem with violence, they have abandoned any critical engagement with the relationship between religion and violence and veered into the territory of Islamophobia.

A second troubling assumption relates to whether the teachings of Islam play a role in terrorism and violence. While prominent Muslim terrorists like bin Laden often invoke religious language and symbols, it is doubtful that religious ideology is the main driving force behind their violent acts. John Esposito argues that the causes of terrorism are more often than not rooted in political and economic grievances.[31] Statements from bin Laden and other terrorists often refer to the long history of Western interventionism in Muslim-majority regions and to larger political grievances, such as the Israeli-Palestinian conflict, the presence of US military troops in the Middle East, US exploitation of the Middle East's oil and energy resources, and the legacy of European colonialism. Even if we consider the possibility that the religious convictions articulated by Muslim terrorists are genuine, religion alone cannot explain their actions. The political context of their statements and actions must be taken into account. Unfortunately, many Western politicians leap to the easy conclusion that Muslims who commit violence do so only because of religion, whereas "we" reluctantly employ force as a last resort and even then for more enlightened secular reasons such as to defend human rights.[32]

We must also remember that jihad, which literally means "struggle," has a long, complex history and cannot be reduced to the category of "holy war." Jihad may connote the use of force,

---

31. Esposito, *Future of Islam*, 71–81; see also Arun Kundani, *The Muslims Are Coming! Islamophobia, Extremism, and the Domestic War on Terror* (London: Verso, 2014), 115–52.
32. William T. Cavanaugh, *The Myth of Religious Violence: Secular Ideology and the Roots of Modern Conflict* (New York: Oxford University Press, 2009).

though whether this force is understood as defensive—to protect Muslims from external attack or threat—or expansionist has been a subject of debate in Islamic history. From the colonial period onward, many Muslim reformers and intellectuals argued that jihad means just or defensive war. On the other end of the spectrum, more radical Muslim thinkers, such as Sayyid Qutb, have understood jihad as permitting the violent overthrow of established governments in Muslim countries. All of these disagreements, moreover, reflect what some Muslim scholars call "the lesser jihad." "The greater jihad," they insist, pertains to the internal struggle against one's own evil inclinations or desires.[33] Some Muslims even insist that nonviolent jihad is the only legitimate kind.[34]

A third problematic and widespread assumption is that Muslims are either silent about or indifferent to terrorist attacks. A frequent complaint heard in the months and years after 9/11 is that most Muslims did not denounce the attacks.[35] Thomas Friedman, a foreign affairs columnist for the New York Times, famously echoed this sentiment in a column four years after 9/11: "To this day—to this day—no major Muslim cleric or religious body has ever issued a fatwa condemning Osama bin Laden."[36] He was wrong. His own newspaper published a full-page ad one month after the attacks that contained statements from prominent Muslim leaders denouncing the attacks, including the Grand Mufti of Saudi Arabia, the king of Jordan, and the Organisation of the Islamic Conference.[37]

33. Rudolph Peters, "Jihad," in The Oxford Encyclopedia of the Islamic World, ed. John L. Esposito (New York: Oxford University Press, 2009), 3:252–56.
34. Jeffry R. Halverson, Searching for a King: Muslim Nonviolence and the Future of Islam (Washington, D.C.: Potomac Books, 2012).
35. Esposito, Future of Islam, 29–33.
36. Thomas L. Friedman, "If It's a Muslim Problem, It Needs a Muslim Solution," New York Times, July 8, 2005, http://www.nytimes.com/2005/07/08/opinion/08friedman.html.
37. Esposito, Future of Islam, 31. The organization changed its name in 2011 to the Organisation of Islamic Cooperation.

There were plenty of other examples. Three days after the attacks, more than forty prominent Muslim scholars released a statement in which they unequivocally repudiated the attacks: "We condemn, in the strongest terms, the incidents, which are against all human and Islamic norms." Signatories included the general guide of the Muslim Brotherhood in Egypt, a prominent leader of the Pakistani political party Jamaat-e-Islami, and a founder of Hamas in Palestine. On September 27, 2001, two prominent Muslim scholars, the chairman of the Sunna and Sira Council in Qatar and the chairman of the North America Fiqh Council, issued a fatwa that was signed by many other Muslim leaders. The fatwa condemned bin Laden and sanctioned Muslim participation in US military action in Afghanistan.[38] Many other Muslims condemned the

fatwa: an unbinding legal opinion issued by a religious scholar (mufti).

9/11 attacks outright; moreover, according to a Gallup Poll, 93 percent of Muslims in Muslim-majority countries believed the attacks to be unjustified.[39] The real question is not why prominent Muslim leaders failed to condemn bin Laden and the 9/11 attacks but rather why so few people in the West know about the many condemnations. More problematically, why are so many people, including politicians, inclined to believe assertions like Friedman's? Is it because of the common conviction, often encouraged by the Western media, that Muslims are guilty by association and thus the horrible deeds committed by a minority are attributable to the majority?

38. Charles Kurzman, a sociologist at the University of North Carolina at Chapel Hill, has compiled and reproduced a substantial list of statements by Muslim leaders against terrorism and the 9/11 attacks, including the statements discussed here. See Charles Kurzman, "Islamic Statements against Terrorism," http://kurzman.unc.edu/islamic-statements-against-terrorism/.
39. Esposito, *Future of Islam*, 155; Esposito and Mogahed, *Who Speaks for Islam?*, 69–70.

Finally, for all of the concerns expressed by Western political and public figures about Islam's violent tendencies, these concerns were all but absent in certain episodes involving Muslims and violence prior to 9/11. During the Soviet-Afghan War of the 1980s, the United States was actively involved in training the mujahideen in guerilla warfare tactics. In the same decade, the United States assisted Saddam Hussein and Iraq's military in the Iran-Iraq War. This assistance included intelligence about Iranian military deployments, the means to develop chemical weapons, and diplomatic support to protect Iraq from UN condemnation in the use of poisonous gas against Iran.[40] When it has served American interests, particularly in winning the Cold War and extending political and military influence in the Middle East, the US government has had no qualms about facilitating and contributing to violence in Muslim-majority regions.

Introducing Democracy

The second justification for the War on Terror was to introduce democracy to Iraq and the broader Middle East. During the year prior to the Iraq War, the Bush administration made the case for invading Iraq by touting the need to remove Saddam Hussein from power because of his supposed links to al-Qaeda and his possession of weapons of mass destruction. One month before the invasion, with no evidence for either charge forthcoming, the administration began pushing a new justification. In a speech to the American Enterprise Institute in February 2003, Bush argued that "the world has a clear interest in the spread of democratic values" and that Iraq in particular "is fully capable of moving toward democracy and living in freedom." He suggested that "success in Iraq could also begin a new

---

40. Khalidi, *Resurrecting Empire*, 42–43; Jarrett Murphy, "U.S. and Iraq Go Way Back," *CBS News*, August 2, 2009, http://www.cbsnews.com/2100-202_162-534798.html.

stage for Middle Eastern peace, and set in motion progress toward a truly democratic Palestinian state."[41] This speech revealed Bush's increasing dependence on neoconservative doctrines, including the use of US military force to impose democracy abroad, in order to make the broader case for war with Iraq. Democracy in Iraq would have a domino effect and inspire the people of other countries in the region to follow suit.

Others in the Bush administration began preaching the gospel of democracy, and this message continued long after the initial invasion was over and the occupation was underway. However, by 2006, with popular support dwindling in the United States and among its allies, the administration began invoking new terms such as "Islamic fascists" and "Islamo-fascism" to characterize the threat to democracy in Middle East. Bush himself stated, "This nation is at war with Islamic fascists," and on one occasion he described Israel's conflict with Lebanon as "the beginning of a long struggle against an ideology . . . [called] Islamo-fascism." Others in the administration, including Bush's press secretary, invoked this language, as did staunch allies in his party such as Senator Rick Santorum.[42] This rhetoric was intended to mobilize popular support for the war by constructing a larger-than-life Islamic enemy, no longer confined to scattered terrorist organizations, bent on the destruction of freedom and democracy in a manner reminiscent of Nazi Germany. The language suggested that Islam itself was the true enemy of democracy. The new vocabulary was controversial from the beginning, but the decision to employ it was likely a political

---

41. Quoted in "George Bush's Speech to the American Enterprise Institute," *Guardian* (UK), February 27, 2003, http://www.guardian.co.uk/world/2003/feb/27/usa.iraq2.
42. Kari Huus and Tom Curry, "The Day the Enemy Became 'Islamic Fascists,'" *NBC News*, August 11, 2006, http://www.nbcnews.com/id/14304397/ns/politics/t/day-enemy-became-islamic-fascists/#.UexQRL-oVUx.

calculation that depended on larger assumptions held by many in the West about the inability of Islam to embrace democracy.

On the surface, the perception that Islam is incompatible with democracy may seem justified. After all, democracy has had a rough go of it in many Muslim-majority countries. With decolonization, most Muslim nations shed the yoke of European colonial domination only to find themselves under strong authoritarian regimes ranging from monarchies to military dictatorships. These regimes, past and present, have consistently restricted or outlawed political opposition and violated human rights, including the rights of women and religious minorities. Such regimes continue to be the rule and not the exception. John Esposito estimates that only one in four Muslim-majority nations have some form of democratic government.[43]

Without denying the real difficulties of democracy taking root in the Muslim world, we should assume neither that Muslim nations are unique in wrestling with the full implications of democracy nor that there is something inherently antidemocratic about Islam. In the first place, Western nations faced challenges in implementing democracy. In the case of the United States, the ratification of the Constitution and the Bill of Rights in the late eighteenth century after a hard-fought war with Britain did not magically create a society in which the voices and the participation of all were embraced. From the Civil War to the civil rights movement, from women's suffrage to the women's liberation movement, US history is replete with examples of violent and nonviolent struggles to develop a more fully democratic process and to protect the rights of minority populations against the majority. One could argue that the birth pangs of democracy and equal rights for all American citizens are still felt, as in the debate over the legal recognition of same-sex marriage and in the surveillance,

43. Esposito, *Future of Islam*, 65.

profiling, and detention of Muslim and Arab Americans. Democracy does not come easy, even in the West, and it should come as no surprise that Muslim nations that have not been at this nearly as long should also struggle.

It is also important to recognize that democracy has found its way into some Muslim countries, albeit in fits and starts. In 2012, Mohamed Morsi of the Muslim Brotherhood became the first democratically elected president of Egypt, though his removal from power one year later by the Egyptian military left unanswered the question about democracy's status in that country. Other Muslim countries, including Turkey, Bangladesh, Indonesia, and Malaysia, have embraced democracy in varying degrees, even if each has a long way to go. At the very least, these countries can be described as emerging democracies.

Despite the challenges facing the Muslim world when it comes to democracy, Gallup polling reveals that majorities in countries with substantial Muslim populations have a strong desire for democracy. Most of those surveyed agreed that if they were to help draft a new constitution for their country, they would defend the right to free speech, "allowing all citizens to express their opinion on the political, social, and economic issues of the day." In Lebanon, 99 percent agreed with this statement, while in Egypt and Iran, 94 percent and 92 percent, respectively, agreed. At the same time, many Muslims do not want a separation of religion and state but rather prefer some role for Sharia. In some countries, majorities want Sharia to serve as the only source of legislation (66 percent in Egypt, 60 percent in Pakistan), but in most Muslim nations majorities want Sharia to be *a* source but not the only source of legislation (65 percent in Morocco, 54 percent in Indonesia, 66 percent in Iran).[44] Many Muslims do

---

44. Dalia Mogahed, *Islam and Democracy* (Princeton: Gallup Organization, 2006), 2.

not see a conflict between adopting democracy and embracing the principles of Islam in governance. Their desires for democracy and for a place for religion in public life are not viewed as mutually exclusive.

At the same time, however, the majority of people in many Middle Eastern countries are skeptical that the United States is committed to supporting democracy. For example, 80 percent in Iran, 76 percent in Egypt, and 74 percent in Lebanon disagreed with the following statement: "The U.S. is serious about encouraging the establishment of democratic systems of government in this region."[45] Plenty of Muslims in the Middle East desire democracy and yet feel that the United States is part of the problem when it comes to realizing this desire.

The Iranian Coup of 1953 involved the overthrow of Iran's democratically elected prime minister, Mohammad Mossadegh, with the assistance of the British and US intelligence agencies. The coup paved the way for the Shah's unopposed rule until the Iranian Revolution of 1979.

What is the source of this skepticism? One needs to look no further than the history of US involvement in the Middle East since World War II. In 1953, the CIA conspired with Britain's MI6 to back a coup that led to the overthrow of Iran's democratically elected prime minister, Mohammad Mossadegh. Mossadegh's great "crime" was to nationalize Iran's petroleum resources. In his place, the United States supported the

45. Mohamed Younis, "Iranians Have Doubted U.S. Commitment to Democracy," *Gallup World*, July 2, 2009, http://www.gallup.com/poll/121370/iranians-doubted-commitment-democracy.aspx.

increasingly oppressive rule of the westernized Shah, who, as we have already discussed, undermined democracy and eliminated political opposition in order to maintain his power.[46] In Iraq, Hussein's Ba'ath Party—the party that the United States targeted for destruction in the War on Terror—was the same party that the United States had supported off and on since the 1960s. In particular, for a decade after the Iranian Revolution the Reagan administration gave significant support to Iraq and to the Ba'ath Party during the war with Iran.[47] In Egypt, President Hosni Mubarak benefited from US support for three decades despite his autocratic rule. Even as the Arab Spring emerged in 2011, the Obama administration initially continued its support for Mubarak, backing off only when it was clear that Mubarak would not be able to maintain power.

The United States has overlooked the violation of democratic principles and human rights by many governments beyond those just mentioned, including Algeria, Morocco, Jordan, and Saudi Arabia.[48] All of this illustrates that the United States has frequently chosen alliances with regimes and parties in the Middle East that have thwarted democracy.

The reason the United States has supported authoritarian regimes for so long is not difficult to discern. In its Cold War confrontation with the Soviet Union, the United States did everything in its power to establish alliances with governments that both supported its battle against communism and provided vital access to oil and energy reserves. Many of these governments were autocratic, but this mattered little when the stakes were so high. After the Cold War, the United States continued its support for repressive rulers in order to maintain its sole superpower status, and it did so frequently at

---

46. Cole, *Engaging the Muslim World*, 11.
47. Khalidi, *Resurrecting Empire*, 40–43.
48. Ibid., 54.

the expense of democracy. To support grassroots democracy was oftentimes to risk having democratically elected governments that were not as friendly to the United States and its imperial interests as were dictatorial regimes in the region.

This history explains why Muslims are suspicious of US pledges to support democracy in the Middle East and beyond. It also undermines any Western political narrative that depicts Islam as an inherent enemy of democracy. Given both the democratic aspirations of many Muslims and the numerous ways that the United States and some European powers have undercut democratic processes in Muslim countries, Western politicians who suggest that Islam is the real obstacle to democracy are likely driven more by Islamophobia or ulterior political motives than by any genuine desire to promote and defend democracy in these regions.

Liberating Women

The third justification feeding the United States' Islamophobic narrative invoked the need to liberate oppressed Muslim women. The US government already promoted this justification during its early involvement in Afghanistan. In December 2001, Bush signed a congressional bill known as the Afghan Women and Children Relief Act. The purpose of the act was to assist Afghan women and children in the areas of health care and education. The act contained a long list of congressional findings about the oppressive conditions faced by Afghan women under Taliban rule, including restrictions or outright prohibitions on freedom of expression, leaving home without male supervision, working outside the home, attending school, and receiving adequate health care.[49]

49. Afghan Women and Children Relief Act, S. 1573, 107th Congress, November 28, 2001, http://www.govtrack.us/congress/bills/107/s1573/text.

At the signing ceremony for the relief act, Bush painted a dark picture of the conditions faced by Afghan women and children:

> America is beginning to realize that the dreams of the terrorists and the Taliban were a waking nightmare for Afghan women and their children. . . .
>
> Afghan women were banned from speaking, or laughing loudly. They were banned from riding bicycles, or attending school. They were denied basic health care, and were killed on suspicion of adultery. . . .
>
> In Afghanistan, America not only fights for our security, but we fight for values we hold dear. We strongly reject the Taliban way. We strongly reject their brutality toward women and children. They not only violate basic human rights, they are barbaric in their indefensible meting of justice. It is wrong. Their attitude is wrong for any culture. Their attitude is wrong for any religion.[50]

Bush insisted that the oppression of women is a fundamental goal of all terrorism and that the United States must do everything in its power to prevent terrorists from enacting their brutality on women beyond Afghanistan. In many ways, he echoed the case that his wife, First Lady Laura Bush, made in a radio address one month earlier: "Because of our recent military gains in much of Afghanistan, women are no longer imprisoned in their homes. They can listen to music and teach their daughters without fear of punishment. Yet the terrorists who helped rule that country now plot and plan in many countries. And they must be stopped. The fight against terrorism is also a fight for the rights and dignity of women."[51]

In the name of women's rights, the Bush administration, backed by the US Congress, transformed a war of self-defense into a war

50. Quoted in "President Signs Afghan Women and Children Relief Act," The White House, December 12, 2001, http://georgewbush-whitehouse.archives.gov/news/releases/2001/12/20011212-9.html.
51. "Radio Address by Mrs. Bush," The American Presidency Project, November 17, 2001, http://www.presidency.ucsb.edu/ws/?pid=24992.

of liberation. The United States now had a moral imperative to battle terrorism in order to ensure the rights and dignity of women and to liberate oppressed women from vicious Muslim men. The connection between Islam and misogyny became a subtext for many speeches about the need to fight the War on Terror and to intervene in the political affairs of other nations, including Iraq.

Employing this particular justification for the war was once again a political calculation rooted in common assumptions in the West about the incompatibility between women's rights and Islam. On one level, it is certainly true that women in many Muslim-majority countries encounter significant obstacles when it comes to human rights, and any effort to combat Islamophobia should not do so by turning a blind eye to these realities. Traditional interpretations of Islamic law have allowed polygamy, child marriages, and husbands' unilateral right of divorce, and these practices continue in parts of the Muslim world. Female genital mutilation (FGM) is practiced in some Muslim countries such as Egypt and the Sudan. Prohibitions on driving and traveling without the permission of a male exist in countries such as Saudi Arabia. Education and literacy levels are very low for women in countries such as Yemen and Pakistan. And, of course, Islam itself has a history of prohibiting women from assuming the position of imam or prayer leader in mixed-gender congregations. It is also common to segregate the sexes during communal prayers in mosques, with women worshipping either behind men or in separate spaces altogether.

The list of obstacles to women's rights in Muslim countries is a long one. Moreover, Islam definitely has a long history of patriarchy and patriarchal interpretations of sacred texts. But do these observations mean that Islam is inherently misogynistic and that Muslim women cannot find freedom or full personhood in Islam? To conclude that Islam is by definition misogynistic is to risk promoting

Islamophobia by ignoring the larger historical, political, and cultural realities both in Muslim countries and in the West. For starters, patriarchy and the oppression of women are not unique to Muslim societies or to practices within Islam. The history of Western Christianity is also one of patriarchy. Until the modern era, most Christian theologians, including towering figures such as Augustine and Martin Luther, promoted the belief that women were more bodily and carnal and therefore lacked the same capacity for reason as men. Women were sexual temptresses that led virtuous men astray, and men were to be on their guards against the "Eves" of the world. Prominent theologians also endorsed the view that God created women primarily if not solely to function as wives and mothers and thus to serve their husbands, fathers, and other male family members.[52]

These common theological convictions found their way into the political and social orders of the West and beyond, resulting in the frequent exclusion of women from formal education and employment outside the home until the last century. At times, such convictions laid the foundation for systematic violence against women. Women, for example, were the primary targets in the European witch trials that resulted in anywhere from fifty thousand to one hundred thousand executions.[53] The physical and sexual abuse of women, often by husbands and fathers, also found support in Christian history from men and male church leaders who appealed to the household codes in the New Testament to keep women "in line."[54] For women enduring such violence in marriage, divorce was

---

52. See, for example, Augustine, *City of God*, XIV.3; Martin Luther, "Lectures on Genesis," in *Luther on Women: A Sourcebook*, ed. Susan C. Karant-Nunn and Merry E. Wiesner-Hanks (Cambridge: Cambridge University Press, 2003), 147–48; and Luther, "A Sermon on the Estate of Marriage," in Karant-Nunn and Wiesner-Hanks, *Luther on Women*, 89–92.

53. Approximately 80 to 85 percent of those executed were women. See Susan C. Karant-Nunn and Merry E. Wiesner-Hanks, "Witchcraft and Magic," in Karant-Nunn and Wiesner-Hanks, *Luther on Women*, 228.

either not an option or a very difficult option in much of the West until the nineteenth and twentieth centuries.

Church teachings on the inferiority of women also led to the exclusion of women from leadership. Many Christian communities began opening the door to women's ordination only in the mid-twentieth century. Plenty of churches still prohibit women's ordination. The largest Christian community in the world, the Roman Catholic Church, continues to exclude women from the priesthood, as does the largest Protestant denomination in the United States, the Southern Baptist Convention.[55] As we see, patriarchy has been a prominent feature of Christian history just as it has in Islamic history, and we would find many of the same problems in a historical survey of other major religions such as Hinduism or Judaism.

We must also realize that many oppressive and patriarchal practices popularly connected to Islam by Westerners either have roots outside Islam or are practiced by only a limited number of Muslim communities. FGM, for example, not only predates Islam but is also found among Christian communities in Egypt, the Sudan, and Kenya. Female circumcision, moreover, is not mentioned in the Qur'an, which may also explain why the practice is limited geographically within the Muslim world. In fact, about half of all Muslim women who have endured the procedure live in Egypt and Ethiopia—hardly evidence that FGM is an Islamic practice.[56] To take another example, polygamy predates Islam, and, while the

54. See, for example, Eph. 5:22-24; 1 Pet. 3:1-6. See also Elisabeth Schüssler Fiorenza and M. Shawn Copeland, eds., *Violence against Women* (Maryknoll, NY: Orbis Books, 1994).

55. The Southern Baptist Convention (SBC) states in *The Baptist Faith and Message* (2000) that "the office of pastor is limited to men as qualified by Scripture" (VI). However, the SBC also acknowledges that its official position on restricting ordination to men is nonbinding on local congregations. For the full text of *The Baptist Faith and Message*, see http://www.sbc.net/bfm/bfm2000.asp#vi.

56. World Health Organization, *An Update on WHO's Work on Female Genital Mutilation (FGM): Progress Report*, 2011, http://whqlibdoc.who.int/hq/2011/who_rhr_11.18_eng.pdf.

Qur'an does open the door to this practice, it is not as widespread as Westerners often assume. Some Muslim countries, such as Tunisia and Turkey, prohibit it altogether, whereas in many others it is confined mainly to the middle and upper classes. The limited practice of polygamy indicates that there is not a monolithic understanding or uniform model of marriage within Islam. Nonpatriarchal or less patriarchal models are also viable options for many Muslims.

The prevalent Western perception that Muslim women are only passive victims completely lacking agency and having no major influence in their otherwise male-dominated societies also becomes problematic when one looks beyond the Bush administration's rhetoric of oppressed and imprisoned women. In politics, organizations such as Malaysia's Sisters in Islam challenge male privilege, combat discriminatory practices, and present alternative interpretations of Islam that further women's rights and egalitarianism.[57] In recent decades, Muslim women have also served as heads of state, including Benazir Bhutto in Pakistan, Megawati Sukarnoputri in Indonesia, and Khaleda Zia and Sheikh Hasina in Bangladesh. In fact, in 2013, women occupied three of the top four posts in Bangladesh.[58] These examples are a stark contrast to a Western country such as the United States where, at the time of this writing, a woman has yet to be elected president or vice president. And, of course, there are many more Muslim women at the grassroots level who have energized and publicly promoted prominent political organizations, including Islamist parties such as Hamas and the Muslim Brotherhood.[59]

---

57. Esposito, *Future of Islam*, 118–19, 151.
58. "Women Elected Speaker of Bangladesh's Parliament," *BBC News Asia*, April 30, 2013, http://www.bbc.co.uk/news/world-asia-22355383.
59. Sophia Jones, "The Sisters of the Muslim Brotherhood," *Daily Beast*, July 9, 2013, http://www.thedailybeast.com/articles/2013/07/09/the-sisters-of-the-muslim-brotherhood.html.

Educational attainment for Muslim women differs from country to country. The poor literacy rates for women in countries such as Pakistan or Yemen are not indicative of all Muslim countries or of Muslim women globally. In Iran and Saudi Arabia, 70 percent of women are literate, while 85 percent of women in Jordan and Malaysia are literate. The percentage of women with higher education degrees isalso quite substantial in some countries: 52 percent in Iran, 37 percent in Lebanon, 34 percent in Egypt, and 32 percent in Saudi Arabia. In the United Arab Emirates and Iran, the majority of students in universities are women.[60] In the United States, Muslim women are more educated than the overall population of women. Whereas 29 percent of American women have a college or postgraduate degree, 43 percent of Muslim women hold such degrees. In fact, a larger percentage of Muslim women in the United States possess higher education degrees than do Christian women, whether Protestant or Catholic.[61]

Muslim women have participated in feminist and reform movements within Islam for much longer than most Westerners realize. Already at the end of the nineteenth century and well throughout the twentieth century, Muslim women in Egypt promoted feminist goals and worked for egalitarianism in the public sphere. While some of the feminist activity was secular in orientation, there are plenty of examples of Islamic feminist work. The latter came on the scene in a powerful way with the rise of political Islam in the 1970s.[62] Examples of prominent women reformers and activists include Nawal El Saadawi and Heba Raouf Ezzat. El Saadawi has been a strong opponent of FGM for decades, arguing that the

60. Esposito, *Future of Islam*, 151.
61. Jane Lampman, "US Muslims: Young, Diverse, Striving," *Christian Science Monitor*, March 3, 2009, http://www.csmonitor.com/USA/Society/2009/0303/p02s02-ussc.html.
62. For a helpful survey of contemporary feminist movements among Muslim women, see Margot Badran, *Feminism in Islam: Secular and Religious Convergences* (Oxford: Oneworld, 2009).

practice reflects patriarchal control of women's bodies and has little to do with authentic Islam.[63] Ezzat has challenged many dominant male interpretations of the Qur'an and has stressed the prominent role of Muslim women as authors, hadith scholars, and educators in Islamic history.[64] These two Egyptian reformers are simply the tip of the iceberg. Much could be written on prominent Muslim women engaged in reform efforts across the globe, including preeminent scholars such as Amina Wadud and Asma Barlas in the United States.

The views of these activists and scholars are not exceptions. In fact, according to Gallup polling, majorities in most Muslim countries support the equal rights of women. For instance, 90 percent of those polled in Malaysia, 86 percent in Turkey, and 85 percent in Egypt believe that women should have the right to work outside the home if they otherwise qualify for the job. Large majorities also believe women should have the right to vote without interference from male family members: 93 percent in Turkey, 90 percent in Bangladesh, 89 percent in Iran, and 80 percent in Indonesia. Overall, countries with large Muslim populations favor women and men enjoying the same legal rights: 90 percent or more in Turkey, Lebanon, Indonesia, and Bangladesh.[65]

The preceding discussion challenges Islamophobic narratives that present Islam as inherently misogynistic and Muslim women as passive victims with no agency or impact beyond the household. By moving away from such simplistic stereotypes, we can focus more clearly on critical questions often avoided by politicians and the Western media when justifying military intervention under the pretext of liberating women. In particular, it is worth asking the question posed by anthropologist Lila Abu-Lughod in an article titled

63. Ibid., 130–31.
64. Esposito, *Future of Islam*, 119.
65. Ibid., 153.

"Do Muslim Women Really Need Saving?"[66] Abu-Lughod rightly calls into question the very presumption that Muslim women in Afghanistan should be reduced to objects of liberation by Western powers. She raises ethical concerns about using women as justification for wars that frequently have larger imperialist motives, noting that such justification has a deep and tangled history with Western colonialism. If anything, Abu-Lughod argues, "Projects of saving other women depend on and reinforce a sense of superiority by Westerners."[67] Such arrogance opens the door to the exploitation, not the liberation, of women, and this does not even begin to address the many adverse ways that women are affected by war.

Abu-Lughod's argument is easily sustained when one starts asking why: Why did the Bush administration justify a war in Afghanistan and later Iraq by focusing on the liberation of women? If the administration was so convinced that the brutality of Taliban rule over women compelled the United States and its allies to take action, why was this action not taken before 9/11? Were women in Afghanistan better off in March 2001 than in October 2001? When the Bush administration was negotiating with the Taliban prior to 9/11 about the development of oil pipelines in the region, was it unaware that women were suffering from Taliban rule, or did such concerns simply fail to override a more pressing economic concern?[68] Similar questions can be asked of Iraq. And if liberating oppressed Muslim women is such a vital part of the United States' mission abroad, why does the United States not target other Muslim countries known for their restrictions on women's rights and freedoms, such

---

66. Lila Abu-Lughod, "Do Muslim Women Really Need Saving? Anthropological Reflections on Cultural Relativism and Its Others," *American Anthropologist* 104 (2002): 783–90.
67. Ibid., 789.
68. Krista Hunt and Kim Rygiel, "(En)Gendered War Stories and Camouflaged Politics," in *(En)gendering the War on Terror: War Stories and Camouflaged Politics*, ed. Krista Hunt and Kim Rygiel (Burlington, VT: Ashgate, 2008), 9–10.

as Saudi Arabia? Why has the United States continually supported governments in many Muslim countries that have undermined women's rights and freedoms?

It we take such questions seriously, it is difficult not to conclude that the idea of what Gayatri Spivak calls "white men saving brown women from brown men" was popular with the Bush administration because it masked ulterior motives.[69] In reality, the US government both manufactured and exacerbated fears of menacing Muslim men oppressing helpless Muslim women in order to expand its military presence and to create regimes that were friendlier to US economic and political interests. As we will see below, these overriding interests led not to the liberation of women but rather to a decline in their safety and livelihood.

The Casualties of the War on Terror

These three justifications for the War on Terror sustained an Islamophobic narrative that claimed Islam and the West were engaged in an unavoidable clash of civilizations. To be sure, the Bush administration frequently distinguished the "good Muslim" from the "bad Muslim" in an ostensible attempt to signal that not all Muslims are terrorists. But the rhetoric employed against terrorism all too often pointed toward an inherent connection between Islam on the one hand and violence, tyranny, and misogyny on the other. As a result, the door was opened for a war that could target Muslim nations and populations and not just a small minority of terrorists.

The impact of the war on Muslims abroad under both the Bush and Obama administrations has been catastrophic. Estimating the death toll in the War on Terror is difficult, but one conservative

---

69. Gayatri Chakravorty Spivak, "Can the Subaltern Speak?," in *Social Theory: The Multicultural, Global, and Classic Readings*, ed. Charles Lemert (Boulder, CO: Westview, 2013), 402.

estimate puts the number of casualties from the eight-year conflict in Iraq at almost 117,000 civilians and 4,800 coalition troops.[70] Many of the civilian deaths stemmed from violent episodes such as the ethnic cleansing of Sunni Arabs, tribal feuds, criminal gang activity, guerrilla warfare, and "collateral damage" from coalition attacks. Many civilian deaths came at the hands of other Iraqis, yet the US-led invasion of Iraq generated the conditions, including the weakening of state-sponsored police and security forces, that led to the widespread violence in the first place.[71] The same holds true for Afghanistan, where upwards of 19,000 civilians and 3,400 coalition troops perished between 2001 and 2013.[72] The war's impact on the infrastructures of Afghanistan and Iraq resulted in limited access to health care, malnutrition, lack of clean drinking water, poor sanitation, and widespread disease, all of which took their toll on the populations of both countries, resulting in additional deaths.[73]

The war also displaced significant numbers of people. By 2008, an estimated four million Iraqis were displaced internally and externally by the war.[74] As of 2013, Afghanistan led all nations as a source of refugees, with approximately 2.7 million refugees scattered over eighty countries.[75] Displaced populations are often those most susceptible to the poor living conditions that lead to death and disease.

70. David Blair, "Iraq War 10 Years On: At Least 116,000 Civilians Killed," *Telegraph* (UK), March 15, 2013, http://www.telegraph.co.uk/news/worldnews/middleeast/iraq/9932214/Iraq-war-10-years-on-at-least-116000-civilians-killed.html.
71. Cole, *Engaging the Muslim World*, 125–27.
72. "Human Costs of War: Direct War Death in Afghanistan, Iraq, and Pakistan October 2001–Feburary 2013," Costs of War, http://costsofwar.org/; "Coalition Military Fatalities by Year," accessed August 4, 2013, http://icasualties.org/oef/.
73. Cole, *Engaging the Muslim World*, 127; "Afghanistan: 16,725–19,013 Civilians Killed," Costs of War, http://costsofwar.org/article/afghan-civilians.
74. Cole, *Engaging the Muslim World*, 122.
75. "2013 UNHCR Country Operations Profile–Afghanistan," UNHCR: The UN Refugee Agency, http://www.unhcr.org/cgi-bin/texis/vtx/page?page=49e486eb6.

Finally, in light of the great concern expressed by the US government for women in Afghanistan and Iraq, it is worth addressing the war's impact on Muslim women. Despite promises of liberation, the US invasion of Afghanistan did not eliminate all or even most of the challenges faced by women in the country, particularly violence and abuse. According to an Amnesty International report in 2003, coalition forces were unable to protect women even after the end of Taliban rule. Women continued to face considerable violence and injustice, including rape and other forms of sexual violence, domestic abuse, forced marriages, abductions, and significant discrimination in the criminal justice system.[76] The fact that the United States continued to fund Afghan warlords such as the Northern Alliance exacerbated the problem because the warlords had a record of violence against women.[77] Malalai Joya, a prominent Afghan activist and politician, has been and continues to be particularly vocal on this point, insisting that US and NATO support for fundamentalist warlords has made the situation of Afghan women worse, not better, since the overthrow of the Taliban in 2001.[78]

In Iraq, women have also suffered from considerable violence since the US–led invasion in 2003. As the US occupation of Iraq began, Human Rights Watch reported an escalation in violence against women. Rape, abductions, forced marriages, "honor killings," and unjust applications of laws favoring men over women in cases of sexual abuse or violence were prevalent, particularly in Baghdad. The organization explained: "Many of the problems in addressing sexual violence and abduction against women and girls derive from

---

76. "'No-One Listens to Us and No-One Treats Us as Human Beings.' Justice Denied to Women," *Amnesty International*, October 5, 2003, http://www.amnesty.org/en/library/info/ASA11/023/2003/en.

77. Hunt and Rygiel, "(En)Gendered War Stories and Camouflaged Politics," 9–10.

78. Elsa Rassbach, "'The Afghan People Are Fed Up': An Interview with Malalai Joya," *Common Dreams*, January 10, 2013, https://www.commondreams.org/further/2013/01/10-0.

the U.S.-led coalition forces and civilian administration's failures to provide public security in Baghdad."[79]

♦ ♦ ♦ ♦ ♦

Much more could be said about the devastating effects of the War on Terror on Muslims outside the West, including the torturing of suspected terrorists and the civilians killed by drone attacks in countries such as Pakistan and Yemen.[80] What is clear is that much of the suffering and devastation described here is inexplicable apart from the Islamophobic narrative employed by US political elites to justify a war that was intended largely to further the United States' political, economic, and military hegemony over strategic parts of the Muslim world.

79. "Climate of Fear: Sexual Violence and Abduction of Women and Girls in Baghdad," Human Rights Watch, July 16, 2003, http://www.hrw.org/reports/2003/07/15/climate-fear-0.
80. Spencer Ackerman, "US Drone Strikes More Deadly to Afghan Civilians than Manned Aircraft–Adviser," *Guardian* (UK), July 2, 2013, http://www.theguardian.com/world/2013/jul/02/us-drone-strikes-afghan-civilians.

Image Gallery

1. Jean Auguste Dominique Ingres, *The Turkish Bath* (1862)

2. Jean-Léon Gérôme, *The Slave Market* (1866)

3. Auguste Renoir, *Odalisque* (1870)

4. Iranian hostage crisis protest in Washington, DC (1979)

5. President Reagan meeting with Afghan mujahideen (1983)

6. Park51 Islamic Center protest in New York City (2010)

7. English Defence League protest in Newcastle, England (2010)

8. Scene in Oslo, Norway, after the Breivik bombing (2011)

9. American Freedom Defense Initiative billboard, Larchmont train station in New York (2012); photo by Cynthia Miller-Idriss

5

The "Islamic Threat" in Modern Europe

The 9/11 attacks on the United States had a profound effect on the American political and cultural landscape, leading to worries about a powerful Muslim enemy that would stop at nothing to destroy Western values and freedoms. But the United States was not alone in succumbing to fears of an "Islamic threat." Similar fears took hold of Europe, stemming in part from the new realities in global terrorism but also arising from a series of events on European soil that heightened concerns about the internal threat to security and Western values posed by the growing number of Muslim immigrants and residents.

In this chapter, I survey five key events in Europe that not only fueled fears of the Muslim enemy "within" but also had reverberations well beyond the European countries in which they occurred.[1] Four

---

1. In time, a sixth episode undoubtedly will be added to this list – the Paris terrorist attacks in early January 2015. On January 7, two Muslim extremists opened fire at the offices of the French satirical magazine *Charlie Hebdo*, a publication with a history of publishing controversial cartoons that ridiculed Islam and other religions. Twelve people were killed. The following day, another Muslim extremist killed a police officer in the suburb of Montrouge. On January 9,

of these events—the murder of Theo van Gogh (2004), the Madrid bombings (2004), the London bombings (2005), and the Danish cartoon controversy (2005–2006)—took place in the decade following 9/11; only one, the Rushdie Affair (1988–1989), preceded 9/11. Yet all five stoked the flames of Islamophobia, exacerbated already existing tensions between Muslim minorities and the non-Muslim majority, and contributed to a climate in which it became increasingly acceptable to question whether Muslims and Islam belong in the European social and political order.

Muslim Immigration and Migration

Before addressing these five events, I will first provide a brief sketch of the changing demographics in Europe since World War II. The rapid growth of Muslim populations in postwar Europe must be kept in mind when making sense of why these particular events have generated so much tension and controversy.

In 1950, some three hundred thousand Muslims lived in the twenty-seven countries that today make up the European Union (EU). Most Muslims at this time came from former European colonies. As a result, most lived in Britain or France, the two largest colonial powers in Muslim-majority regions during the nineteenth and twentieth centuries.[2] But the pressing need for unskilled labor to rebuild European countries after World War II led to the first wave of Muslim immigration in the 1950s and 1960s. Much of this immigration came at the invitation of European governments through labor and guest worker programs. Both the host

---

a Muslim terrorist took the lives of four hostages in a Jewish grocery store. In all, seventeen victims died in the three attacks.

2. Doug Sanders, *The Myth of the Muslim Tide: Do Immigrants Threaten the West?* (New York: Vintage Books, 2012), 40.

governments and the immigrants operated under the assumption that the latter would stay and work for some years and then return home. For this reason, most of the immigrants in this first wave consisted of men, some single and others with families that they left behind.

In time, many Muslim immigrants from the first wave chose to stay. A second wave of immigration ensued in the 1970s with family reunification. Wives and children reunited with husbands and fathers, and the Muslim population experienced significant growth. A third wave of Muslim immigration, from the 1980s onward, witnessed considerable numbers of asylum seekers and refugees seeking safe haven from the conflicts and instability in their countries of origin, including Afghanistan, Iran, Iraq, Somalia, and the former Yugoslavia.[3]

According to the Pew Research Center, in 2010, the Muslim population in EU countries, plus Switzerland and Norway, was 18.2 million, or 4.5 percent of the population. Table 5.1 provides an overview of the Muslim population in select European countries.

The Pew study also projects that, based on current immigration levels and extrapolations from birth rate trends, the Muslim population in Europe by 2030 will be 29.8 million, or 7.1 percent of the population.[4]

3. Jocelyne Cesari, *When Islam and Democracy Meet: Muslims in Europe and in the United States* (New York: Palgrave Macmillan, 2004), 13–15.
4. Pew Research Center, *The Future of the Global Muslim Population: Projections for 2010–2030* (Washington, DC: Pew Forum on Religion and Public Life, 2011), 124.

Table 5.1 Europe's Muslim Population in 2010		
Countries	Estimated Muslim Population (2010)	Estimated Muslim Percentage of Overall Population (2010)
Austria	475,000	5.7%
Belgium	638,000	6.0%
Denmark	226,000	4.1%
France	4,704,000	7.5%
Germany	4,119,000	5.0%
Italy	1,583,000	2.6%
Netherlands	914,000	5.5%
Norway	144,000	3.0%
Spain	1,021,000	2.3%
Sweden	451,000	4.9%
Switzerland	433,000	5.7%
United Kingdom	2,869,000	4.6%

Source: Pew Research Center, *The Future of the Global Muslim Population: Projections for 2010-2030* (Washington, DC: Pew Forum on Religion and Public Life, 2011), 124.

This growth in Europe's Muslim population is significant for two reasons. First, it means that most European countries have a much higher percentage of residents with a Muslim background than the United States. The Pew Research Center estimated that, in 2010, there were 2.6 million Muslims in the United States, comprising 0.8 percent of the population. Projections for 2030 indicate there will be 6.2 million Muslims, constituting 1.7 percent of the population.[5] The Muslim presence in Europe, comparatively speaking, is and will continue to be much more substantial and visible.

5. Ibid., 141–42.

Second, the growth in Muslim populations across Europe since the mid-twentieth century runs parallel to secularization or, perhaps more aptly, de-Christianization. As Muslim populations grow and assert their religious identities in the public sphere, Christianity's public role and influence fade. In other words, the increasing presence and vitality of Islam is accompanied by the decreasing influence and presence of traditional Christianity. This trend is important because many Europeans have grown accustomed to thinking of religion as a private matter, not because they long to return to a period in which Christian leaders and institutions wielded greater power. Islam's presence and growth thus creates tension because it calls into question the secular values and assumptions that govern much of public and political life in Europe today. This tension feeds most contemporary conflicts between Muslim minorities and the majority populations of Europe.

The Rushdie Affair

The event that triggered the first major conflict between Muslim and non-Muslim populations in Europe was the so-called Rushdie Affair, which followed the publication of *The Satanic Verses* (1988), a novel by Salman Rushdie. Rushdie was born into a Muslim family in Bombay (now Mumbai), India, but has spent the better part of

Salman Rushdie is a British-Indian writer best known for his controversial book *The Satanic Verses* (1988), which satirized Islam, sparked global protests and a call from the Ayatollah Khomeini for Rushdie's death.

his life in Britain. Rushdie's ties to Islam throughout his adult life have been more cultural than religious. He has never considered himself a believer in or practitioner of Islam.

Rushdie began writing novels in the 1970s and earned great acclaim for his 1981 book *Midnight's Children*. This novel also engendered controversy, with the former prime minister of India, Indira Gandhi, suing Rushdie for defamation of character as a result of a not-so-flattering sentence about her in the book. In fact, Rushdie was no stranger to controversy throughout the 1980s, serving as a major voice against racism in Britain and a strong critic of the ruling Conservative Party. *The Satanic Verses*, published on September 26, 1988, transformed Rushdie into the most controversial figure in Britain.

The Rushdie Affair (1988–1989) was a controversy that erupted after the publication of *The Satanic Verses* (1988), a fictional novel by the British-Indian author Salman Rushdie. After its publication, the book generated protests and condemnations from Muslims in Britain and beyond due to its provocative portrayal of Muhammad and the origins of Islam.

The Satanic Verses is not an easy read, nor is it easy to summarize. The book, blending myth and magic with everyday life, focuses on the two survivors of a hijacked jetliner that has exploded over the English Channel: Gibreel, a famous Indian movie star, and Chamcha, a well-known voiceover artist for British radio. The two characters develop opposite personas. Gibreel becomes an angelic figure, Chamcha a devil, though, as the book unfolds, their journeys, both exterior and interior, greatly complicate these personas.

The controversial portion of the book comprises a series of dream sequences in the mind of Gibreel. One of these involves a retelling of the origins of Islam, with a particular interest in the story behind the novel's title.[6] This story of the "satanic verses" derives from a disputed tradition, recorded by two early Muslim commentators, about Muhammad's efforts to persuade residents in Mecca to accept Allah. According to this story, Satan places false words in the mouth of Muhammad so that he concedes to the Meccans that the three goddesses they already worship have the power of intercession. The story suggests that Muhammad was willing to compromise with the pre-Islamic polytheistic beliefs of Mecca in order to persuade the Meccans to submit to Allah. In Islamic history, this story never made it into the authoritative collection of *hadith*, accounts of Muhammad's sayings and deeds.[7] However, Rushdie plays with this alternative narrative in the novel and reimagines other places and figures in Islam's origins and history, from the holy city of Mecca to Muhammad's wives.

hadith: a collection of reports or accounts of Muhammad's words and deeds.

The significance of the allusions to Islam in *The Satanic Verses* was largely lost on Western readers, but, for many Muslims, the novel came across as an endeavor to ridicule and insult Islam in the most provocative ways. Muslim critics typically pointed to the following four aspects of the novel as proof that Rushdie was intent on offending Muslims. First, Rushdie gave the "satanic verses" story a prominent place in the novel, reinforcing older anti-Islam narratives in Christian history that labeled Muhammad as an imposter inspired

---

6. The controversial retelling of this and other early stories in Islamic history can be found in Salman Rushdie, *The Satanic Verses* (New York: Random House, 2008), 93–129.

7. Paul Weller, *A Mirror for Our Times: "The Rushdie Affair" and the Future of Multiculturalism* (London: Continuum, 2009), 13–14.

by Satan and the Qur'an as the product of Muhammad's devilish collaboration. Second, Rushdie substituted the name "Mahound" for Muhammad. "Mahound" was used by medieval Christians to malign Muhammad as a false prophet and an agent of the devil. Third, Rushdie named twelve prostitutes in a brothel after Muhammad's wives. Muhammad's wives have a revered status in Islam, connected with purity, honor, and modesty, yet Rushdie associated them with the exact opposite. Finally, Rushdie referred to Islam's holiest city, Mecca, as "Jahilia," a name Muslims associate with the period of ignorance before the revelation to Muhammad.[8] Taken together, these four features appeared to mock Islam as a malevolent, ignorant, and sexually deviant religion.

jahiliyah: the period of ignorance prior to Islam.

The events that unfolded in the aftermath of the novel's publication ignited a controversy felt throughout the world. Already on October 6, 1988, India became the first country to ban the novel, with many other countries, including Bangladesh, South Africa, Sri Lanka, and the Sudan, following suit in the next couple of months.[9] While these bans did not generate considerable attention within Britain, things changed on January 14, 1989, when the media reported a major demonstration in Bradford, a city in the north of England with a large Muslim population. Protestors burned the book, and this inspired other demonstrations around the country and the world, some of which turned deadly, such as those in Pakistan and India.

8. Leonard W. Levy, *Blasphemy: Verbal Offense against the Sacred, from Moses to Salman Rushdie* (New York: Alfred A. Knopf, 1993), 559–60; The Islamic Defence Council, "Memorandum of Request," in *The Rushdie File*, ed. Lisa Appignanesi and Sara Maitland (Syracuse, NY: Syracuse University Press, 1990), 64 – 66; Weller, *Mirror for Our Times*, 14.

9. Weller, *Mirror for Our Times*, 33–34.

The most pivotal event in the Rushdie Affair occurred on February 14, 1989. The Ayatollah Khomeini of Iran issued a fatwa ordering the death of Rushdie and anyone involved in the publication of *The Satanic Verses*. Khomeini's fatwa not only brought the book firmly into the orbit of Middle Eastern politics, which was undoubtedly one of his motives for issuing it, but also resulted in Rushdie going into hiding for the better part of a decade. During this time, Rushdie adopted an alias, Joseph Anton, inspired by the first names of two favored authors: Joseph Conrad and Anton Chekhov.[10]

In the early years of hiding, the stress on Rushdie was enormous. The fatwa and the fear of assassination certainly were a large part of that, as was the continued violence, which included the bombing of bookstores in Britain and the United States and the murder of the book's Japanese translator.[11] In one effort to put an end to the controversy, Rushdie announced at the end of 1990 that he had converted to Islam. As a sign of his renewed faith, he stated that he would not support the publication of a paperback version of the novel. The "conversion" did not have any effect on the fatwa, as Khomeini's successor reaffirmed the fatwa's irrevocable nature. Rushdie later renounced his conversion, describing it as the biggest mistake of his life.[12]

In the course of the Rushdie Affair, two broad camps developed in opposition to one another. The first advocated fiercely for freedom of expression as a nonnegotiable Western principle. This camp consisted primarily of Rushdie, the publishers of his novel, numerous Western journalists, and many high-profile authors. In fact, thousands of authors signed their names to a statement condemning

10. In his memoirs, Rushdie provides an autobiographical account of his years in hiding after the fatwa. See Salman Rushdie, *Joseph Anton: A Memoir* (New York: Random House, 2012).
11. Steven R. Weisman, "Japanese Translator of Rushdie Book Found Slain," *New York Times*, July 13, 1991, http://www.nytimes.com/books/99/04/18/specials/rushdie-translator.html.
12. Weller, *Mirror for Our Times*, 49–51.

the fatwa and unequivocally supporting Rushdie's freedom to express his beliefs without fear of punishment or death. Signatories included Samuel Beckett, Joan Didion, William Golding, Norman Mailer, Ian McEwan, James Michener, Harold Pinter, Philip Roth, Edward Said, Susan Sontag, and Kurt Vonnegut.[13] Many such statements also expressed regret over the hurt and violence caused by the book but noted that freedom of speech was a principle that could not be abandoned.

The other camp prioritized the rights and sensitivities of Muslim minority communities and insisted that any resolution to the controversy must ensure that Muslims are treated fairly, justly, and respectfully. This camp consisted primarily of Muslim organizations in Britain such as the Islamic Defence Council, Muslim organizations outside of Britain, prominent religious leaders in Britain such as the chief rabbi and the archbishop of Canterbury, and even some notable political figures such as former US president Jimmy Carter.[14] Some in this camp upheld the author's right to freedom of expression while also condemning the offensive nature of Rushdie's novel.

For some Muslim organizations within Britain, however, the focus was on the insult alone. In an effort to have their concerns addressed, these organizations invoked a variety of tactics. In the early months after publication, Muslim leaders and organizations lobbied for the book to be withdrawn from publication voluntarily or for a statement to be inserted into the novel clarifying that it did not contain a historical or factual account of Islam. When these calls went unheeded, the focus turned to extending Britain's existing blasphemy laws, which technically applied only to Christianity, to include Islam. While many in the British government expressed sympathy with

13. For the text of the statement and a longer list of signatories, see Appignanesi and Maitland, *Rushdie File*, 109–12.
14. Weller, *Mirror for Our Times*, 82–86, 89–92; Appignanesi and Maitland, *Rushdie File*, 236–38.

Muslim concerns, the Home Office responded that it had no intention of changing the laws.[15] Under such circumstances, Khomeini's fatwa found sympathy among some British Muslims.

Many of the tensions resulted from each side talking past the other. Both camps also exercised poor judgment and made significant mistakes along the way that exacerbated the controversy. Not all Muslim critics of Rushdie's novel, for example, took the time to read the book, relying instead on hearsay or small excerpts circulated in the media. The burning of Rushdie's novel, while legally permissible, also made matters worse, as book burning raises memories of more sordid episodes in European history such as the Inquisition and Nazi Germany.[16] While attempts to expand Britain's blasphemy laws were understandable, given what few legal avenues were available at the time, these laws had mostly fallen by the wayside by the 1980s and few in Britain had the stomach for returning to an era in which the state regulated religious orthodoxy of any kind. Finally, the vocal support in some Muslim communities for Khomeini's fatwa eroded sympathy for their cause and contributed to the perception that Muslims were unable to accept or abide by the principles and freedoms embedded in a Western secular political order.

For Rushdie and some of his more ardent defenders, the insistence on freedom of expression often came across as an absolute principle not subject to critical scrutiny. In particular, the Rushdie camp failed to consider that human expression, even when done "freely," does not take place on a level playing field. It arises from individuals and communities who occupy unequal positions of power and privilege as a result of complex social, political, and historical forces. Although Rushdie came from a Muslim family from the Indian subcontinent, he had distanced himself from those in Britain with a similar

15. Weller, *Mirror for Our Times*, 17–18, 32, 135.
16. Ibid., 28.

background by pursing a prestigious university education and accepting a secular worldview. As a celebrated author, Rushdie moved in elite social circles, as did many of his more prominent supporters. His access to media outlets and publishers provided him with a potent platform from which he could express his views and shape public opinion. All of this made a difference whenever he chose to articulate his positions on issues from racism to religion. Rushdie possessed not only the freedom to voice his convictions but also the power to make his voice heard. Most British Muslims, by contrast, were members of an underprivileged community, one that had below-average education and income levels, lacked political and social influence, and held to a religious worldview at odds with the dominant culture. Because they possessed neither the power nor the status of a Salman Rushdie, their voices often were ignored or otherwise went unheard, and this reality fueled their frustrations.

Put simply, Rushdie had the power to shape the public narrative of Islam in a manner that British Muslims themselves did not. Ironically, in his recently published memoir Rushdie comments on the difficulty of controlling how a story is told: "At the heart of the dispute over *The Satanic Verses* . . . behind all the accusations and abuse, was a question of profound importance: *Who shall have control over the story? Who has, who should have, the power not only to tell the stories with which, and within which, we all lived, but also to say in what manner those stories may be told?*"[17] Rushdie's answer to these questions is that "*everyone and anyone has, or should have that power,*" and yet the Rushdie Affair is a prime example of the unequal distribution of this power.[18] Rushdie's novel demonstrates how one person can have control over the most sacred stories of a marginalized religious community in Britain. After the publication of *The Satanic Verses*,

17. Rushdie, *Joseph Anton*, 360.
18. Ibid.

many people in Britain, if not the West, were more familiar with Rushdie's version of Islam's origins than they were with the accounts articulated by most Muslims.

One of Rushdie's defenders, Edward Said, noted this irony. While condemning the fatwa and defending Rushdie's right to freedom of expression, Said observed that Rushdie's decision to tell the story of Islam in the manner that he did created the perception among many Muslims that he was aligning himself with the colonial power reflected in Orientalist narratives and not with the victims of such power: "Above all, however, there rises the question that people from the Islamic world ask: Why must a Moslem, who could be defending and sympathetically interpreting us, now represent us so roughly, so expertly and so disrespectfully to an audience already primed to excoriate our traditions, reality, history, religion, language, and origin? Why, in other words, must a member of our culture join the legions of Orientalists in Orientalizing Islam so radically and unfairly?"[19] The failure of Rushdie and his more fervent supporters to consider and grapple with these issues and questions resulted in the perpetuation of harmful stereotypes and led to intransigence that impaired efforts at fruitful dialogue.

The Rushdie Affair's impact on Muslims in Britain and beyond has been significant in many ways, though I will focus primarily on two areas. First, in the realm of politics, the affair exposed the weaknesses in political mobilization that existed among many Muslim minority communities across Europe. During and after the affair, Muslims created organizations to facilitate political involvement and to wield greater influence in European governments so that they would not be solely dependent on a handful of sympathetic allies in the political establishment.[20] Muslims in Europe also began privileging their

---

19. Quoted in Appignanesi and Maitland, *Rushdie File*, 165.

religious identities over their national ones, a development that contributed to tensions with majority populations who had grown accustomed to religion playing an increasingly smaller role in Europe.[21]

The Rushdie Affair also made a significant impact in the growth of systemic bias toward Muslims minorities in the West, what we now call Islamophobia. The anger and resentment expressed by many Muslims during the Rushdie Affair, combined with vocal support for Khomeini's fatwa from some Muslims in the West, created the impression that Muslims were incapable of accepting the values and ideals of a secular political order. This impression, in turn, gave rise to a political climate in which it became increasingly common to question multiculturalism—that is, the commitment of many European governments to accommodate the cultural, ethnic, and religious diversity of immigrant populations, particularly Muslims.

multiculturalism: the practice of acknowledging, accepting, and accommodating cultural and religious differences in the public sphere.

The British novelist Fay Weldon put it bluntly in 1989: "Our attempt at multiculturalism has failed. The Rushdie affair demonstrates it."[22] Roy Jenkins, former home secretary in Britain and an architect of some of Britain's early multiculturalist policies, noted in response to the Rushdie Affair that "in retrospect we might have been more cautious

20. Sophie Gilliat-Ray, *Muslims in Britain: An Introduction* (Cambridge: Cambridge University Press, 2010), 252; Jytte Klausen, *The Islamic Challenge: Politics and Religion in Western Europe* (New York: Oxford University Press, 2005), 33–34; and Jørgen Nielsen, *Muslims in Western Europe* (Edinburgh: Edinburgh University Press, 2004), 160–61.
21. Weller, *Mirror for Our Times*, 106, 111.
22. Quoted in ibid., 103.

about allowing the creation in the 1950s of substantial Muslim communities here."[23]

Of course, raising questions about multiculturalism is not in itself tantamount to endorsing Islamophobia. Even today, Europeans across the political spectrum believe that multiculturalist policies have generally not succeeded in building bridges between Muslim minority communities and the majority population, though there is plenty of disagreement about why these policies have failed and whether they are worth revamping. However, once it became politically and culturally permissible to question the efficacy of multiculturalist policies, the door was opened for some in the majority population, including prominent politicians, to blame Muslims for most social ills and to question whether the dominant culture should tolerate a segment of the population that adhered to a backward, intolerant religion. The Rushdie Affair was thus a catalyst that generated the conditions in which first multiculturalism and then Islamophobia became such politically and culturally divisive issues in Britain, if not Europe.

The Rushdie Affair not only created a climate conducive to Islamophobia, it also produced one of the most outspoken opponents of the very concept of Islamophobia—Salman Rushdie himself! The concept has plenty of detractors, particularly in far right circles, but, among Western intellectuals, Rushdie is one of its most consistent critics. In the first chapter, I noted that in 2006 Rushdie joined a number of other prominent thinkers in authoring a statement that referred to Islamophobia as a "wretched concept."[24] In his more recent memoir, Rushdie expands on his contempt: "A new word had been created to help the blind remain blind: *Islamophobia*. To

23. Quoted in ibid., 104.
24. See Ayaan Hirsi Ali, Chahla Chafiq, Caroline Fourest et al., "Together Facing the New Totalitarianism," *BBC News* (UK), March 1, 2006, http://news.bbc.co.uk/2/hi/europe/4764730.stm.

criticize the militant stridency of this religion in its contemporary incarnation was to be a bigot. A *phobic* person was extreme and irrational in his views, and so the fault lay with such persons and not with the belief system that boasted over one billion followers worldwide. One billion believers could not be wrong, therefore the critics must be the ones foaming at the mouth."[25] The irony, according to Rushdie, is that the ones who are truly phobic and bigoted are those Muslims who are protected by the concept of Islamophobia, whereas enlightened individuals committed to criticizing Islam's intolerance and narrow-mindedness are the ones labeled bigots.

Rushdie's reflections on Islamophobia are provocative, but this is hardly surprising, given that Rushdie authored one of the most provocative books in modern literary history. Nor is it surprising that the fallout from Rushdie's controversial novel continues to resonate in the ongoing debates about the place of Muslims in the European social and political order. These debates show no sign of subsiding. If anything, they have intensified in light of more recent events.

The Murder of Theo Van Gogh

In November 2004, a young Dutch-Moroccan Muslim named Muhammad Bouyeri murdered the filmmaker Theo van Gogh in broad daylight on the streets of Amsterdam. The murder sent shockwaves throughout the Netherlands and the rest of Europe, unsettling so many who had viewed the Netherlands as a model of multiculturalism and religious tolerance. The murder was retaliation for a short but incendiary film directed by Van Gogh called *Submission*. The film accused Islam of promoting the physical and

25. Rushdie, *Joseph Anton*, 144.

sexual abuse of women. Van Gogh's collaborator was a Somalian refugee turned Dutch politician, Ayaan Hirsi Ali, who was already known as one of Europe's most outspoken critics of Islam. Hirsi Ali was also the object of Bouyeri's fury. After killing Van Gogh, Bouyeri pinned a note to Van Gogh's body that condemned Hirsi Ali for engaging in a crusade against Islam.

It is difficult to grasp the significance of Van Gogh's murder without surveying some of the events and circumstances preceding it. Van Gogh and Hirsi Ali, after all, did not land in the spotlight overnight with their warnings about the dangers of Islam. They followed in the footsteps of a politician who paved the way for them and many others to raise questions openly about whether the Dutch should be afraid of the growing Muslim population in the Netherlands.

The politician in question was Pim Fortuyn. Fortuyn was a sociology professor and former communist who eventually set his sights on Dutch politics. He became a prominent critic of Islam in the Netherlands in 1997 with his book *Against the Islamization of Our Culture: Dutch Identity as Foundation*.[26] He was also an outspoken

> **The murder of Theo van Gogh (2004) was a retaliatory act carried out by a radical Dutch-Moroccan Muslim, Muhammad Bouyeri, for a provocative short film that Van Gogh and Ayaan Hirsi Ali made called *Submission*. *Submission* portrayed Islam as a religion that condoned the oppression and abuse of women.**

26. This title is my English translation. The book was published, however, in Dutch. See Pim Fortuyn, *Tegen de islamisering van onze cultur: Nederlandse identiteit als fundament* (Utrecht: A. W. Bruna, 1997).

opponent of the Dutch commitment to multiculturalism at a time when this was not a popular position politically. The populist Livable Netherlands Party elected Fortuyn as its leader in November 2001, though he soon lost his leadership position after making critical comments about Muslims, including accusations that Muslims were incapable of respecting women, lesbians, and gays.[27] He formed his own party, Pim Fortuyn List, and prepared for the national elections, but he was assassinated on May 6, 2002, just prior to the elections. People immediately speculated that the killer was a radical Muslim, an assumption bolstered by Fortuyn's outspoken views on Islam. As it turned out, the murderer was an animal rights activist, but this fact did not let Muslims off the hook. The initial speculation alone reinforced the Western narrative that connected Islam and violence. Fortuyn's murder thus heightened scrutiny of Muslims in the Netherlands.

Van Gogh and Hirsi Ali owed some of their success as provocative commentators on Islam to the fertile soil created by Fortuyn. Other circumstances in the years preceding 2004 also helped their cause. For example, in May 2001, Imam Khalil el-Moumni of Rotterdam made controversial statements on a television program concerning homosexuality. When asked what Muslims believed about homosexuality, he responded: "It is a sickness." On the topic of same-sex marriage, he argued: "If men continue to marry men, and women marry women, then Dutch society will disappear."[28] The statements brought considerable scrutiny both to the imam and to Muslims in the Netherlands, with prominent politicians and public figures calling for the imam to be prosecuted under antidiscrimination laws or even

27. "Pim Fortuyn op herhaling: 'De islam is een achterlijke cultuur,'" *De Volkskrant* (Netherlands), February 9, 2002, http://www.volkskrant.nl/vk/nl/2686/Binnenland/article/detail/611698/2012/05/05/Pim-Fortuyn-op-herhaling-De-islam-is-een-achterlijke-cultuur.dhtml.
28. Quoted in Sam Cherribi, *In the House of War: Dutch Islam Observed* (New York: Oxford University Press, 2010), 143–44.

expelled from the country. El-Moumni was eventually prosecuted but acquitted on the grounds of freedom of expression. Nonetheless, the reputation of Muslim minorities took a major hit, and, with the 9/11 attacks happening roughly in the same time frame, Muslims became the object of increasing hostility.

By the time Van Gogh and Hirsi Ali began their work on *Submission*, the cultural and political landscape of the Netherlands was already primed for openly critical debates about Islam and the ability of Muslims to fit into Dutch society. But Van Gogh and Hirsi Ali were able to push these debates further and bring them more fully into the national spotlight through their collaborative film.

Van Gogh was not a lifelong antagonist of Islam, but he was a professional provocateur. He was born in 1957 into one of the most famous families in the Netherlands. His great-grandfather, also named Theo van Gogh, was the brother of the famous painter Vincent van Gogh. Theo van Gogh dropped out of law school and devoted his career to filmmaking, though he also served as a columnist for the newspaper *Metro*. He was a friend and strong supporter of Pim Fortuyn. In 2003, Van Gogh authored a book highly critical of Islam called *Allah Knows Better*.[29] In the book, he accuses Dutch imams of promoting wife abuse and homophobia.[30] His provocative statements were not limited to Islam. He also made derogatory statements against Jews, including Amsterdam's Jewish mayor Job Cohen. Van Gogh viewed himself as an equal opportunity critic of all forms of political correctness.

Hirsi Ali, in contrast to Van Gogh, had strong, intimate ties with Islam in her past that not only shaped her particular criticisms but also

29. The title is my English translation. The Dutch title is *Alla weet het beter*.
30. Ambrose Evans-Pritchard and Joan Clements, "Film-Maker Killed in Islamic Revenge," *Telegraph* (UK), November 3, 2004, http://www.telegraph.co.uk/news/worldnews/europe/netherlands/1475758/Film-maker-killed-in-Islamic-revenge.html.

gave her a special "insider status" that lent more credibility to her criticisms.[31] Born in Somalia in 1969, Hirsi Ali spent her childhood years on the move, living in Saudi Arabia, Ethiopia, and Kenya. By her own account, she was a devout and even radical Muslim in these years, protesting perceived insults against Islam, such as the publication of *The Satanic Verses*.[32] In 1992, her father arranged a marriage for her with a cousin in Canada. Hirsi Ali reluctantly agreed, but on her way to Canada she took a detour to Europe and eventually applied for asylum in the Netherlands.[33]

Ayaan Hirsi Ali (1969–) is a prominent politician and critic of Islam. Born in Somalia and raised a devout Muslim, she sought asylum in the Netherlands in 1992. She eventually abandoned Islam, became a member of the Dutch parliament, and served as one of Europe's most vocal critics of Islam's treatment of women. She currently resides in the United States and works for the American Enterprise Institute.

Hirsi Ali quickly learned Dutch, became a citizen, and obtained an advanced degree in political science from Leiden University. She also gained experience working with Muslim and immigrant women in abuse shelters and asylum centers. She drew on this experience as a

31. Ayaan Hirsi Ali, *Infidel* (New York: Free Press, 2008), 170–99; Eyerman, *Assassination of Theo Van Gogh*, 87.
32. Ron Eyerman, *The Assassination of Theo Van Gogh: From Social Drama to Cultural Trauma* (Durham, NC: Duke University Press, 2008), 86–87.
33. Ayaan Hirsi Ali, *Infidel* (New York: Free Press, 2008), 170–99; Eyerman, *Assassination of Theo Van Gogh*, 87.

researcher for the Labor Party, her first foray into Dutch politics.[34] In 2002, she switched to the People's Party for Freedom and Democracy, claiming that the Labor Party had failed to integrate Muslims and had succumbed to multiculturalism.[35] She successfully ran for parliament and shot to political stardom as an outspoken critic of Islam and previous Dutch policies on immigration. By this time, Hirsi Ali had abandoned Islam and become an atheist.

Central to Hirsi Ali's career, then and now, is her criticism of Islam as a backward religion that is incompatible with the West. She has a particular concern for what she perceives as the abuse and oppression of women sanctioned by Islam. Hirsi Ali claims the mantles of feminism and the Enlightenment to challenge Islam's patriarchy, misogyny, and intolerance. Many conservative commentators and politicians view her both as a courageous heroine in the battle against Islam and as a beloved "Daughter of the Enlightenment."[36] While her career as a member of the Dutch parliament came to an end in 2006, largely because she falsified information on her original asylum application, she continues to weigh in on political affairs as part of the neoconservative American Enterprise Institute in the United States. She is also a fellow at the Belfer Center's Future of Diplomacy Project at the Harvard Kennedy School of Government.

A fuller account of Hirsi Ali's criticisms of Islam can be found in chapter 6, but her core views on the abuse and oppression of Muslim women are on full display in the 2004 short film *Submission*. Directed by Van Gogh with Hirsi Ali as the scriptwriter, *Submission*, a title

---

34. Cherribi, *In the House of War*, 166–67.

35. Eyerman, *Assassination of Theo Van Gogh*, 36–37; Cherribi, *In the House of War*, 167.

36. Christopher Caldwell, "Daughter of the Enlightenment," *New York Times Magazine*, April 3, 2005, http://www.nytimes.com/2005/04/03/magazine/03ALI.html?_r=0; see also Ayaan Hirsi Ali, *The Caged Virgin: An Emancipation Proclamation for Women and Islam* (New York: Free Press, 2008).

that refers to the literal translation of the word *Islam*, provides a fictional portrayal of five Muslim women. One woman stands at the center of the room. She is veiled, but the veil is transparent in the front and shows much of her body. Inscribed on her body are the opening verses of the Qur'an. After reciting these verses, the camera reveals that the woman has been flogged, and we hear her talk about receiving punishment for engaging in a forbidden love affair. As the film unfolds, we learn the stories of the other women, all victims of physical or sexual violence. One woman is beaten by her husband weekly, another is raped and impregnated by her uncle, still another is forced to marry a man who repulses her and to submit sexually to him. All of the women have Qur'anic verses inscribed on their bodies, verses that presumably support the submission and oppression of women.[37]

The film aired on a late-night television program in August 2004. Hirsi Ali was a guest on the show, and the host invited her to show a clip from the film and then to discuss it. She indicated on the program that the movie was aimed at Muslim women to facilitate their liberation.[38] In her autobiography *Infidel*, Hirsi Ali elaborated on her intentions in the film, arguing that a slavish obedience to the Qur'an as Allah's literal word perpetuated the types of violence against women dramatized in the film. The liberation of Muslim women—and men—could only come about by the liberation of the mind from allegiance to rigid dogmatism.[39]

Submission provoked considerable debate in the Netherlands about Islam and the treatment of women. It also reinforced the perception that Hirsi Ali was the Dutch version of Salman Rushdie, and comparisons between the two were common, for understandable

37. Hirsi Ali, *Infidel*, 313–14.
38. Cherribi, *In the House of War*, 197–98.
39. Hirsi Ali, *Infidel*, 313–14.

reasons. Both were born into Muslim families but ultimately left Islam and embraced a secular worldview. Both used their insider status to lend greater credence to their criticisms of Islam. Both were accused by various Muslims of committing blasphemy. And both became symbolic representatives of freedom of speech.

Hirsi Ali owes her revered status in some political circles, not to mention her reputation as a media star, in part to *Submission*. Even so, the problematic assumptions and portrayals in *Submission* open Hirsi Ali to significant criticisms. First, the dialogue in the film is in English. If Hirsi Ali were really serious about reaching her supposed target audience, Muslim women, the characters would speak languages such as Dutch, Arabic, or Turkish. The use of English leaves Hirsi Ali susceptible to the charge that her real audience consists of those who are already either anxious or hostile toward Islam, at home and throughout the West. She wants the film to be accessible not to Muslims but to Islam's critics.[40]

Second, Hirsi Ali's decision to show Muslim women almost nude, with Qur'anic texts inscribed on their bodies, does not further her stated goal of supporting women's liberation. A case can be made that Hirsi Ali herself is guilty of exploiting the bodies of women for political gain.[41] Moreover, the prevalence of nudity points to the larger problem of a hypersexualized West in which women's power resides in their sexuality alone.

Third, Hirsi Ali gives names to the women in the film that many Muslims see as a direct insult to Islam. The names of the characters are the same as the names of some of Muhammad's family members, including Amina (Muhammad's mother), Aisha (one of Muhammad's wives), and Fatima (Muhammad's daughter).[42] The implication is that

40. Cherribi, *In the House of War*, 202.
41. Ibid.
42. Ibid.

what Muslim women suffer today is what those women closest to Muhammad suffered in his day. In other words, Islam's most revered figure, either through his teachings or actions, has been and continues to be the source of the physical and sexual abuse experienced by Muslim women.

Finally, *Submission* resurrects all sorts of Western stereotypes and Orientalist tropes about the oppression of women by sexually depraved Muslim men. The film promotes Islamophobia by suggesting that the only way to interpret the Qur'anic texts invoked in the film is in the manner portrayed by Hirsi Ali. It is as if Muslim men are somehow programmed or brainwashed to oppress women simply by reading the Qur'an. The film implies that all or most Muslim men are prone to abuse women and that all or most Muslim women are victims of abuse. The film offers no other explanation for why men, Muslim or otherwise, might abuse women, nor does the film give any hint that the physical and sexual abuse of women is a problem that exists globally, occurring in all cultures and religious traditions.

In making the film, Hirsi Ali clearly wanted her audience to be afraid of Islam's power to perpetuate the abuse of women. She wanted her audience to recognize and accept that Islam was a threat to Western values. In her quest to manufacture a large-scale fear of Islam, she received help from an unlikely source—Muhammed Bouyeri. His decision to hunt down and kill Van Gogh seemed to confirm Hirsi Ali's warning that Islam was a danger to the West.

Bouyeri was born and raised in Amsterdam. His father, Hamid, emigrated from Morocco to France and then to the Netherlands in the 1960s. As a child, Bouyeri seemed well adjusted and even ambitious. He graduated from high school and studied accounting and business information technology at Inholland University, though he left before finishing his degree. Bouyeri was also active in his community, volunteering at a neighborhood youth center.[43]

As Bouyeri entered adulthood, his behavior changed and he began to have more confrontations with Dutch authorities and law enforcement, including a couple of arrests. Bouyeri also began to embrace more radical forms of Islam, and this led him to adopt an increasingly hostile rhetoric and attitude toward perceived opponents of Islam in the Netherlands. It is unclear what precipitated this shift in behavior and identity: perhaps it was the closing of the neighborhood youth center that meant so much to him as a teenager, the death of his mother, or the decreasing health of his father.[44]

Bouyeri grew weary of attacks on Islam in the Netherlands and took matters into his own hands. On November 2, 2004, while Van Gogh was bicycling to work, Bouyeri opened fire and wounded the filmmaker. Van Gogh tried to elude his attacker by running around a parked car, all the while pleading for his life, but to no avail. Bouyeri fired the final shots that killed Van Gogh and then approached his body, cut his throat with a small machete, and drove a knife deep into his corpse. Attached to the knife was a note that included threats to Van Gogh's collaborator, Hirsi Ali, accusing her of operating as an "infidel fundamentalist" who "terrorizes Islam."[45]

The murder left the Netherlands and much of Europe in disbelief and seemed to confirm the suspicions of those who believed that Europe was very much in the throes of a clash of civilizations.[46] One

43. Eyerman, *Assassination of Theo Van Gogh*, 56–57.
44. Ibid., 58–59.
45. Ian Buruma, *Murder in Amsterdam: Liberal Europe, Islam, and the Limits of Tolerance* (London: Penguin Books, 2006), 2–6; Eyerman, *Assassination of Theo Van Gogh*, 6.
46. Bouyeri was tried, convicted, and sentenced to life without parole. A second trial took place concerning the possibility that coconspirators, members of the so-called Hofstad Network, aided Bouyeri. The network was labeled a terrorist network as a result of the trial, though it remains unclear what sort of involvement members of the network had in the murder. See Eyerman, *Assassination of Theo Van Gogh*, 2.

headline from the newspaper *De Volkskrant* read: "Murder Starts Holy War in the Netherlands."[47] Bouyeri's actions became grounds for suspecting that Muslims were out to destroy the nation in the name of Islam.

In reflecting on the larger impact of Van Gogh's murder on the place of Muslims and Islam in the Netherlands and Europe more generally, four observations can be made. First, multiculturalism suffered a huge setback with the murder. Pim Fortuyn may have paved the way for questioning multiculturalist policies, but, after Van Gogh's murder, many in the Netherlands and throughout Europe felt that multiculturalism and tolerance of diversity had gone too far. Polls taken in the Netherlands within a year after the murder reflected the turning tide, with 40 percent of Dutch citizens expressing the hope that Muslim immigrants "no longer feel at home in the Netherlands," and more than 80 percent desiring greater restrictions on immigration. Another poll indicated that 51 percent of so-called native Dutch held unfavorable views of Muslims.[48]

Second, as in the Rushdie Affair, freedom of expression became the primary framework within which major political and public figures interpreted the murder and the controversy over *Submission*. Legitimate criticisms of the film took a backseat to louder calls to defend this Western freedom at all costs. The Dutch prime minister identified Van Gogh as "a champion of freedom of expression."[49] On the evening of November 2, members of Van Gogh's family told a massive crowd gathered on Amsterdam's Dam Square to "make as much noise as possible in support of freedom of speech." At the same gathering, Amsterdam's mayor referred to Van Gogh as a symbol of

47. "Moord begin heilige oorlog in Nederland," *De Volksrant* (Netherlands), November 6, 2004, http://www.volkskrant.nl/vk/nl/2824/Politiek/article/detail/691841/2004/11/06/Moord-begin-heilige-oorlog-in-Nederland.dhtml.
48. Eyerman, *Assassination of Theo Van Gogh*, 12.
49. Quoted in ibid., 46.

free speech, insisting that "freedom of speech is a foundation of our country and that foundation was tampered with today."[50] An editorial in *De Volkskrant* argued: "Muslims have to learn, in a democracy, religion, too, is open to criticism."[51] The Dutch commitment to freedom of expression was pitted against the failure of immigrants and Muslims to recognize and cherish this principle.

Third, Van Gogh's murder and the resulting suspicion of Muslims paved the way for a stronger far right presence in the political arena. In the Netherlands, the best example of this was the formation of the Party for Freedom in 2005, led by Geert Wilders. Wilders will be discussed in greater detail in the next chapter, but what is important to note at this point is that his party quickly grew and became the third-largest party in the parliament in 2010. The party maintains a strong anti-immigrant platform, and Wilders is probably the most recognizable and controversial critic of Islam in Europe today. To be sure, other Dutch politicians, including Fortuyn, helped create a climate in which criticizing Islam could score political points. But Wilders and his party managed to capitalize on the growing misgivings toward Muslims in the Netherlands arising in the aftermath of the Van Gogh murder.

Finally, the murder reinforced one of the core Western stereotypes of Islam: its inherently violent nature. Bouyeri articulated his motives in the context of his Muslim faith, giving the impression that Islam promotes violence against anyone who disagrees with its teachings. The fact that the media sometimes framed Bouyeri's actions as a "holy war" bolstered the perception that Islam was at war with the West and that the battleground was now Europe. But the Van Gogh murder was not the only episode on European soil to give this impression. Just before and after the murder, two other events—the

50. Quoted in ibid., 47.
51. Quoted in ibid., 49.

Madrid bombings of 2004 and the London bombings of 2005—fed the narrative of a grave and violent "Islamic threat."

The Madrid Bombings

On March 11, 2004, ten bombs on four commuter trains in Madrid exploded during morning rush hour, killing 191 people and injuring at least 1,800. Until the Madrid bombings, referred to as "11-M" in Spain, terrorist attacks on European soil had primarily been carried out by individuals and organizations involved in larger national conflicts, including the Irish Republican Army in the United Kingdom and Spain's Euskadi Ta Askatasuna (ETA).[52]

ETA, a separatist organization that seeks independence for the Basque Country, a region in northern Spain, is especially relevant for the story that developed in the immediate aftermath of the Madrid attacks. Immediate suspicion was cast on ETA by

> **The Madrid bombings (2004) refer to a series of bombs set off on four commuter trains in Madrid on the morning of March 11, 2004. The bombings, referred to as "11-M" in Spain, resulted in almost two hundred deaths and close to two thousand injuries. Just over twenty people, many with a Moroccan background, were found guilty of aiding or carrying out the bombings.**

52. Kate Friesen, "The Effects of the Madrid and London Subway Bombings on Europe's View of Terrorism," in "Human Rights and the War of Terror," supplement to *Human Rights and Human Welfare* (2007): S10–S17, http://www.du.edu/korbel/hrhw/researchdigest/terror/europe_2007.pdf.

journalists, politicians, and even the broader public, but within hours of the bombings police discovered some evidence suggesting that ETA was not the culprit, including detonators of a type not typically used by ETA and a cassette tape of Qur'an readings. Despite this evidence, the minister of the interior, Ángel Acebes, insisted at an afternoon press conference: "The government has no doubt ETA is responsible."[53] In an evening press statement, Acebes confirmed that ETA was still the primary suspect, though he also indicated that other lines of investigation were still open.[54]

In the days that followed, the Popular Party, Spain's conservative ruling party, came under increasing attack from political opponents and the broader public. The government's ETA hypothesis was lacking solid evidence, and an anonymous caller claimed that al-Qaeda was responsible. Protests erupted on March 13 as critics accused the government of obscuring the truth behind the attacks for political gain.

Under different circumstances, the Popular Party might have recovered from its initial mishandling of the 11-M story, but the timing of the attacks made this impossible, given that national elections were held three days later on March 14. Despite polls prior to the bombings that predicted the Popular Party would win against its rival, the center-left Spanish Socialist Workers' Party, the latter won by a significant majority.[55]

The results may seem odd in light of conventional political wisdom. With terrorist attacks, it is not uncommon for voters, perhaps feeling vulnerable, to rally behind the ruling government and

---

53. Quoted in Cristina Flesher Fominaya, "The Madrid Bombings and Popular Protest: Misinformation, Counter-Information, and Mobilisation and Elections after '11-M,'" *Contemporary Social Sciences* 6 (2011): 292.
54. Ibid., 292, 294.
55. Teemu Sinkkonen, *Political Responses to Terrorism: Case Study of the Madrid Terrorist Attack in March 11, 2004, and Its Aftermath* (Tampere, Finland: Tampere University Press, 2009), 13–14; Fominaya, "Madrid Bombings and Popular Protest," 289.

avoid significant change. For example, after 9/11, public approval for President Bush in the United States rose dramatically.[56] This did not happen in Spain. Opposition to the Popular Party's position on the War on Terror (which it firmly supported) increased rapidly in the days following 11-M, as did frustration over the party's insistence that ETA was responsible for the Madrid attacks. With trust in the ruling government depleted, the Spanish people reversed course on March 14. The new prime minister, José Zapatero, immediately set about withdrawing Spanish troops from the US-led war in Iraq.

Who were the perpetrators behind the attacks that so dramatically altered Spain's political landscape and its support for the War on Terror? In the weeks after 11-M, Spanish authorities rounded up and arrested an array of suspects, many of whom had a Moroccan background. This background is significant in light of the fact that on May 16, 2003, a group of fourteen radicalized Moroccan Muslims, motivated in part by anti-Spanish sentiment, bombed several sites in downtown Casablanca, including a Spanish restaurant. Eleven of the fourteen men died in the attacks, as did thirty-three victims.[57] A similar Moroccan anti-Spanish sentiment may have contributed to the motives of the 11-M attackers as well, though, as we shall see, mystery remains concerning the full range of motives behind the Madrid bombings.[58] Either way, the Moroccan backgrounds of the perpetrators connect both attacks, and Moroccans traditionally have not been associated with radical Islamism.[59]

In all, twenty-nine suspects were arrested and charged for the 11-M attacks. They went on trial in 2007, and, by the end, twenty-one were found guilty of crimes that ranged from forgery to

---

56. Sinkkonen, *Political Responses to Terrorism*, 14–15.
57. Alison Pargeter, *The New Frontiers of Jihad: Radical Islam in Europe* (Philadelphia: University of Pennsylvania Press, 2008), 120–21.
58. Ibid., 138.
59. Ibid., 115.

collaboration to murder. Two of the convicted murderers received prison sentences amounting to thousands of years.

No hard evidence surfaced in the trial linking the defendants to al-Qaeda.[60] While one can reasonably assume that al-Qaeda's ideology and methodology served as a source of inspiration for the 11-M attacks, the actual financing and carrying out of the bombings seems to have been independent of formal al-Qaeda support. Moreover, given the defendants' insistence on their innocence throughout the trial, we have no confession from those convicted that points to a clear motivation.[61] The timing of 11-M suggests that the perpetrators wanted to disrupt Spain's national elections and to undermine its involvement in the War on Terror, but, in the end, it is impossible to move beyond speculation concerning the motives.

The London Bombings

Just over one year after the Madrid bombings, London experienced a similar tragedy. In the morning hours of July 7, 2005, four bombs exploded in the heart of London's transportation system. Three of the four bombs detonated within one minute of each other on three different London Underground trains. The fourth bomb exploded almost one hour later on a double-decker bus in central London's Tavistock Square. In addition to the four suicide bombers, fifty-two people were killed in the coordinated attacks, and over seven hundred were injured. The London attacks, subsequently referred to as "7/7," constituted the most devastating bombings in London since World War II.[62]

60. Ibid., 137–38.
61. Ibid., 133.
62. Nafeez Mosaddeq Ahmed, *The London Bombings: An Independent Inquiry* (London: Duckworth, 2006), 12.

The London bombings (2005) involved four bombs set off in the London transportation system on the morning of July 7, 2005. The bombings, known as "7/7" in Britain, killed just over fifty people and injured hundreds. The four perpetrators, all Muslim, were raised in Britain, and three of the four were born there.

Within a few days after 7/7, police pieced together the identities of the four men responsible for the initial attacks. Three of them were of Pakistani descent, the fourth of Jamaican origin. All four lived in or near Leeds in northern England.[63] Three of the four were born in Britain, and all four were raised there.[64] This fact surprised many in Britain since it meant these were not disaffected outsiders but rather "homegrown terrorists." More surprisingly, as details emerged about their backgrounds, it seemed as if most of the perpetrators were well integrated into British society. One of the perpetrators served as a teaching assistant in a primary school, and another came from a family that operated a butcher shop and two eateries.[65]

Why four young men who called Britain their home and who enjoyed the rights and privileges of British citizenship would carry out such horrific attacks is a question not easily answered. It is possible that they wrestled with an identity crisis. As second-generation British Muslims (for three of the four at least), they perhaps felt alienated both from mainstream British society and from the home country of their parents, victims of what Rushdie refers

---

63. Yasmin Hussain and Paul Bagguley, "Securitized Citizens: Islamophobia, Racism and the 7/7 London Bombings," *Sociological Review* 60 (2012): 715–34.
64. Milan Rai, *7/7: The London Bombings, Islam and the Iraq War* (Ann Arbor, MI: Pluto, 2006), 23.
65. Ibid., 25, 31.

to as "double unbelonging," and this may have made them more susceptible to radical Islamist teachings.[66] But this is merely speculation.

We do know their declared reasons for carrying out the attacks pertained to Britain's involvement in Afghanistan and Iraq as well as a larger concern to protect fellow Muslims throughout the world who were suffering. Two of the bombers left videotape confessions indicating as much. One of the bombers, Mohammed Siddique Khan, stated: "Your democratically elected governments continuously perpetuate atrocities against my people all over the world. And your support of them makes you directly responsible, just as I am directly responsible for protecting and avenging my brothers and sisters. . . . [U]ntil you stop the bombing, gassing, imprisonment and torture of my people we will not stop this fight."[67] Another bomber, Shehzad Tanweer, insisted that the bombings were "only the beginning of a string of attacks that will continue and become stronger until you pull your forces out of Afghanistan and Iraq and until you stop your financial and military support to America and Israel."[68] Beyond these stated reasons, we cannot be sure about the social, political, religious, or cultural forces that put these men on such a violent path. We cannot even confirm the degree to which al-Qaeda was involved in the attacks, though documents have surfaced that may suggest an al-Qaeda operative was instrumental in planning the attacks.[69]

What we can assert is that the 7/7 bombings, along with the 11-M attacks, gave rise to greater hostility toward Muslims and Islam

---

66. Pargeter, *New Frontiers of Jihad*, 140–41; Rushdie, *Joseph Anton*, 54.
67. Quoted in "London Bomber: Text in Full," *BBC News* (UK), September 1, 2005, http://news.bbc.co.uk/2/hi/uk_news/4206800.stm.
68. Quoted in Pargeter, *New Frontiers of Jihad*, 152.
69. Nic Robertson, Paul Cruickshank, and Tim Lister, "Documents Give New Details on Al Qaeda's London Bombings," *CNN*, April 30, 2012, http://www.cnn.com/2012/04/30/world/al-qaeda-documents-london-bombings/.

in Europe. Both Spain and Britain witnessed a rise in anti-Muslim incidents following the bombings. Long-term data on racially motivated crimes against Muslims does not exist in Spain, but information provided by the director of the National Police Force and the director of the Civil Guard for the period from January 2004 to May 2005 indicates a rise in Islamophobic incidents after 11-M. Examples of more egregious incidents include vandalism of mosques, a violent assault on a Muslim woman wearing a headscarf, the murder of a Moroccan pedestrian by a automobile driver, and the murder of a Moroccan farm laborer.[70]

As for the London bombings, the data recorded by the London Metropolitan Police Service on what are called "faith-hate" incidents, or incidents motivated by the perceived religious identity of the victim, witnessed a sharp increase in the weeks following 7/7.

70. European Monitoring Centre on Racism and Xenophobia, *Muslims in the European Union: Discrimination and Islamophobia* (Vienna: EUMC, 2006), 71–72, http://fra.europa.eu/sites/default/files/fra_uploads/156-Manifestations_EN.pdf.

Table 5.2 "Faith Hate" Crimes in London, 2004–2005		
Weeks	2004	2005
June 20 – June 26	14	16
June 27 – July 3	8	15
July 4 – July 10	11	68
July 11 – July 17	22	92
July 18 – July 24	20	67
July 25 – July 31	19	79
August 1 – August 7	7	60
August 8 – August 14	9	35
August 15 – August 21	10	28
August 22 – August 28	6	21
August 29 – September 4	8	19
September 5 – September 11	23	17
Source: European Monitoring Centre on Racism and Xenophobia, *Muslims in the European Union: Discrimination and Islamophobia* (Vienna: EUMC, 2006), 86, http://fra.europa.eu/sites/default/files/fra_uploads/156-Manifestations_EN.pdf		

The data in the table do not distinguish between different kinds of faith-related incidents or crimes; for example, it is not possible to determine from these statistics which crimes were rooted in anti-Semitism and which in Islamophobia. Even so, given the timing of the spike in incidents, most of which involved verbal and physical assaults along with property damage, and in light of the corroborating evidence provided by various nongovernmental organizations on anti-Muslim incidents in this period, it is reasonable to conclude that many of the victims during the weeks immediately after 7/7 were Muslims or those otherwise presumed to be Muslims.[71]

71. Ibid., 86.

In addition to outright Islamophobic incidents, negative perceptions of Muslims and Islam increased sharply immediately after the London bombings. A poll taken by the *Telegraph* one day after 7/7 revealed a significant degree of hostility toward Muslims. Forty-six percent of the British population felt that Islam itself presented a threat to liberal democracy, an increase of 14 percent since shortly after September 11, 2001.[72] Polls in subsequent years reinforced such negative perceptions. For example, a poll taken in May 2008 indicated that 51 percent of the British population felt that Islam was either partly or fully to blame for the 7/7 attacks.[73]

This last poll reflects how the London bombings fueled the perception that Islam is inherently violent and that Muslims are internal security risks against whom additional if not extraordinary measures need to be taken. In the wake of these attacks, raising critical questions about multiculturalism, not to mention the place of Muslims in the cultural and political landscape of Europe, has become commonplace. We see this in the rhetoric of far right political parties and even in the comments made by mainstream European politicians. For example, David Cameron, the current prime minister in the UK, has pointed to the failure of "state multiculturalism" and has argued for stronger measures to reinforce British identity and to combat Muslim extremists. He has also invoked the guilt-by-association principle by indicating that Muslim organizations that fail actively to tackle Islamic extremism should not receive public funds and should be subject to greater government scrutiny.[74] These sentiments from the head of the British government make sense only when one considers the altered political and security climate in post-7/7 Britain,

72. Rai, 7/7, 59.
73. Hussain and Bagguley, "Securitized Citizens," 716.
74. "State Multiculturalism Has Failed, Says David Cameron," *BBC News* (UK), February 5, 2011, http://www.bbc.co.uk/news/uk-politics-12371994.

even if concerns about multiculturalism were raised as far back as the Rushdie Affair.

An even clearer post-7/7 critique of multiculturalism and the menacing "Islamic threat" comes from Melanie Phillips. A prominent British journalist, Phillips penned a vitriolic diatribe against British Muslims in her book *Londonistan* (2006). In the book, she argues that the London attacks "revealed a terrible truth about Britain." The bombings "finally lifted the veil on Britain's dirty secret in the war on terrorism—that for more than a decade, London had been the epicenter of Islamic militancy in Europe. Under the noses of successive British governments, Britain's capital had turned into 'Londonistan' . . . and become the major European center for the promotion, recruitment, and financing of Islamic terror and extremism."[75] Phillips counters those who believe that most Muslims in Britain are law-abiding citizens by arguing that the 7/7 attacks took place because many British Muslims have established a separate identity and a parallel legal system that creates the conditions for the extremism of the London bombings.

Phillips has plenty of harsh words for the British government as well. "Driven by postcolonial guilt and, with the loss of empire," she writes, "Britain's elites have come to believe that the country's identity and values are by definition racist, nationalistic and discriminatory."[76] These ruling elites have opted for a multicultural society, turning a blind eye to Islamic extremism and failing to challenge the many Muslims in their midst who explicitly or implicitly condone violence and terrorism. According to Phillips, these elites must abolish multiculturalism as a government policy and "set about the remoralization and reculturation of Britain" by

---

75. Melanie Phillips, *Londonistan* (New York: Encounter Books, 2006), x–xi.
76. Ibid., xix–xx.

restoring the country's Judeo–Christian values, without deference to the almost three million Muslims who call Britain home.[77]

The purpose of *Londonistan* is not to offer a nuanced analysis of immigration policy or the complex factors that contribute to the violent extremism embraced by a very small minority of Muslims. The book's larger intent is to stir up resentment and hostility toward Muslims and to warn readers of the threat posed by Muslims to British and Western values and identity. Most politicians and journalists in Britain or other European countries would never embrace the harsh rhetoric employed by Phillips, but, without a doubt, her book and the larger narrative it endorses is the product of a political climate in which targeting Muslims and Islam as the ultimate "enemy within" has become mainstream. Such a climate is unimaginable apart from the adverse impact of the Madrid and London bombings on public and political opinions toward Muslim minorities in Europe.

The Danish Cartoon Controversy

Tensions between Muslim minorities and the non-Muslim majority in Europe were already at a boiling point by the end of the summer of 2005. In light of Van Gogh's murder and the two deadly attacks in Madrid and London, the last thing Muslims needed was another major controversy to fuel the perception that Muslims were a menace to Western values and ideals. But when a Danish newspaper decided to publish a series of cartoons of the Prophet Muhammad in September 2005, controversy once again erupted, this time extending from a small Scandinavian country all the way to the Middle East and South Asia.

77. Ibid., 188.

The cartoon controversy's origins lie in the desire of two editors of a right-leaning Danish newspaper, *Jyllands-Posten*, to test whether self-censorship and concerns for political correctness regarding Muslims had gone too far in the Danish press and larger society.[78] In particular, the editors were concerned that a children's author was having difficulty finding someone to illustrate the Prophet Muhammad for a book, presumably because of the offense this would give to Muslims in light of the perception that Islam prohibits images of the Prophet.[79] Flemming Rose, the newspaper's culture editor, sent a letter to forty-two illustrators on September 19, 2005, requesting that they submit an illustration of Muhammad that would be published in the newspaper. The illustrators were "to draw Muhammad as you see him."[80] In the end,

> **The Danish cartoon controversy (2005–2006) began with the publication of twelve cartoons of the Prophet Muhammad in the *Jyllands-Posten* newspaper on September 30, 2005. Some of the cartoons mocked Muhammad and Islam; they generated a global controversy, including violent protests outside of Danish embassies in countries such as Iran, Pakistan, and Syria.**

---

78. For a detailed overview of the Danish cartoon crisis and its global repercussions, see Jytte Klausen, *The Cartoons That Shook the World* (New Haven, CT: Yale University Press, 2009).

79. Despite common assumptions among Muslims and non-Muslims alike that Islam prohibits outright any images of the Prophet, there are plenty of examples of such depictions in Islam's history, particularly in popular art. Moreover, the primary factor leading to Muslim protests over the Danish cartoons was not the perceived violation of some fixed Islamic law but rather the perceived insult of some of the caricatures of Muhammad. See Ibid., 137–43.

80. Quoted in ibid., 7.

only twelve artists submitted cartoons or caricatures of Muhammad to the newspaper.

The newspaper published the twelve cartoons on September 30, under the heading, "The Face of Muhammad." Carsten Juste, the editor in chief, included an editorial to explain the reason behind publishing the cartoons. He argued that Muslim leaders in Denmark were too sensitive to criticism. He took particular aim at "mad mullahs" who were quick to interpret any criticism directed at them as criticism of the Prophet or the Qur'an. He characterized these leaders as belonging to "a dark and violent middle age."[81] Rose added in his own commentary that some Muslims "are demanding a special position when they insist that special consideration should be given to their religious sensitivities." He insisted that such consideration "is incompatible with secular democracy and freedom of expression."[82]

> *Shahada*: the Islamic declaration of faith in which believers proclaim, "There is no god but God, and Muhammad is His messenger."

The cartoons themselves were a mixed bag. One ridiculed the children's author whose initial request led to the newspaper's solicitation of the cartoons. Another implied that Muslims were victims. Several mocked the newspaper and its editors. But without a doubt, some contained problematic if not racist depictions. The most controversial cartoon, submitted by Kurt Westergaard, depicted Muhammad wearing a turban containing a huge bomb. Inscribed on the bomb in Arabic was the *Shahada*, the Islamic declaration of faith: "There is no god but God, and Muhammad is His messenger."

---

81. Quoted in ibid., 13.
82. Quoted in Jørgen Nielsen, "Danish Cartoons and Christian-Muslim Relations in Denmark," *Exchange* 39 (2010): 223.

Whatever Westergaard's intentions, both critics and supporters of the *Jyllands-Posten* experiment interpreted the cartoon as associating Muhammad and thus Islam with violence.

The cartoons generated some anger among Danish Muslims as well as Muslims from other countries. On October 12, ambassadors and representatives from eleven Muslim countries wrote a letter to Anders Fogh Rasmussen, Denmark's prime minister, criticizing what they believed was a campaign to demean Muslims. They argued that publishing the cartoons "goes against the spirit of Danish values of tolerance and civil society."[83] They asked the prime minister to apply Danish law to those responsible for the cartoons, and they concluded the letter with a request for a meeting with the prime minister. Rasmussen responded a week later. He affirmed the importance of freedom of the press in Denmark and ignored the request for a meeting.

A small delegation of Danish imams traveled to the Middle East in December to generate international Muslim support for their opposition to the cartoons. They met with representatives of the Egyptian government and the Arab League. Around the same time, the Organisation of the Islamic Conference (OIC) held a summit in Mecca. While the original purpose of the meeting was to address the image of Islam in light of 9/11 and the Madrid and London bombings, the agenda was amended to incorporate the topic of Islamophobia in light of the cartoons. The OIC condemned the cartoons as a sign of "the rising hatred against Islam and Muslims" and urged governments to respect all religions and not to use freedom of expression as a pretense for disparaging religions.[84] The OIC also

---

83. Quoted in ibid., 224.
84. Organization of the Islamic Conference, "Meeting the Challenges of the 21st Century, Solidarity in Action," final communiqué of the Third Extraordinary Session of the Islamic Summit Conference, December 7–8, 2005, http://www.oic-oci.org/ex-summit/english/fc-exsumm-en.htm.

established the Islamophobia Observatory at the meeting in order to monitor and counteract Islamophobia. The OIC summit marked the internationalization of the controversy: because of this meeting, the global Muslim population became aware of the Danish cartoons.[85]

By January 2006, the situation was deteriorating rapidly. In a speech early in the new year, Prime Minister Rasmussen reaffirmed Denmark's commitment to freedom of expression, even as he also condemned the demonization of people based on their religious or ethnic identities. In a letter to the secretary-general of the Arab League on January 6, Denmark's foreign minister insisted: "Freedom of expression is absolute."[86] By the end of the month, the prime minister and even the editor of *Jyllands-Posten* began adopting a more apologetic tone, but, by this time, the controversy was out of hand. Demonstrations materialized in many Muslim countries in February, leading to attacks on Danish embassies in cities such as Damascus, Beirut, Tehran, and Islamabad. Some of the demonstrations turned deadly. The worst of the violence lasted into March, though some violence persisted beyond this time. In 2008, for example, al-Qaeda attacked the Danish embassy in Islamabad, ostensibly in response to the cartoons.

In addition to the demonstrations, a boycott on Danish goods swept through the Middle East beginning in late January 2006 and lasting into the spring. Danish companies such as Arla, Scandinavia's largest dairy producer, suffered significantly from the boycott. In fact, Danish exports across the board suffered huge losses during that period, decreasing between March 2006 and June 2006 by 88 percent in Libya, 47 percent in Iran, and 40 percent in Saudi Arabia. One estimate put the export losses on the one-year anniversary of the cartoon publications at one billion Danish kroner.[87]

---

85. Klausen, *Cartoons That Shook the World,* 74–75.
86. Quoted in Nielsen, "Danish Cartoons," 225.

Both support for and criticism of the cartoons surfaced across the globe. A number of European newspapers republished the cartoons as a gesture of solidarity with Denmark and *Jyllands-Posten*. Westergaard's cartoon in particular found its way into many newspapers from Europe, Latin America, and India. Even some newspapers in the Middle East, such as the Egyptian newspaper *Al-Fagr*, republished some of the cartoons. A handful of American newspapers and publications, such as the *Philadelphia Inquirer* and the *New York Sun*, republished one or more of the cartoons, but these newspapers were definitely the exception and not the rule. In fact, British and American newspapers were among the least likely in the West to republish the cartoons.

The cartoon controversy did lead to some positive developments for Danish Muslims. The more conservative imams whose lobbying campaign in the Middle East contributed to the tensions between Denmark and Muslim-majority countries began to lose support from many Danish Muslims who felt that the imams were exacerbating anti-Muslim feelings in Denmark. Existing Muslim organizations that were more moderate, including Muslims in Dialogue and the Forum for Critical Muslims, were given more attention and support by Danish Muslims. The controversy also gave rise to one of Denmark's first umbrella organizations for Muslims, the Federal Council of Muslims. In Denmark's Lutheran state church, greater support for Christian-Muslim relations and dialogue emerged.[88]

But there is little doubt that the cartoon controversy reinforced negative perceptions of Muslims within the West. Evidence of this can be found in a Pew Research Center poll from 2006. The poll revealed that many non-Muslims in the West blamed the controversy

87. Ibid., 227.
88. Safet Bektovic, "Interreligious Relations," in *Islam in Denmark: The Challenge of Diversity*, ed. Jørgen Nielsen (Lanham, MD: Lexington Books, 2012), 236–37.

on Muslims and their inability to respect different viewpoints. In France, 67 percent of those surveyed felt that Muslims and their intolerance were primarily at fault for generating the conflict over the cartoons. Similar majorities existed in other countries: 62 percent in Germany, 60 percent in the United States, and 59 percent in Britain.[89]

The cartoon controversy provides an intriguing bookend to this chapter in light of the many similarities it shares with the Rushdie Affair. Both controversies witnessed Western politicians and media portraying Muslim reactions to perceived insults as monolithic, with little attention to the diversity of Muslim responses and perspectives. Both controversies included Muslim minority communities with very little political representation responding to what they perceived to be demeaning and insulting representations of Islam by the cultural elite. Both controversies involved Muslims initially looking to existing laws, including blasphemy laws, to address their grievances, but to no avail. Both controversies eventually got out of hand as the conflicts played out on an international stage with the attention and participation of Muslim-majority nations.

The most significant overlap in the two controversies involves their framing. The newspaper editors and their supporters, like Rushdie's staunchest advocates, framed the conflict as a battle between freedom of expression and respect for religion and religious sensibilities. But the problematic assumptions behind such framing are worth addressing in some detail, given how they feed Islamophobic discourses and perpetuate the narrative of Muslims as the ultimate "Other." My focus here will be on the Danish cartoons, but many of the following points apply to the Rushdie Affair as well.

89. Pew Research Center, "Most in France Blamed Muslim Intolerance for 2006 Cartoon Controversy," September 20, 2012, http://www.pewresearch.org/daily-number/most-in-france-blamed-muslim-intolerance-for-2006-cartoon-controversy/.

The first problem with this framing, one that I addressed earlier in the Rushdie Affair discussion, is that it assumes that freedom of expression is a principle that benefits everyone equally. The *Jyllands-Posten* editors, like many other Western journalists and politicians, have access to media outlets and other platforms from which they can make their voices and perspectives heard. Marginalized religious and racial communities often lack this kind of access and privilege. Danish Muslims during the controversy did not have any of the country's major newspapers or media outlets at their disposal. As in the case of the Rushdie Affair, Danish Muslims found themselves subject to criticism and ridicule by cultural and political elites who were in a position to shape the narrative of Islam in a harmful fashion.

Second, this framing makes freedom of expression a central component of Western identity, thereby minimizing or even disregarding the importance of a Western commitment to religious toleration and diversity. But is not the affirmation of greater respect for religious pluralism and the great variety of religious beliefs and practices also a significant Western commitment? After all, the Enlightenment itself gave rise to greater religious toleration and diversity, and much of Western history over the past two or three centuries has moved toward greater inclusivity of the world's many religions and religious expressions. To set respect for religious expressions and diversity against freedom of expression, under the assumption that the latter symbolizes the West and the former does not (or does not as much), is to place two principles at odds that should, in fact, complement one another. It is ironic that, in the cartoon controversy, the eleven ambassadors of Muslim countries are the ones to make this exact point to Prime Minister Rasmussen when they write that "casting aspersions on Islam as a religion and publishing demeaning caricatures of the Holy Prophet Muhammad

(PBUH) goes against the spirit of Danish values of tolerance and civil society."[90]

Third, this framing suggests that Muslims are simply incapable of accepting freedom of expression and that their religion forces them to react negatively and at times violently to criticism. An example of such an assumption is found in a story from the US-based Associated Press during the cartoon controversy: "So far the West and Islamic nations remain at loggerheads over fundamental, but conflicting cultural imperatives—the Western democratic assertion of a right to free speech and press freedom, versus the Islamic dictum against any representation of the Prophet Muhammad."[91] The media was also quick to report on Muslims within Europe whose protests over the cartoons seemed to confirm the belief that Islam and the West were "at loggerheads." For example, in February 2006, some Muslim protestors took to the streets of London with placards calling for the deaths of the cartoonists. The protest attracted lots of media attention. And yet, one week later, even more Muslim protestors, possibly upwards of five thousand people, came out in force to reject the violent messages from the previous presentation. They poured into Trafalgar Square and held placards that read, "United against Islamophobia, united against incitement, mercy to mankind and Muhammad, symbol of freedom and honour." Some of these protestors also held British flags and banners that reflected their pride in being British.[92]

In a similar vein, a spokesperson for the Muslim Council of Britain voiced clear support for freedom of expression: "Of course, no one

90. Quoted in Nieslen, "Danish Cartoons," 224.
91. Quoted in Peter Gottschalk and Gabriel Greenberg, *Islamophobia: Making Muslims the Enemy* (Plymouth, UK: Rowman and Littlefield, 2008), 146.
92. Anushka Asthana, "Muslims Fly Flag for Peaceful Protest against Cartoons," *Guardian* (UK), February 11, 2006, http://www.theguardian.com/uk/2006/feb/12/muhammadcartoons.religion.

disputes the freedom of speech in Europe. Newspapers and broadcasters have the right to publish these offensive cartoons."[93] Many Muslims had similar sentiments during the controversy, and, of course, many other Muslims simply had no strong reaction to the cartoons and never thought to protest. Western journalists, however, generally lacked interest in incorporating such diverse responses (and nonresponses) into their overarching narrative. Islam's opposition to freedom of expression remained the dominant media story.

Finally, the problem with defining freedom of expression as an absolute, nonnegotiable principle in the West overlooks the fact that *all* Western societies regulate freedom of expression. Many European countries, for example, have hate speech laws. Denmark's Criminal Code prohibits individuals from threatening or degrading a group of people "because of their race, skin color, national or ethnic background, [and] faith or sexual orientation."[94] Punishment by fine or imprisonment is warranted under the law. Similar laws exist in other European countries such as Britain, France, the Netherlands, Norway, and Sweden.

Blasphemy laws, vestiges of a Christian past, also remain on the books in many European countries. Denmark's Criminal Code threatens with punishment, including possible imprisonment, anyone who "publicly mocks or insults the religious doctrines or acts of worship of any lawfully existing religious community."[95] Other countries with blasphemy laws include Austria, Finland, Germany, the Netherlands, Spain, and Switzerland. Britain abolished its blasphemy laws in 2008. Even some US states, such as Massachusetts

---

93. Michael McDonough and Mark Oliver, "British Muslims Protest over Cartoons," *Guardian* (UK), February 3, 2006, http://www.theguardian.com/world/2006/feb/03/religion.uk.

94. Danish Criminal Code, Section 226(b), https://www.retsinformation.dk/Forms/R0710.aspx?id=142912. The English translation from the original Danish is mine.

95. Danish Criminal Code, Section 140, https://www.retsinformation.dk/Forms/R0710.aspx?id=142912. The English translation from the original Danish is mine.

and Pennsylvania, have blasphemy laws, though the Constitution itself does not prohibit blasphemy. In truth, blasphemy laws are rarely applied anymore, and their scope historically has not extended beyond Christianity.[96] Some Muslims in both the Rushdie Affair and the Danish cartoon controversy appealed to the government to apply the existing blasphemy laws to the offending parties, but political and legal authorities in both cases declined to pursue this route.

More examples could be given of regulated speech in the West, including laws that prohibit publicly denying the Holocaust in countries such as Austria, Belgium, and France. The very existence of these laws illuminates the contradiction in ridiculing Muslims for not embracing freedom of expression while praising the West for its unyielding commitment to it. We can certainly debate the prudence or necessity of regulating certain forms of expression, just as we can argue about whether the less restrictive position on freedom of expression in the United States is preferable to the European tendency to impose greater regulations on hate or defamatory speech. But we should not pretend that Muslims who complain about being ridiculed for their religious convictions or who want existing laws to protect them from such ridicule are somehow violating cherished Western norms and values.

We should also not forget that there are prominent examples in modern Western history of other religious communities, particularly Christian ones, advocating for restrictions on freedom of expression in light of perceived offenses to religious sensibilities. Some Christian groups accused *Monty Python's Life of Brian* (1979), a British satirical film about a mistaken messiah, of promoting blasphemy and other offensive views on Christianity. The film was banned in Norway and Ireland as well as in some cities in the UK.[97]

---

96. Klausen, *Cartoons That Shook the World*, 144.

Martin Scorsese's *The Last Temptation of Christ* (1988) also evoked charges of blasphemy for portraying Jesus as a man who was tempted to abandon the cross and live a normal human life. One particularly controversial scene showed Jesus consummating his marriage to Mary Magdalene. Various Christian communities throughout the world protested the movie and called for bans. Several major movie theater chains in the United States, overseeing close to four thousand theaters, responded to protests by refusing to show the movie. Some US cities, including New Orleans, Oklahoma City, and Savannah, imposed bans on the film.[98] Bomb threats were made against theaters in the United States and Europe, with one conservative Catholic group setting a Parisian theater on fire while it was showing the film.[99] Other countries with clear Christian majorities, such as Chile, Brazil, and Argentina, banned the film. The Israeli Film Censorship Board initially banned the movie out of fear that it would upset Christians and insult religious sensibilities, but the nation's highest court overturned the board's decision.[100]

In an ironic twist to this modern history of Western censorship, just two-and-a-half years before the Muhammad cartoons, *Jyllands-Posten* refused to publish cartoons satirizing the resurrection of Jesus because the Sunday editor feared the Jesus cartoons would "provoke an outcry."[101] The same newspaper that decried self-censorship and

97. Tony Roche, "The Life of Brian: When Monty Python Took on God," *Telegraph* (UK), October 19, 2011, http://www.telegraph.co.uk/culture/tvandradio/8833320/The-Life-of-Brian-When-Monty-Python-took-on-God.html.

98. "Martin Scorsese's *The Last Temptation of Christ*," PBS, http://www.pbs.org/wgbh/cultureshock/flashpoints/theater/lasttemptation.html.

99. James M. Markham, "Religious War Ignites Anew in France," *New York Times*, November 9, 1988, http://www.nytimes.com/1988/11/09/world/religious-war-ignites-anew-in-france.html.

100. "Israel Lifts 'Last Temptation' Ban," *Los Angeles Times*, June 15, 1989, http://articles.latimes.com/1989-06-15/news/mn-2691_1_israeli-film-censorship-board-lifts-ban.

lampooned Muslim oversensitivity to ridicule did not waver in practicing censorship in deference to Christian sensibilities.

The dominant Western portrayal of the Danish cartoon controversy as a conflict between Western commitment to freedom of expression and Muslims' unreasonable demands for respecting religious sensitivities at best overlooks the complexities of freedom of expression as it exists in Western contexts and among Muslim minority communities. At worst, this portrayal reflects a hypocritical and even Islamophobic motif that ignores relevant instances in which the West either restricts freedom of expression or shows concern for Christian sensibilities while refusing to do the same for Muslims.

◆ ◆ ◆ ◆ ◆

As indicated in chapter 1, a key component of Islamophobia is the tendency to portray Muslims as a monolithic bloc. Once Muslims are regarded as fundamentally sharing the same attitudes and commitments, it is not difficult to conclude that one violent Muslim, or one intolerant Muslim, makes all Muslims violent or intolerant. The events discussed in this chapter demonstrate how the actions of a few—Muhammad Bouyeri in Amsterdam, four young men in the London bombings, or a handful of imams from Denmark—are often presumed to be representative of all or most Muslims. Such episodes contribute to an anti-Muslim atmosphere in which Muslim Europeans are collectively viewed as the "enemy within" and thus a serious threat to Western values and security. In the next chapter, we will take a closer look at how this atmosphere on both sides of the Atlantic provides fertile ground for some of the most dedicated

101. Gottschalk and Greenberg, *Islamophobia*, 2–3, 146. Gwladys Fouché, "Danish Paper Rejected Jesus Cartoons," *Guardian* (UK), February 6, 2006, http://www.theguardian.com/media/2006/feb/06/pressandpublishing.politics.

opponents of Islam, those who participate in the Islamophobia industry, to demean if not demonize Muslims for professional gain.

6

Professional Islamophobia

As objects of suspicion if not overt hostility, Muslims often cannot speak for themselves to Western audiences or, perhaps more accurately, are not heard when they do speak. They lack the power to control the public narrative of Islam. We have already seen how prominent politicians drive negative views of Islam in the context of foreign political and military endeavors as well as domestic security. We have also encountered examples of the media dictating the narrative of Islam in light of key events such as the Danish cartoon controversy, though a more thorough analysis of the media's portrayal of Muslims will take place in the next chapter.

In this chapter, I analyze the arguments, motivations, and influence of prominent individuals and organizations that deliberately drown out the diversity of Muslim voices and consciously manufacture and exploit the fear of Islam in a manner unprecedented in mainstream political and media circles. I refer to this enterprise as "professional Islamophobia." Professional Islamophobia is constituted by a cadre of conservative politicians, right-wing activists and bloggers, and even disgruntled Muslims or ex-Muslims who make a career of demonizing Muslims and Arabs. Nathan Lean refers to this cadre as the "Islamophobia Industry," whereas the Center for American Progress labels it the "Islamophobia Network."[1] Whatever we call it, what matters is that those who participate in and profit from professional Islamophobia have powerful political, media, and publishing platforms from which to generate and exacerbate Western anxieties toward the Muslim "Other."

Far Right Activists and Bloggers in the United States

In the post-9/11 era, a host of far right academics, activists, and bloggers have emerged and become prominent voices in US debates about Islam. Three individuals in particular—Daniel Pipes, Pamela Geller, and Robert Spencer—have made a huge impact on the misinformation about Islam that circulates so freely on the Internet, in the media, and in political circles.

Daniel Pipes

The most prominent of the three, and the one who was already a known commodity in far right circles prior to 9/11, is Daniel Pipes.[2] Pipes received a PhD in medieval Islamic history from Princeton University in 1978. He entered government service in the early 1980s, serving on the policy planning staff for the US State Department. He also tried his hand at university teaching, but he left the academic world permanently in 1986 and entered the world of

1. Nathan Lean, *The Islamophobia Industry: How the Right Manufactures Fear of Muslims* (London: Pluto, 2012); Ali Wajahat et al., *Fear, Inc.: The Roots of the Islamophobia Network in America* (Washington, DC: Center for American Progress, 2011).
2. For a brief biography of Daniel Pipes, see Eyal Press, "Neocon Man," *Nation*, May 10, 2004, http://www.thenation.com/article/neocon-man.

political think tanks, directing the Foreign Policy Research Institute from 1986 to 1993 and then assuming the leadership of the Middle East Forum in 1994. Pipes established the Middle East Forum to foster a conservative response to perceived threats to US interests in the Middle East.

Pipes authored numerous books and articles prior to 9/11. His most famous, "The Muslims Are Coming! The Muslims Are Coming!," was published by the *National Review* in 1990. In it, he argued that "West European societies are unprepared for the massive immigration of brown-skinned peoples cooking strange foods and not exactly maintaining Germanic standards of hygiene."[3]

His political and cultural influence rose significantly after 9/11. In the year following the attacks, he appeared on 450 radio shows and 110 television programs and wrote op-ed pieces for prominent newspapers.[4] In 2002, he solidified his public reputation as an "expert" on Islamic terrorism with his book *Militant Islam Reaches America*. In the book, he argues that Muslim Americans present a serious threat to

Daniel Pipes (1949–) is a former academic who heads the Middle East Forum, a conservative think tank that is highly critical of Islam and of the academic study of the Middle East in American universities. Pipes created a website in 2002 called Campus Watch in order to keep track of professors whose approach to Middle East studies did not align with his conservative position.

3. Daniel Pipes, "The Muslims Are Coming! The Muslims Are Coming!," *National Review*, November 19, 1990, http://www.danielpipes.org/198/the-muslims-are-coming-the-muslims-are-coming.
4. Press, "Neocon Man."

the United States because they are sympathetic with the goals of al-Qaeda.[5] In 2003, Pipes received an appointment to the US Institute of Peace from President Bush, despite numerous objections from politicians and organizations who feared that Pipes was more committed to conflict than to peace with Muslims and Muslim-majority countries.

Pipes used his post-9/11 status to create the Campus Watch website in 2002.[6] The purpose of the site was to keep track of so-called activist scholars on US college campuses whose views on the Middle East did not align with a neoconservative perspective. He wanted to ostracize scholars critical of US foreign policy in the Middle East, including the case for war in Iraq, and of the Israeli occupation of Palestine. Pipes even encouraged students to report "problematic" professors to the website. In September 2002, the site posted the dossiers of eight "suspect" scholars. When news of this blacklist became known, over one hundred scholars contacted the Middle East Forum and asked to be added to the Campus Watch list in an act of solidarity. The list was removed by the end of the month, at least in part as a result of criticisms that Pipes was engaged in McCarthyism.

In many ways, Pipes is the figurehead of professional Islamophobia in the United States, though, unsurprisingly, he rejects the very concept of Islamophobia. He asks, "What constitutes an 'undue fear of Islam' when Muslims in the name of Islam today make up the premier source of worldwide aggression?" He encourages Muslims to discard the term and to stop blaming "the potential victim for fearing his would-be executioner."[7] In other words, Pipes insists that because

5. Daniel Pipes, *Militant Islam Reaches America* (New York: Norton, 2002).
6. For an overview of *Campus Watch*, see Kristine McNeil, "The War on Academic Freedom," *The Nation*, November 25, 2002, http://www.thenation.com/article/war-academic-freedom.
7. Daniel Pipes, "Islamophobia?," *New York Sun*, October 25, 2005, http://www.danielpipes.org/3075/islamophobia.

Muslims worldwide pose an existential threat to everyone else, the Western fear of Muslims is completely justified.

Pamela Geller and Robert Spencer

Whereas Pipes's reputation as a harsh critic of Muslims antedated 9/11, others engaged in professional Islamophobia owe their careers solely to 9/11 and its aftermath. Two clear examples are Pamela Geller and Robert Spencer. Geller, a native of New York City, spent her early career working first as a financial analyst and later as a publisher and columnist for newspapers in the city. After 9/11, she entered the professional Islamophobia business, launching the website Atlas Shrugs in 2005. The website focused on drawing attention to the dangers of Islam.

Spencer, like Pipes, has some academic training in religion. He received his MA in religious studies from the University of North Carolina in 1986, though his focus was on early Christian history, not Islam. He taught some years at a Catholic high school in the Bronx before assuming the mantle of public intellectual after 9/11.[8] His breakthrough book, *Islam Unveiled* (2003), gave Spencer the chance to claim expertise in Islam and to warn of the dangers Islam posed to the United States in light of the religion's inherent violence, backwardness, and misogyny.[9] He has continued to author and coauthor books with incendiary titles, including *The Truth about Muhammad: Founder of the World's Most Intolerant Religion* (2007), *Stealth Jihad: How Radial Islam Is Subverting America without Guns or Bombs* (2008), and *The Complete Infidel's Guide to the Koran* (2009). He has made the rounds on US and European news programs and

---

8. Lean, *Islamophobia Industry*, 58.
9. Robert Spencer, *Islam Unveiled: Disturbing Questions about the World's Fastest-Growing Faith* (San Francisco: Encounter Books, 2003).

written articles for prominent Western newspapers. His views have also found wider circulation through his website, Jihad Watch.

Geller and Spencer were already rising stars in the professional Islamophobia network before the controversy over a proposed Islamic center near Ground Zero erupted in 2010, but this controversy turned them into rock stars within conservative anti-Islam factions in the United States. In fact, Geller is one of the main reasons the center, also known as the Park51 Islamic Center (see image 6), became the focus of so much controversy. In May 2010, Geller wrote a blog entry for Atlas Shrugs that ignited the national controversy over the center. The title of the entry left no doubt concerning Geller's fears: "Monster Mosque Pushes Ahead in Shadow of World Trade Center Islamic Death and Destruction." In the piece, she associates plans to build the center with Islamic terrorism, employing the guilt-by-association principle that serves as the bedrock of Islamophobia: "Islamic jihad took down those buildings when they attacked, destroyed and murdered 3,000 people in an act of conquest and Islamic supremacism. What better way to mark your territory than to plant a giant mosque on the still-barren land of the World Trade Center? Sort of a giant victory lap. Any decent American, Muslim or otherwise, wouldn't dream of such an insult."[10] Despite the fact that the developer and organization behind the proposed center had no ties to al-Qaeda or extremist forms of Islam, Geller connects them to the 9/11 attacks without hesitation.

Geller and Spencer became partners around the time this controversy emerged. They became the coleaders in April 2010 of Stop Islamization of America (SIOA), the US branch of a European anti-Islam organization. SIOA joined the fray quickly and helped

---

10. Pamela Geller, "Monster Mosque Pushes Ahead in Shadow of World Trade Center Islamic Death and Destruction," May 6, 2010, http://pamelageller.com/2010/05/monster-mosque-pushes-ahead-in-shadow-of-world-trade-center-islamic-death-and-destruction.html/.

organize a "Stop the 911 Mosque" rally on June 6. Geller and others in SIOA chose the date because it coincided with D-Day and the invasion of Normandy in World War II. She connected the American fight against Nazism with the ongoing fight against Islamic supremacism that was symbolized in the resistance to the Park51 Center.[11] Neither the rally nor the overall campaign by Geller, Spencer, and SIOA prevented plans for the center from moving forward, but their efforts did succeed in making the project, and the Muslims who supported it, very unpopular in many political and media circles. SIOA built on this momentum and quickly began work on other anti-Islam projects, including advertisements condemning Islam that appeared in New York City buses and subways. SIOA continues to attract notoriety and publicity, and their campaigns have prompted the Southern Poverty Law Center and the Anti-Defamation League to label the organization as a hate group.

Pipes, Geller, and Spencer are the tip of the iceberg of anti-Muslim bloggers and activists in post-9/11 America. Much more could be said about other prominent participants in professional Islamophobia, such as Brigitte Gabriel, a Lebanese-born Christian and founder of ACT for America who equates all practicing Muslims with radical Islam, and Frank Gaffney and David Yerushalmi, both of whom head organizations that are responsible for spreading misinformation about Islam and that seek to enact anti-Muslim laws, including the infamous anti-Sharia legislation that began sweeping through state legislatures in 2010. Readers interested in learning more about this network of right-wing bloggers and activists, including the network's sources of funding, amounting to over $40 million, from hardline conservative foundations and donors, would do well to read

11. Lean, *Islamophobia Industry*, 51–53.

the Center for American Progress's report from 2011 titled *Fear, Inc.: The Roots of the Islamophobia Network in America.*

Anti-Muslim Politicians in the United States

Far right bloggers and activists in the United States have succeeded in promoting Islamophobia through effective websites, media strategies, and publications. But their success has also depended on powerful politicians who spread misinformation about Islam and Muslims in order to garner media attention, enhance their political standing, and mobilize voters. They have proven to be powerful allies to many of the right-wing individuals and organizations discussed in the previous section.

Peter King, a congressional representative from New York, is the embodiment of a politician whose post-9/11 career has been enhanced by his ability to stir up fear of Muslim Americans and to capitalize on this fear. For example, when King took over as chairman of the House Homeland Security Committee in 2010, he immediately announced his intention to sponsor hearings on the radicalization of Muslim Americans. The hearings, which began in March 2011, ignited controversy as King repeated a claim he had made years before that 80 to 85 percent of mosques in the United States are controlled by Islamic fundamentalists. King cited right-wing "experts," including Daniel Pipes and Steven Emerson, to verify these bogus statistics, reflecting his dependence on the professional Islamophobia industry to help bolster his anti-Muslim campaign.[12]

King's hearings did not go unchallenged. Representative Keith Ellison of Minnesota, the first Muslim ever elected to Congress, testified at the hearings and put a human face on the community

12. Deepa Kumar, *Islamophobia and the Politics of Empire* (Chicago: Haymarket Books, 2012), 185–86.

King characterized as broadly supportive of terrorism. Ellison became particularly emotional when telling the story of Salman Hamdani, a Muslim and one of the first responders who died in the World Trade Center on 9/11. Despite such opposition, the hearings moved forward as King insisted that to "back down would be a craven surrender to political correctness and an abdication of what I believe to be the main responsibility of this committee; to protect America from a terrorist attack."[13]

The guilt-by-association tactic has proved attractive to other politicians. Representatives Michele Bachmann of Minnesota and Allen West of Florida both attempted to accuse their political opponents of having ties to the Muslim Brotherhood in an effort to strike fear among voters that the United States was being infiltrated by an Islamist organization. In 2012, Bachmann accused Huma Abedin, a senior aide to Secretary of State Hilary Clinton, of having ties to the Muslim Brotherhood and of potentially participating in a conspiracy to influence US policy in light of these ties. Bachmann also insinuated that the Muslim Brotherhood had already infiltrated the US government, including the Department of Homeland Security and the Department of Justice.[14] The charges were completely made up. In 2013, she traveled with congressional colleagues to Egypt to hold a press conference in which she condemned the spread of the Muslim Brotherhood. "We stand against this great evil," she insisted. "We are not for them. We remember who caused 9/11 in America. We remember who it was that killed 3,000 brave Americans."[15] The fact that the Muslim

---

13. Quoted in Huma Khan and Z. Byron Wolf, "Muslim Congressman Gets Emotional in House Hearing on Radicalization," *ABC News*, March 10, 2011, http://abcnews.go.com/Politics/peter-king-defends-house-radicalization-hearing-keith-ellison/story?id=13103800.

14. Jason Linkins, "Michele Bachmann Points to Huma Abedin as Muslim Brotherhood Infiltrator," *Huffington Post*, July 17, 2012, http://www.huffingtonpost.com/2012/07/17/michele-bachmann-huma-abedin-muslim_n_1680083.html.

Brotherhood has ties neither to al-Qaeda nor the 9/11 attacks mattered little to Bachmann. The very mentioning of the organization in the context of 9/11 was her attempt to heighten suspicions back home about the possibility of radical Muslims infiltrating America.

In July 2011, West, who previously referred to Keith Ellison as the "antithesis of the principles upon which this country was established," held a briefing known as "Homegrown Jihad in the USA: Culminating of the Brotherhood's 50-year History of Infiltrating America."[16] Prior to the briefing, he promised to reveal a list of thousands of names of individuals and organizations in the United States with ties to the Muslim Brotherhood. He ultimately did not release the list at the briefing, but he managed to reinforce the narrative that the Muslim Brotherhood had penetrated deeply into the United States and that Muslim Americans posed a serious threat to the nation.

The demonization of Muslims in national politics has not been limited to the US Congress. Prominent presidential candidates, including Newt Gingrich and Herman Cain, have appealed to prospective voters through anti-Muslim fearmongering. In 2011, Gingrich compared Muslim Americans to Nazis in the 1940s, arguing that just as the latter attempted to infiltrate the United States during World War II, so might the former be doing the same to promote an anti-American agenda.[17] Cain told a reporter in 2011 that, if elected, he would not consider appointing a Muslim to his

15. Quoted in Paige Lavender, "Michele Bachmann Suggests Muslim Brotherhood to Blame for 9/11, Thanks Egyptian Military for Coup," *Huffington Post*, September 9, 2013, http://www.huffingtonpost.com/2013/09/09/michele-bachmann-911_n_3893575.html.
16. Quoted in Nick Wing, "Allen West: Keith Ellison 'The Antithesis of Principles upon Which Country Was Founded," *Huffington Post*, January 24, 2011, http://www.huffingtonpost.com/2011/01/24/allen-west-keith-ellison_n_813159.html.
17. Huma Khan and Amy Bingham, "GOP Debate: Newt Gingrich's Comparison of Muslims and Nazis Sparks Outrage," *ABC News*, June 14, 2011, http://abcnews.go.com/Politics/gop-debate-newt-gingrichs-comparison-muslims-nazis-sparks/story?id=13838355.

cabinet or as a federal judge. He justified his position by claiming that Muslim Americans are engaged in a "creeping attempt . . . to gradually ease Sharia law and the Muslim faith into our government."[18] Gingrich and Cain articulated these and other anti-Muslim views during a Republican presidential debate in June 2011, and, in most instances, they were met with applause from the audience.[19] Neither Gingrich nor Cain won their party's nomination, but their rhetoric indicated that, to some extent, Muslim-bashing was acceptable for those aspiring to the highest political office in the nation.

Radical Right Politics in Europe

While US politicians such as Peter King and Newt Gingrich enhance their careers by promoting anti-Muslim sentiment, the careers of some politicians in Europe depend almost exclusively on their ability to manufacture and exploit anxieties toward Europe's growing Muslim population. These politicians are frequently found in nativist, right-wing political parties, most of which have platforms that are strongly anti-immigrant and anti-Muslim.[20]

The rise of radical right parties in Europe has gone hand in hand with the migration and immigration of Muslims in the postwar era. Particularly since the 1980s, the presence and visibility of Muslims and Islam have increased dramatically, which has contributed to some of the changing political fortunes of radical right parties. One study

18. Quoted in Scott Keyes, "Herman Cain Tells ThinkProgress 'I Will Not' Appoint a Muslim in My Administration," *ThinkProgress*, March 26, 2011, http://thinkprogress.org/politics/2011/03/26/153625/herman-cain-muslims/#.

19. Doug Mataconis, "Herman Cain and Newt Gingrich Bring Out the Anti-Muslim Hysteria," *Outside the Beltway*, June 14, 2011, http://www.outsidethebeltway.com/herman-cain-and-newt-gingrich-bring-out-the-anti-muslim-hysteria/.

20. Much of the following discussion is dependent on Todd H. Green, "Who Speaks for Europe's Muslims? The Radical Right Obstacle to Dialogue," *CrossCurrents* 62 (2012): 337–49.

indicates that the radical right more than quadrupled its support in two decades. They moved from an average of 2 percent of the popular vote in 1985 to 8.5 percent of the vote by 2006.[21] In the past fifteen years, they have constituted the second- or third-largest party in the parliaments of the Netherlands, Norway, and Denmark. In Switzerland, the Swiss People's Party, a radical right party, has the largest representation in parliament. In other countries, including Belgium, Germany, France, and Austria, radical right parties have had a strong presence in both local and national politics.

The radical right is making an impact on Europe's most prominent and powerful politicians, leading some of them to move to the right on immigration and Islam. Chancellor Angela Merkel of Germany now claims that multiculturalism in her country has "utterly failed," while Prime Minister David Cameron of the UK blames multiculturalism for "the weakening of our collective identity."[22] Merkel and Cameron have plenty of company when it comes to rejecting the merits of multiculturalism, and one must keep in mind that in a European context, criticism of multiculturalism is tantamount to criticism of immigrants and Muslims. Radical right parties and politicians alone have not changed the conversation about multiculturalism, but they have definitely been a contributing factor.

The radical right's popularity enables it to co-opt the narrative of Islam and to drown out the voices of Europe's diverse Muslims. But what narrative does the radical right promote? How does the radical right tell the story of Islam? The dominant motifs in this narrative are similar to many of the Islamophobic themes we have

21. Antonis A. Ellinas, *The Media and the Far Right in Western Europe: Playing the Nationalist Card* (New York: Cambridge University Press, 2010), 4–5.
22. Quoted in Matthew Weaver, "Angela Merkel: German Multiculturalism Has 'Utterly Failed,'" *Guardian* (UK), October 17, 2010, http://www.theguardian.com/world/2010/oct/17/angela-merkel-german-multiculturalism-failed. For a transcript of the speech from which this quote is taken, see David Cameron, "PM's Speech at Munich Security Conference," February 5, 2011, https://www.gov.uk/government/speeches/pms-speech-at-munich-security-conference.

encountered in previous chapters, particularly the focus on Islam as violent, antidemocratic, and misogynist.

Geert Wilders, founder and leader of the Party for Freedom in the Netherlands, is notorious for his views on the inherently violent nature of Islam. When Anders Breivik, motivated by a hatred of Muslims, went on a killing rampage in Norway in July 2011, Wilders responded by not only condemning Breivik but also heightening the contrast between Islam and the West on violence: "The Oslo murderer falsely claims to be one of us. But he is not one of us. We abhor violence. We are democrats. We believe in peaceful solutions. The reason why we must reject Islam is exactly Islam's violent nature. We believe in democracy. We fight for the force of our convictions, but we never use violence."[23] What makes Wilders's words all the more astounding is that the Norway murders were not committed by a Muslim but by a self-proclaimed Christian and opponent of multiculturalism. For Wilders, such details are insignificant. Whether Muslims are involved in violence or not, any opportunity to portray Islam as violent is an opportunity that Wilders takes.

Geert Wilders (1963–) is the leader of the far right Party for Freedom in the Netherlands. He has become the de facto spokesperson on Europe's far right when it comes to criticizing Islam and the threat it poses to European values and culture.

Wilders's public statements on Islam's violent nature, however, have not gone unchallenged. In 2009, Wilders was charged with hate

23. Geert Wilders gave the speech that includes this excerpt in Berlin on September 3, 2011. The full text is available online at http://geertwilders.nl/index.php/component/content/article/87-news/1764-speech-geert-wilders-in-berlin-3-September-2011-english-version.

speech and eventually tried under Dutch law for some of these statements and for his short film *Fitna* (2008). *Fitna* intersperses

fitna: trial or temptation.

citations from the Qur'an with newspaper headlines and film clips that depict extremist Muslims engaged in acts of violence, including the 9/11 attacks. Although Wilders was acquitted, thanks in part to the financial assistance provided to his legal defense by Daniel Pipes's Middle East Forum, the media coverage of the trial helped to publicize and reinforce *Fitna*'s (and Wilders's) central message that Islam's violent nature is why we have terrorism.

Islam's violence goes hand in hand with its rejection of democracy, according to many right-wing politicians. Filip Dewinter, a leader in the Flemish Interest Party in Belgium, describes Islam as a "religion of conquest, which despises and rejects our values, norms and way of life." Islam threatens "democracy with its free expression, its separation of church and state and equality between men and women."[24] Islam is a political ideology about domination and conquest, and if steps are not taken, Sharia law, not democracy, will rule Europe: "This introduction of *sharia*, of Islamic law, is only the first phase. Second, Muslims will demand that *sharia* become a part of our civil code. And at the end, there is only *sharia*. The holy war—the *jihad*—against the Western enemy is a duty for every Muslim."[25]

For many radical right politicians, the inability of Islam to embrace peace and democracy is rivaled only by its oppressive treatment of women. Pia Kjæsgaard, former leader of the Danish People's Party, accuses Muslims of having "the deepest contempt for all things

---

24. Quoted in Hans-Georg Betz, "Against the System: Radical Right-Wing Populism's Challenge to Liberal Democracy," in *Movements of Exclusion: Radical Right-Wing Populism in the Western World*, ed. Jens Rydgren (New York: Nova Science, 2005), 35.

25. Filip Dewinter, "De sharia is al in Antwerpen," September 24, 2009, http://www.filipdewinter.be/filip-dewinter-in-gva-de-sharia-is-al-in-antwerpen.

Western, for all things Danish and for all things Christian. They come with baggage filled with male chauvinism . . . the circumcision of girls and clothes and traditions that are oppressive to women, all of which belong more in the darkest part of the Middle Ages."[26]

Other radical right politicians manipulate this narrative into public campaigns to "save" Muslim women. Dewinter, for example, launched a campaign in Belgium in 2012 called "Women Against Islamization." "Women are always the first victims of Islam," he maintained. "We want to make clear that they have a choice." To illustrate this choice, he arranged for his teenage daughter to be photographed wearing a burqa that covered her head and backside, while the rest of her body was exposed except for a bikini. The photograph was plastered on posters with Dutch words written across her bikini top that, translated into English, read: "Freedom or Islam?" The words across her bikini bottom read: "You choose!"[27]

The anti-Islam rhetoric employed by Europe's right wing is not innovative. It relies on many of the same stereotypes and tropes discussed throughout this book. But it is much more overt and aggressive than that encountered among mainstream politicians on either side of the Atlantic. Europe's right-wing politicians also stake their careers, successfully it seems, on this rhetoric and on gimmicks like Dewinter's. It is safe to conclude that we would not even be familiar with Europe's more famous right-wing personalities if not for their demonization of Muslims. In a *New York Times* editorial, Ian Buruma notes the following: "If not for his hatred of Islam, Geert Wilders would have remained a provincial Dutch parliamentarian of

---

26. Quoted in "Vi i DF satte vort folk og fæderland over alt andet," *Dansk Folkeblad* 5 (1999): 5.
27. Rick Dewsbury, "Belgian Politician Risks Muslim Backlash after Using Teenage Daughter Dressed in Burqa and Bikini for Campaign against Islam," *Daily Mail* (UK), February 3, 2012, http://www.dailymail.co.uk/news/article-2095862/Belgian-Vlaams-Belang-risks-Muslim-backlash-picture-daughter-burka-bikini.html.

little note."[28] Buruma's observation holds for a whole host of radical right politicians.

Native Informants

A final group of individuals whose careers and fame depend on denigrating Islam are referred to by scholars as "native informants."

> **native informants: Muslim and ex-Muslim "insiders" who draw on their personal knowledge and experience of Islam to promote the belief that Islam is at odds with Western values and to reassure Western audiences that their fear of Islam is justified.**

Native informants are Muslim "insiders" who either have become disgruntled with Islam or have rejected it altogether. They draw on their personal knowledge and experience of Islam to "inform" the West about Islam's "true" nature and to air the dirty laundry of Muslim communities. Native informants acquire considerable authority because their insider status gives them the credentials necessary to speak "authentically" about Islam. While they sometimes appear to address other Muslims in their writings and speeches, by and large their audience is the non–Muslim majority in the West. Their overall purpose is to reassure non-Muslims that Western misgivings and anxieties about Islam are justified, that Islam really is as bad and as dangerous as many Westerners suspect.

28. Ian Buruma, "Totally Tolerant, up to a Point, *New York Times*, January 29, 2009, http://www.nytimes.com/2009/01/30/opinion/30buruma.html?_r=0.

Professional native informants flourished after 9/11. They took advantage of the overwhelming desire for an answer to the question articulated by President Bush: "Why do they hate us?" Using their insider status, native informants began writing tell-all books about Islam and its hostility toward all things Western. While the list of influential native informants is long, the two most prominent since 9/11 are Ayaan Hirsi Ali and Irshad Manji.

We met Hirsi Ali in the previous chapter's discussion of *Submission* and the subsequent murder of Theo van Gogh in Amsterdam. Born in Somalia and raised in Ethiopia, Kenya, and Saudi Arabia, Hirsi Ali fled to Europe and sought asylum in the Netherlands as a young woman. She eventually made her way into politics and was elected to the Dutch parliament in 2002 by presenting herself as an outspoken opponent of Islam's treatment of women. After a controversy over her asylum application, she resigned from parliament in 2006 and moved to the United States, where she currently works for the neoconservative American Enterprise Institute and serves as a fellow at Harvard's Kennedy School of Government.

Hirsi Ali's opposition to Islam, particularly its treatment of women, has served as the foundation of her political career and has also provided her a platform from which to write. She has authored three books. Her first book, *The Caged Virgin* (2006), is a collection of essays on the need for Muslim women's liberation. The other two books are memoirs: *Infidel* (2007) and *Nomad* (2010).

Hirsi Ali's efforts have resulted in numerous awards and recognitions. Various organizations, from Sweden's Liberal People's Party to the American Jewish Committee, have given Hirsi Ali awards for her moral courage and commitment to women's rights and human rights. In 2005, she was named one of the one hundred most influential people in the world by *Time* magazine.

Irshad Manji was the author of the *Time* article that praised Hirsi Ali as a leader and revolutionary and as someone who "knows the risks of standing up for one's beliefs."[29] Manji was born in Uganda into a Pakistani family. When the military dictator Idi Amin came to power in 1972, he ordered the expulsion of Uganda's South Asian minorities. Manji's family moved to Canada. She grew up in Vancouver, British Columbia, and, by her own account, struggled to fit in with the Muslim community there. As a teenager, she repeatedly challenged her conservative madrassa teacher and was eventually expelled. Manji studied Islam on her own and concluded that Muslims had forsaken reason. Unlike Hirsi Ali, Manji did not abandon Islam, but she describes her Muslim identity as on shaky ground.

Manji pursued a career in journalism and professional writing. She has also ventured into television, producing and hosting programs that include discussions of Islam. In the late 1990s, she hosted *QT: Queer Television*, a program focusing on LGBT issues that included stories on lesbian and gay Muslims. These stories intersected with her own story as a lesbian Muslim. Manji's international fame took off with the publication of her first book, *The Trouble with Islam Today* (2003). She later authored *Allah, Liberty, and Love* (2011).

Like Hirsi Ali, Manji has received numerous awards and accolades for her efforts to initiate reform within Islam. *Ms. Magazine* recognized her as a "Feminist for the 21st Century." Oprah Winfrey's magazine gave Manji its first Chutzpah Award for her "audacity, nerve, boldness and conviction."[30] Manji's reform efforts have also been rewarded by academic institutions, including New York

---

29. Irshad Manji, "Ayaan Hirsi Ali," *Time*, April 18, 2005, http://content.time.com/time/specials/packages/article/0,28804,1972656_1972691_1973029,00.html.
30. Quoted in "Faith without Fear," *PBS*, http://www.pbs.org/weta/crossroads/about/show_faith_without_fear_film.html.

University, which recruited her to head its Moral Courage Project in order "to develop leaders who will challenge political correctness, intellectual conformity and self-censorship."[31]

Hirsi Ali is the more famous and influential of the two, though Manji probably has broader appeal across the political spectrum. Even with such broad appeal, Manji attracts the same sort of allies on the far right as Hirsi Ali does. Daniel Pipes, for instance, praises both as refreshing voices on Islam.

The personal accounts of Hirsi Ali and Manji share two important features. First, their stories conform to a common narrative involving a journey from bondage (Islam) to liberation (the West), from being a victim of Islam to fighting the oppression of Islam. Second, each draws on her experience as a woman who has experienced firsthand the abysmal treatment Islam affords women.[32] These two characteristics feature prominently in many native informant biographies. This is not to say that all native informants are women, but the ones who attract the most attention oftentimes are.

Beyond the similarities in their personal journeys, Hirsi Ali and Manji invoke many of the same themes in their quest to inform audiences about the stark differences between Islam and the West. Three overlapping themes stand out: Islam's lack of critical thinking and reason, Islam's oppression of women, and the superiority of Western values and freedoms.

Hirsi Ali argues that one of the fundamental flaws of Islam is its lack of critical thinking. There may be some diversity in Islam, notes Hirsi Ali, but "all Muslims share the conviction that the fundamental principles of Islam cannot be criticized, revised, or in any way contradicted."[33] When it comes to interpreting the Qur'an and the

31. Toor Saadia, "Gender, Sexuality, and Islam under the Shadow of the Empire," *Scholar and Feminist Online* 9 (Summer 2011), http://sfonline.barnard.edu/religion/print_toor.htm.
32. Evelyn Alsutany, *Arabs and Muslims in the Media: Race and Representation after 9/11* (New York: New York University Press, 2012), 84–85.

223

Sunna, or the example of the Prophet Muhammad, there is no diversity, she argues. Manji agrees, adding that the problem stems from an Arab tribal mentality that has thrown out *ijtihad*, or independent reasoning, and replaced it with mindless imitation of Islam's founders, a preoccupation she labels "foundamentalism."

> **Sunna: the example established by Muhammad's words and deeds that is recorded in the hadith.**

Lavish praise for the European Enlightenment combined with calls for reform feature prominently in both Hirsi Ali's and Manji's writings. "The history of the West," writes Hirsi Ali, "is the search for enlightenment through self-reflection. This is the source of its democratic practices and its power."[34] Islam, by contrast, has not experienced enlightenment. It will therefore continue to lag behind the West unless it engages in serious rational and scientific analysis. Manji frames her entire book, *The Trouble with Islam Today*, as a call for Muslims to discover reason and reform. Islam is in crisis: "If ever there was a moment for an Islamic reformation, it's now."[35] At the end of her book, she coins the phrase "Operation Ijtihad" to characterize her plan to "jump-start change in Islam" by embracing reason and looking particularly to Muslim women, with Western support and inspiration, to help her.[36]

Hirsi Ali and Manji believe that the failure of Muslims to embrace critical thinking is one of the main reasons so many women suffer abuse within Islam. The oppression of women is linked to Islam's

33. Ayaan Hirsi Ali, *The Caged Virgin: An Emancipation Proclamation for Women and Islam* (New York: Free Press, 2008), 1.
34. Ibid., 143.
35. Irshad Manji, *The Trouble with Islam Today: A Muslim's Call for Reform in Her Faith* (New York: St. Martin's, 2003), 3.
36. Ibid., 160.

inability to question its sources and founder. As a result, argues Hirsi Ali, Muslim men view women through the Arab tribal values that existed at the time of the Prophet Muhammad. Women are basically the property of their fathers, brothers, husbands, or other men. "The essence of a woman," Hirsi Ali adds, "is reduced to her hymen. Her veil functions as a constant reminder to the outside world of this stifling morality that makes Muslim men the owners of women."[37] Hirsi Ali's *The Caged Virgin* emphasizes repeatedly that Islam creates a culture in which women are denied education and employment, are forced into marriages, are victims of female genital mutilation, and are subject to abuse and violence at the hands of brutal Muslim men. All of this is done with justification from the Qur'an and the example of the Prophet Muhammad. Manji affirms many of these observations, insisting that "Muslims constantly exhibit a knack for degrading women."[38]

Islam's horrific treatment of women, combined with its irrationality, present stark contrasts with the West. Western values and freedoms are superior to anything one finds in Islam, according to both writers. Hirsi Ali explains:

> As a woman in the West I have access to education. I have a job, and I can change jobs as I wish. I can marry the man of my choice, or I can choose not to marry. . . . I can have an abortion. I can own property. I can travel wherever I want. . . . I can have an opinion on the moral choices of others and express my opinion, even publish it. . . . I can choose not to vote. I can stand for election to office or go into business. This is what makes the West so great.[39]

She adds that the journey from the bondage of Islam to the freedom of the West is difficult but nonetheless imperative for Muslims: "I

37. Hirsi Ali, *Caged Virgin*, xi.
38. Manji, *Trouble with Islam Today*, 158.
39. Hirsi Ali, *Caged Virgin*, 162.

moved from the world of faith to the world of reason—from the world of excision and forced marriage to the world of sexual emancipation. Having made that journey, I know that one of those worlds is simply better than the other. Not because of its flashy gadgets, but fundamentally, because of its values."[40]

Such effusive praise can imply that native informants are completely incapable of criticizing the West. Not quite. Both Hirsi Ali and Manji take aim at problematic assumptions and attitudes in the West, but even these criticisms serve as veiled compliments. For example, Hirsi Ali and Manji frequently criticize the Western affinity for multiculturalism and for tolerating diverse cultures and religions. Manji maintains that such sentiments are dangerous: "As Westerners bow down before multiculturalism, we often act as if anything goes. We see our readiness to accommodate as a strength—even as a form of cultural superiority. . . . But [Muslim] fundamentalists see our inclusive instincts as a weakness that makes us soft, lardy, rudderless. . . . The ultimate paradox may be that in order to defend our diversity, we'll need to be less tolerant."[41] The West needs to stop apologizing for its greatness and to start claiming the values that make it superior to Islam. The West also needs to intervene more in Muslim reform efforts. "Unshackling the Muslim world," argues Manji, "is an ambitious effort that will require an array of allies, Westerners among them, if only to deal a decisive blow to tribalism."[42]

Native informants such as Hirsi Ali and Manji have very strong opinions about what ails Islam and what needs to be fixed, but is there anything wrong with their arguments? The way they articulate their critiques, not to mention the content of their critiques, has

40. Ayaan Hirsi Ali, *Infidel* (New York: Free Press, 2008), 348.
41. Manji, *Trouble with Islam Today*, 199.
42. Ibid., 160.

the potential to do great harm, particularly to Muslims. The danger in their criticisms is twofold: they promote an irrational view of Islam, and they encourage an uncritical view of the West and its relationship to Islam.

For all of their touting of Enlightenment-based reason, Hirsi Ali and Manji manage to draw firm conclusions about Islam that ignore any evidence that would complicate or contradict their views. One example involves their assumption that Islam has abandoned reason (ijtihad) and completely lacks self-criticism and reform. Even a cursory survey of modern Islamic history proves such claims to be false.[43] From nineteenth-century intellectuals such as Muhammad Abduh and Sayyid Ahmad Khan to the contemporary European scholar Tariq Ramadan, plenty of examples exist of Muslims advocating for ijtihad.[44] Neither Hirsi Ali nor Manji are the first to "discover" the concept, much less to invoke it. Nor are they lone voices calling for reform. Contemporary Muslim reformers abound, including Leila Ahmed, Mohja Kahf, Nurcholish Madjid, Fatima Mernissi, Tariq Ramadan, and Amina Wadud. These voices are not given much attention in the writings or speeches of Hirsi Ali and Manji, probably because the views endorsed by these reformers reinforce neither a simplistic, unnuanced view of Islam nor an uncritical perspective of the West and its relationship to Islam.

> *ijtihad*: the use of independent reasoning and judgment in matters of Islamic law.

43. For an account of the debates over "the closing of the gates of ijtihad," see Wael B. Hallaq, "Was the Gate of Ijtihad Closed?," *International Journal of Middle East Studies* 16 (1984): 3–41; see also Moustafa Bayoumi, "The God that Failed: The Neo-Orientalism of Today's Muslim Commentators," in *Islamophobia/Islamophilia: Beyond the Politics of Enemy and Friend*, ed. Andrew Shryock (Bloomington: Indiana University Press, 2010), 82–83.

44. Todd Green, "Does Islam Really Need a Martin Luther?," *Huffington Post*, July 5, 2011, http://www.huffingtonpost.com/todd-green-phd/islam-martin-luther_b_884264.html; Tariq Ramadan, *Western Muslims and the Future of Islam* (New York: Oxford University Press, 2004).

Another example of Hirsi Ali's and Manji's failure to attend to evidence that counters their point of view involves the oppression of Muslim women, a theme that features prominently in their work. They are eager to point out the lack of education and the exclusion from political power that many Muslim women experience, but they make little effort to point to evidence that would complicate this picture. High percentages of women in Iran and Egypt, for example, achieve a college education or greater.[45] In the United States, Muslim women are more likely to have a college or graduate degree than the overall population of women, including Christians.[46] In politics, women have broken the glass ceiling and have served as heads of state in countries such as Pakistan, Bangladesh, and Indonesia.

When it comes to violence against women, Hirsi Ali and Manji seek to convince Western audiences that Muslim women suffer abuse from Muslim men in a manner unparalleled in the West. Hirsi Ali, for example, is willing to admit that such violence exists in Western families, but she qualifies these observations by arguing that "Westerners emphatically repudiate violence, while most Muslim families regard violence against women as something that women themselves provoke."[47] Hirsi Ali frames violence against women as an "Islam thing," something unique to the religion that results in the horrific treatment of Muslim women that Westerners presumably reject.

There is nothing wrong with Hirsi Ali raising the issue of the sexual and physical abuse experienced by Muslim women. It is a problem in Muslim contexts. For example, according to a United Nations report, 33 percent of women in Egypt and 21 percent of women in Jordan have experienced physical abuse from an intimate

---

45. John L. Esposito, *The Future of Islam* (New York: Oxford University Press, 2010), 151.
46. Jane Lampman, "US Muslims: Young, Diverse, Striving," *Christian Science Monitor*, March 3, 2009, http://www.csmonitor.com/USA/Society/2009/0303/p02s02-ussc.html.
47. Hirsi Ali, *Caged Virgin*, 19.

partner. In Bangladesh, almost half of all women reported such abuse.[48] These are troubling statistics, and we should not avoid discussing or confronting these abuses.

But two things are missing from Hirsi Ali's description of violence against Muslim women. First, she reduces *all* Muslim women to victims of violence and abuse, as if there were a universal Muslim female experience that results in all Muslim women undergoing the same hardships. You would never know from reading Hirsi Ali that Muslim women ever experience loving, fulfilling relationships with their fathers, husbands, or other male figures, nor would you know the stories of the many Muslim women whose experiences do not include abuse or violence from male family members. You would not even know that there are Muslim women throughout the world who find within Islam the resources to combat patriarchy, oppression, and domestic violence.

Hirsi Ali's narrative is also missing any effort to place violence against Muslim women in a broader global context or to analyze the many possible factors that generate and perpetuate violence against women throughout the world, not just in Muslim countries. When reading or listening to Hirsi Ali, it is easy to lose sight of the fact that one in four women in the United States have experienced violent abuse from an intimate partner, and one in five have experienced an attempted rape.[49] In Europe, one-third of all women report having experienced a sexual or physical assault.[50] Such statistics are shocking, but they are also indicative of a global problem of violence against

48. Laura Turquet, *Progress of the World's Women, 2011–2012: In Pursuit of Justice* (New York: UN Women, 2011), 136, http://progress.unwomen.org.
49. Roni Caryn Rabin, "Nearly 1 in 5 Women in U.S. Survey Say They Have Been Sexually Assaulted," *New York Times*, December 14, 2011, http://www.nytimes.com/2011/12/15/health/nearly-1-in-5-women-in-us-survey-report-sexual-assault.html.
50. "One-Third of EU Women Suffered Physical or Sexual Assault, Report Says," *Al-Jazeera America*, March 5, 2014, http://america.aljazeera.com/articles/2014/3/5/major-report-revealsextensiveabuseofwomenineu.html.

women that transcends religious and geographical boundaries. The West, like many Muslim-majority countries, is struggling to come to terms with a long-standing culture of violence against women that reflects a variety of historical, political, social, and religious factors. It makes no more sense to reduce this problem in the West to one cause—religion—than it does in Muslim communities. This broader context never factors into Hirsi Ali's accounts of the abuse experienced by Muslim women. Either she is not aware of this larger picture, or, more likely, she is not interested in complicating her narrative of oppressed Muslim women juxtaposed with liberated Western women.[51]

If Hirsi Ali and Manji are going to claim reason as central to their own criticisms of Islam, and if such reason is based on empirical evidence, both authors have a long way to go in drawing reasonable conclusions about Islam that reflect both the diversity of Muslim experiences and the larger global context.

Hirsi Ali's and Manji's refusal to consider the connections between Muslim women and Western women points to the other significant problem with their arguments—their largely uncritical view of the West. Neither author considers how the West has contributed and continues to contribute to problems in Muslim countries, from economic challenges to the struggle for democracy. They brush aside any suggestion that Western colonialism, imperialism, and racism have anything to do with the social, economic, and political problems facing the global Muslim population. Hirsi Ali, echoing Bernard Lewis, claims that Muslim rage and jealousy, not Western imperialism, are to blame for the economic and political woes in the Muslim world. Manji agrees. She adds that, even within the West,

---

51. For an outstanding critique of the rhetoric of saving Muslim women, including that used by native informants, see Lila Abu-Lughod, *Do Muslim Women Need Saving?* (Cambridge, MA: Harvard University Press, 2013).

Muslims really have no basis to complain. She rejects the notion that Western Muslims have experienced a significant backlash since 9/11, insisting that racism and Islamophobia have been hyped by the media to the neglect of all of the good things the West has done for Muslims.

Hirsi Ali and Manji literally "whitewash" the West's colonial history, its past and present racism, and its ongoing intervention in Muslim countries. They downplay or otherwise disregard the evidence that points to the West's historic support of autocratic regimes in the Middle East, its exploitation of the Middle East's energy resources, and its domestic targeting of Muslims for racial profiling and discrimination.

Put simply, Hirsi Ali, Manji, and many other native informants discount the complexity and diversity of global Muslim populations, disregard historical realities, and adopt narrow and decontextualized views of the West's relationship with Islam. In doing so, they perform, in the words of Saba Mahmood, "a quasi-official function in various American and European cabinets today: lending a voice of legitimacy to, and at times leading, the civilizational confrontation between 'Islam and the West.'"[52] In return for performing this service, they receive lucrative book deals, handsome speaking fees, considerable media exposure, and a place among the West's cultural and political elites from which they can continue to promote "the white man's burden" of taming the restless Muslim natives.

◆ ◆ ◆ ◆ ◆

What sets professional Islamophobia apart from the work of many contemporary politicians, journalists, and authors who occasionally

---

52. Saba Mahmood, "Feminism, Democracy, and Empire: Islam and the War on Terror," in *Women's Studies on the Edge*, ed. Joan Wallach Scott (Durham, NC: Duke University Press, 2008), 83.

tap into negative stereotypes of Muslims is its overt and unapologetic demonization of Islam. Participants in professional Islamophobia networks and endeavors cannot afford to be subtle in their characterizations of Muslims. Their careers literally depend on provocative rhetoric, exaggerated claims, and sensational narratives of backward, irrational, misogynist, and violent Muslims threatening the very foundations of the West. Almost every one of the building blocks of Islamophobia appears prominently in their writings, speeches, and interviews: Islam as monolithic, other, inferior, manipulative, and so forth. Nuance, complexity, and critical inquiry, by contrast, are absent from their work. The reason for this is not difficult to pinpoint. The fear of Islam, not the complexity of Islam, is what "sells" in the end.

One can make the case that without the media's attraction to those who traffic in professional Islamophobia, we would know little about Daniel Pipes, Geert Wilders, or Ayaan Hirsi Ali. This begs a larger question, one that is the focus of the next chapter: how much does the media contribute to the problem of Islamophobia?

7

Muslims in the Media and at the Movies

Truth be told, Westerners know very little about Islam. A lack of direct interactions or relationships with Muslims, combined with little if any sustained study of Islamic texts and traditions, creates a vacuum of ignorance in the West concerning the world's second-largest religion. And yet plenty of Europeans and Americans harbor strong and frequently negative opinions about Islam and Muslims. Why is that?

What we know about Islam, or what we think we know, is filtered primarily through the media and the stories and images it provides to audiences and consumers. The media determines who tells the story of Islam, which elements and perspectives are included or excluded, and how the story is packaged and presented. Without a doubt, the media functions as the most powerful and influential conveyor of "knowledge" of Islam.

In what follows, I examine how various forms of Western media, from newspapers to television programs to movies, tell the story of Muslims and Islam. This brief survey demonstrates that the media reduces Islam to a religion that promotes violence and the oppression of women, therefore reproducing the same stereotypes that have existed since the Middle Ages and have dominated modern epochs such as colonialism and the War on Terror. The result is not an expansion of our knowledge but the perpetuation of our illiteracy concerning Islam.

In the News

The stories audiences read in newspapers or see on television about current events are not objective accounts of what happened. Journalists and editors make choices about the angle to adopt in telling a story. Crucial to any analysis of the media's portrayal of Muslims and Islam, therefore, is an understanding of what scholars refer to as "framing." The sociologist Michael Schudson summarizes media framing in this way: "Journalists normally work with materials that real people and real events provide. But by selecting, highlighting, framing, shading, and shaping in reportage, they create the impression that real people—readers and viewers—then take to be real and to which they respond in their lives."[1] The news media creates frames of interpretation through which we understand "reality," but the reality in question is a construction that reflects the biases and ideologies of individual journalists and the media organizations that employ them. The reality created by the media, moreover, is often constructed to attract consumers and to keep a newspaper, news website, or television network in business. The mass media, after all, is part of the corporate world, with ownership of most news organizations held by a handful of companies.[2] Profit

1. Michael Schudson, *The Sociology of News* (New York: Norton, 2003), 2.
2. Brian L. Ott and Robert L. Mack, *Critical Media Studies: An Introduction* (Oxford: Wiley-Blackwell, 2010), 25. Ott and Mack point to five corporations that own most news publications

is always a part of the picture, which means that the media faces immense pressure to present news stories that reinforce the assumptions and ideologies held by the dominant culture and its most powerful institutions.

This concept of framing must be kept in mind when discussing the media's portrayal of Islam and Muslims. When a news network airs stories about militant Muslims in, say, Pakistan, it is choosing to highlight one slice of the Muslim community in that nation, a slice that will appease the appetites of Western audiences who are attracted to stories involving violence or conflict. But by choosing not to air stories about Pakistani Muslims who fight for women's rights or who provide health care to the poor, the network creates the impression that extremist or violent Muslims are the norm in Pakistan. When other news organizations repeat this selective coverage, the result is a constructed reality that reduces all Pakistani Muslims to angry militants.

Scholarly studies of the Western news media's framing of Islam highlight two prevalent themes: terrorism and the oppression of women. Since 9/11, the media's interest in these themes has increased significantly, and its reporting has fortified the widespread conviction that Islam is defined primarily in relation to violence and misogyny.

Framing "Islamic Terrorism"

Terrorism is the most prominent theme in media stories of Islam. In the United States, stories of Muslim terrorism have dominated news coverage since 9/11 and reinforced the link between Islam and violence. The 9/11 attacks represent the most obvious example of this link. For weeks after 9/11, images and videos of the attacks saturated

and media outlets in the United States: Time Warner, Disney, Viacom, News Corporation, and Bertelsmann.

news coverage, as did stories of the hijackers and their motives for taking aim at US targets. The only news story about Islam was the story of "Islamic terrorism." Islam was reduced to a religion that prompted violence against and hatred of the West.

In the years after 9/11, the media continued to focus on the link between Islam and violence, mirroring and reinforcing the US government's own anxieties about "Islamic terrorism." Kimberly Powell's study of US media coverage of terrorism since 9/11 illustrates this media obsession.[3] She analyzes how major print and Internet media sources, from the *New York Times* to CNN, framed terrorist events on US soil since 9/11, and she identifies a number of patterns that emerged in media coverage. Two are worth highlighting for our discussion: media speculation on the Muslim identity of terrorists and the characterization of Muslim terrorist suspects as prone to violence and religious extremism.

Powell notes the frequency with which the media assumes that a suspected terrorist is a Muslim. In some cases, the speculation turns out to be accurate, even though the focus on Muslim identity becomes obsessive. Such was the case when Major Nidal Hasan, a US Army psychiatrist, opened fire at Fort Hood, Texas, in 2009, killing thirteen people. News reports were quick to link Hasan to Islam, to the point that Islam was assumed to be the only relevant factor in understanding his actions. In a two-week period, there were 578 news stories labeling Hasan a Muslim. Many of these stories focused on Hasan's possible connections to the radical Muslim cleric Anwar al-Awlaki. The repetition of Hasan's Muslim identity and links to radical Islam reinforced the relationship between Islam and terrorism.[4]

---

3. Kimberly A. Powell, "Framing Islam: An Analysis of U.S. Media Coverage of Terrorism since 9/11," *Communication Studies* 62 (2011): 90–112.
4. Ibid., 96–97.

In other instances, perpetrators of terrorist acts were suspected of having a Muslim identity without any corroborating evidence. One week after 9/11, letters containing anthrax spores were sent to the offices of two senators and several news organizations. Five people died as a result of the attacks. Media and government speculation of a possible al-Qaeda connection began immediately. The *New York Times*, for example, reported at length on the "possibility that Al Qaeda confederates of the hijackers are behind the incidents," even though the newspaper also noted that investigators "lacked concrete evidence or intelligence to explain who sent the anthrax-contaminated letters."[5] As it turned out, the suspect was later identified as a microbiologist and researcher for the US Army with no ties to Islam or al-Qaeda, but the damage was already done. Islam became a major actor in the story even though it played no part.

The media's willingness to engage in such unfounded speculation is not new to the post-9/11 era. A classic example is the Oklahoma City bombing in 1995. When news first broke of an explosion at the Alfred P. Murrah Federal Building, CBS News dispatched its terrorism expert, Steven Emerson, to the site to offer his analysis for viewers. Emerson reported: "This was done with the attempt to inflict as many casualties as possible. That is a Middle Eastern trait. Oklahoma City, I can tell you, is probably considered one of the largest centers of Islamic radical activity outside the Middle East."[6] Other television news networks and newspapers, including ABC News, the *Chicago Tribune*, and *Newsday*, echoed Emerson's analysis and insisted that the bombing bore the marks of Middle Eastern

---

5. David Johnston and William J. Broad, "A Nation Challenged: The Investigation; Link Suspected in Anthrax and Hijackings," *New York Times*, October 19, 2001, http://www.nytimes.com/2001/10/19/us/a-nation-challenged-the-investigation-link-suspected-in-anthrax-and-hijackings.html.

6. Quoted in Nathan Lean, *The Islamophobia Industry: How the Right Manufactures Fear of Muslims* (London: Pluto, 2012), 72.

terrorism.[7] Although the mainstream media assumed that it was only a matter of time before investigators confirmed the identities of the Muslim culprits, as it turned out, the perpetrator was Timothy McVeigh, a white, Christian American and Gulf War veteran with strong antigovernment convictions. Muslims became central figures in widespread media coverage of a terrorist attack that had nothing to do with them. But the repeated speculation still inflicted damage on the public image of Muslims and ensured that Muslims would be a dominant feature of future media coverage of terrorist attacks.

Powell's study also contrasts the different ways that the media characterizes Muslim terrorists versus non-Muslim domestic terrorists. The media was much more likely to describe Muslim terrorists as violent or motivated by extremist (typically religious) ideology than to describe white non-Muslim terrorists in that way. For example, Luke Helder, a university student who set off pipe bombs throughout the Midwest in 2002, was described by CNN as "an intelligent young man with strong family ties."[8] The media speculated a great deal on his mental instability, a common feature in reports on white, non-Muslim men who participate in domestic terrorism or other mass shootings.[9] The reporting consistently humanized and complexified these perpetrators and their motives.

By contrast, Muslim terrorists were frequently described as angry extremists, motivated primarily if not solely by religion. Speculation on mental health problems was sparse and in most cases nonexistent. When Abdulhakim Mujahid Muhammad opened fire at a US military recruiting office in Arkansas in 2009, killing one, Fox News reported that "Muhammad was targeting U.S. soldiers 'because of what they had done to Muslims in the past' and was angry about the wars in

7. Ibid., 72–73.
8. "FBI, Postal Service Reveal Pipe Bombing Suspect," *CNN*, aired May 7, 2002, transcript at http://transcripts.cnn.com/TRANSCRIPTS/0205/07/bn.09.html.
9. Powell, "Framing Islam," 98–99.

Iraq and Afghanistan." The same report suggested that the shooting "was part of what security experts call an alarming domestic trend" involving Muslim converts carrying out violent attacks in the United States.[10] The *New York Times* initially focused on suggestions from experts, and even the defense lawyer, that Muhammad "was radicalized by Islamic fundamentalists in a Yemeni prison."[11] The media's framing of Muhammad's attack, like other terrorist attacks carried out by Muslims, reduced the perpetrator to a simple-minded, angry Islamic extremist with no complex motivations or forces shaping his actions other than revenge and religion. The media exerts little effort to psychologize, humanize, or nuance Muslim terrorists in the same manner as white non-Muslim perpetrators.

European media coverage of terrorism and violence reflects similar patterns. Scholars have focused particularly on the British media's reporting on Islam. One prominent study dealt with the coverage of British Muslims in the UK press from 2000 to 2008. It concluded that two-thirds of stories about British Muslims invoked one of three angles: terrorism, controversial religious issues (Muslim dress codes, the place of Sharia in the UK, and so forth), or Muslim extremism.[12] Violence, or the tendency to violence, featured prominently in the majority of stories in the UK press concerning British Muslims.

In a separate study, Elizabeth Poole examined two of Britain's more prominent newspapers, the *Guardian* and the *Times*, to determine the effects of 9/11 on how reporting on British Muslims was framed. She found the overwhelming majority of articles in 2003 focused on

---

10. Joseph Abrams, "Little Rock Shooting Suspect Joins Growing List of Muslim Converts Accused of Targeting U.S.," *Fox News*, June 2, 2009, http://www.foxnews.com/story/2009/06/02/little-rock-shooting-suspect-joins-growing-list-muslim-converts-accused/.

11. James Dao, "Suspect's Lawyer Outlines Defense in Killing of Soldier," *New York Times*, June 4, 2009, http://www.nytimes.com/2009/06/05/us/05recruit.html.

12. Justin Lewis, Paul Mason, and Kerry Moore, "'Islamic Terrorism' and the Repression of the Political," in *Media, Religion and Conflict*, ed. Lee Marsden and Heather Savigny (Burlington, VT: Ashgate, 2009), 17–37.

the threat of "Islamic terrorism" in the UK.[13] Her findings echoed previous studies that highlighted how frequently the British media places Muslims, inside and outside of Britain, within a framework centered on violence and conflict.[14]

Poole's findings also foreshadowed the conclusions of a more comprehensive study of the Western media's portrayal of Islam. In a study by Media Tenor, 975,000 news stories pertaining to Islam in both Europe and the United States were analyzed. In 2001, only 2 percent of these stories focused on Muslim militants and extremists, but this figure jumped to 25 percent by 2011. In the same period, the percentage of stories devoted to ordinary Muslims remained at 0.1 percent—no change from 2001 to 2011.[15] This study, combined with the other studies discussed in this section, demonstrates just how fixated the Western media is on constructing Islam as a religion prone to violence and extremism.

Framing Oppressed Muslim Women

Perhaps it goes without saying that many media stories on terrorism and extremism concentrate on Muslim men, but women also feature prominently in reporting on Islam. Stories of Muslim women focus mostly on their oppression and status as victims. The stereotypical Muslim woman in the Western media is depicted as a victim of either violence or sexism (or both) at the hands of angry and misogynist

13. Elizabeth Poole, "The Effects of September 11 and the War in Iraq on British Newspaper Coverage," in *Muslims and the News Media*, ed. Elizabeth Poole and John E. Richardson (New York: I. B. Tauris, 2006), 89–102; see also Elizabeth Poole, *Reporting Islam: Media Representations of British Muslims* (New York: I. B. Tauris, 2002).
14. See John E. Richardson, *(Mis)representing Islam: The Racism and Rhetoric of British Broadsheet Newspapers* (Amsterdam: J. Benjamins, 2004).
15. This study, called "A New Era of Arab Western Relations," is cited in John L. Esposito, "2013 AAR Presidential Address: Islam in the Public Square," *Journal of the American Academy of Religion* 82 (2014): 301.

Muslim men (and sometimes other women). As a victim, the Muslim woman is passive. She lacks agency and frequently even a voice. One would be hard pressed to discover Muslim women in the Western media who make choices and participate in activities that shape their own destinies. One would also have difficulty encountering the great diversity of Muslim women, with occupations including housewives, scientific researchers, and politicians, and with religious orientations ranging from Islamist to progressive. From the media's perspective, Muslim women have no more complexity or nuance than Muslim men.

The media obsession with oppressed Muslim women is best illustrated in the surge of stories involving honor killings or honor-related violence in recent years. Honor-related violence refers to violence against girls or women who have violated the sexual norms and therefore the honor of their families of origin. Such violence includes murder but can include other forms of physical abuse or coercion, such as forced marriage.

In a study analyzing the impact that media coverage of honor killings and violence has on public policy, Anna Korteweg and Gökçe Yurdakul point out how the problematic framing of this violence in some countries resulted in the stigmatization of all Muslims, particularly when the explanations offered for the violence focused narrowly on culture and religion.[16] For example, in the Netherlands, two honor killings in 2003 and 2004 generated intense media coverage of violence against Muslim women. The press gave voices such as Ayaan Hirsi Ali, then a parliamentarian, plenty of coverage. In an interview with *De Volkskrant* newspaper, Hirsi Ali

---

16. Anna C. Korteweg and Gökçe Yurdakul, "Religion, Culture and the Politicization of Honour-Related Violence: A Critical Analysis of Media and Policy Debates in Western Europe and North America," Paper No. 12, Gender and Development Programme, UN Research for Social Development, October 2010, http://korteweg.files.wordpress.com/2010/12/kortewegyurdakul-2010-hrv-unrisd1.pdf.

stated: "You know how it goes. Honour killing is a component of something bigger. It has to do with sexual morality within Islam, the desire to control women's sexuality. A cult of virginity reigns. A woman who doesn't keep to the rules, can be expelled, hit, murdered."[17] Likewise in Germany, the murder of a twenty-three-year-old Muslim woman by her brother in 2005 resulted in newspaper coverage that overwhelmingly depicted the killing as something endemic to Turkish immigrant communities and Islam. All immigrants and Muslims were indicted for supporting a culture in which women's rights were not respected and violence against women was condoned.[18]

Without a doubt, violence against Muslim women, in the West and beyond, is not to be treated lightly, and the incidents described above deserve critical scrutiny. But media framing of such events depends heavily on the classic narrative of helpless Muslim women destined to suffer at the hands of misogynist Muslim men until rescued by enlightened, compassionate Westerners. This narrative ignores the more complex factors involved in honor-related violence. Korteweg and Yurdakul argue that economic and social forces, combined with the immigrant experience and the integration policies of the receiving countries, contribute to the gendered violence from which some Muslim women in the West suffer.[19] Moreover, when the media focuses on cultural or religious explanations for honor-related violence, it fails to connect the victims of this violence to other victims of gendered abuse and violence. It is worth repeating that in EU countries, one in three women have suffered from physical or sexual assault.[20] In the United States, one in five women have been sexually assaulted, and one in four have experienced violent abuse by

---

17. Quoted in Ibid., 9.
18. Ibid., 15–16; see also Katherine Ewing, *Stolen Honor: Stigmatizing Muslim Men in Berlin* (Stanford: Stanford University Press, 2008), 151–79.
19. Kortweg and Yurdakul, "Honour-Related Violence," 3–4.

an intimate partner.[21] Domestic abuse, and even domestic murder, are realities affecting large numbers of women with a wide range of cultural and religious backgrounds.

The media's concern for oppressed Muslim women is also illustrated by stories featuring the veil. The veil, whether in the form of a hijab (covering only the hair) or the burqa (covering the entire face), is a standard symbol for the oppression of women in the Western media. It represents Islam's backwardness and uncivilized nature and is therefore an object of particular concern for the media. Journalists frequently analyze those President George W. Bush referred to as "women of cover."

In Europe, the media's obsession with the supposedly oppressive nature of the veil is most easily seen in France, where a law enacted in 2004 banned the hijab in public schools. In the debate leading up to the ban, the media gave less attention to opponents of the law than it did to those politicians, public figures, and other commentators who argued that the law helped protect women from Islam's sexism. The media rarely solicited opinions from Muslim women or girls who wore the hijab and whose rationale for doing so did not confirm the narrative of oppressed Muslim women.[22] The French media framed the debate as fundamentally about women's rights and equality, with the veil representing the antithesis of such values.

Other instances of Western journalists depicting the veil as oppressive and backward are not difficult to find. Maureen Dowd,

20. "One-Third of EU Women Suffered Physical or Sexual Assault, Report Says," *Al-Jazeera America*, March 5, 2014, http://america.aljazeera.com/articles/2014/3/5/major-report-revealsextensiveabuseofwomenineu.html.

21. Roni Caryn Rabin, "Nearly 1 in 5 Women in U.S. Survey Say They Have Been Sexually Assaulted," *New York Times*, December 14, 2011, http://www.nytimes.com/2011/12/15/health/nearly-1-in-5-women-in-us-survey-report-sexual-assault.html.

22. Nahed Eltantawy, "Above the Fold and beyond the Veil: Islamophobia in Western Media," in *The Routledge Companion to Media and Gender*, ed. Cynthia Cater, Linda Steiner, and Lisa McLaughlin (New York: Routledge, 2014), 384–94.

columnist for the *New York Times*, described Saudi Arabia as a "suffocating, strict, monochromatic world of white-robed men and black-robed women." She characterized the women as "faceless" and "ghostly," suggesting that their humanity is covered up by their black robes.[23] Referring to the "ghostly women" of the United Arab Emirates, a journalist for the *San Francisco Chronicle* made this point more explicitly: "Sometimes you can see their faces. Sometimes just their eyes. Sometimes you see nothing at all of the humans beneath the black shrouds."[24] A reporter for the *Toronto Star* described the horror she felt at the sight of Muslim women wearing chadors in Paris: "Those dead, shuttered, hollowed-eyed faces were the ugliest image of enslavement I have ever seen." She added that such a sight "was literally sickening."[25] All of these descriptions share in common the assumption that Muslim women who wear the veil lack both an individual identity and a full sense of personhood. They are passive, voiceless victims who deserve our pity but otherwise have nothing to offer us except an opportunity to play the role of savior.

Not all Muslim women who make appearances in the Western media seem to fit the stereotype of the helpless, voiceless victim. Consider Malala Yousafzai, the teenage advocate for girls' and women's education in Pakistan who was shot by the Taliban in October 2012. Yousafzai became a media sensation in the West after the attempted assassination. Newspaper headlines hailed her courage in the face of terrorism and her unyielding commitment to girls' and women's rights. Once she began to recover, the honors quickly followed. *Time* magazine heralded her as one of the hundred most influential people in 2013. That same year, she gave a highly

23. Maureen Dowd, "Driving While Female," *New York Times*, November 17, 2002, http://www.nytimes.com/2002/11/17/opinion/driving-while-female.html.
24. Joan Ryan, "The Error of Too Much Tolerance," *San Francisco Chronicle*, August 26, 2004, http://www.sfgate.com/sports/article/The-error-of-too-much-tolerance-2730549.php.
25. Quoted in Eltantawy, "Above the Fold," 389.

publicized speech to the UN on girls' education, met with President Obama at the White House, and received a nomination for the Nobel Peace Prize. In 2014, she became the youngest person ever to receive the Nobel Peace Prize. The media took pains to cover each of these accolades and events in great detail.

On the surface, the media coverage of Yousafzai appears to add complexity to the preceding analysis. She was a female victim of violence committed by Muslim men in the form of the Pakistani Taliban, but she was neither passive nor voiceless. Before and after the attack, she was a strong and vocal activist for girls' education and women's rights, and the media did not shy away from celebrating her strengths and accomplishments. On closer examination, some of the same stereotypes discussed above found their way into the media stories of Yousafzai. For example, to the extent that religion made any appearance in these stories, it was usually the extremist brand of Islam preached by the Taliban.

Yousafzai's Muslim faith received little attention. Western audiences would be hard pressed to learn from most media stories that Yousafzai's activism for girls' education and her opposition to the Taliban are driven by Islam. Many of her speeches and writings, including her autobiography, are replete with references to the Qur'an and her faith in Allah. But why did many Western journalists fail to explore or highlight Yousafzai's religious identity and motivations? One possible explanation is that her story did not conform neatly to the preexisting assumptions about Islam. Islam is a religion that is supposed to oppress women, not empower them. Her story was therefore recast to minimize her own religious identity and to highlight her clash with radical Islam so that the framework for reporting on Islam remained intact.

Of course, one can find exceptions to the general conclusions reached here. There are increasing numbers of newspapers, television programs, and websites that portray the complexity of Islam and allow for diverse Muslim voices and experiences. In addition, a growing number of Muslim journalists and Muslim-run news organizations offer alternative perspectives on Islam. Even so, these competing sources of news are often overshadowed by the overwhelming amount of reporting in the mainstream media that reduces Islam to violence, terrorism, and misogyny.

On Television

Muslims as the threatening "Other" are found not only in the news but also on popular television programming and in films. Arab and Muslim characters have been a part of the American film and television industry's history from the beginning, though depictions of these characters adapted to the times.[26] With the United States' rise to global superpower status after World War II, violence and terrorism became central features in representations of Muslims and Islam, mainly because of events in the Middle East that increasingly occupied the United States' attention, including the establishment of Israel (1948), the Six-Day War (1967), the Arab oil embargo (1973), and the Iranian Revolution and hostage crisis (1979–1980). These events, covered extensively by the news media, fed the popular image of Muslims and Muslim-majority regions as sources of anti-Western, anti-American violence and terrorism.[27]

26. I recognize that "Arab" and "Muslim" are not interchangeable designations—not all Muslims are Arab (the majority, in fact, are not), and not all Arabs are Muslim. However, as Jack Shaheen observes, the American television and film industry frequently conflates the two, with unfortunate consequences for both. For this reason, the following discussion deals with both groups. See Jack G. Shaheen, *Guilty: Hollywood's Verdict on Arabs after 9/11* (Northampton, MA: Olive Branch, 2008), xiii.
27. Evelyn Alsultany, *Arabs and Muslims in the Media: Race and Representation after 9/11* (New York: New York University Press, 2012), 7–8; Jack G. Shaheen, *Reel Bad Arabs: How Hollywood Vilifies a People* (Northampton, MA: Olive Branch, 2009), 34–35.

My focus in this section and the following one will be on television programs and movies that reinforce negative stereotypes of Muslims and Islam, particularly those related to violence and terrorism in the post-9/11 era. Many of the examples I will analyze come from the United States, largely because American television shows and films have massive audiences and extensive influence domestically and internationally.[28]

The Prime-Time Muslim Enemy

The most common type of television show with prominent Muslim characters is prime-time drama. After 9/11, numerous dramas surfaced with Muslim terrorism or the War on Terror as central themes. The pervasive fear of terrorist threats after 9/11 created fertile ground for these dramas to attract audiences. Shows such as *The Agency* (2001–2003), *Threat Matrix* (2003–2004), and *Sleeper Cell* (2005–2006) provided viewers with an outlet in which to see the United States and its representatives successfully conduct the war against terrorism.[29] Two of the more popular and successful shows in this genre, *24* (2001–2010, 2014) and *Homeland* (2011–present), provide an excellent glimpse into the portrayal of Muslims and Arabs in period.

24 follows Jack Bauer, a heroic but troubled agent with the US government's Counter-Terrorism Unit (CTU), as he thwarts terrorist plots at home and abroad. Each episode covers one hour of real time, and Bauer has twenty-four hours (or twenty-four episodes)

---

28. The television show *24*, for example, averaged between eleven and thirteen million viewers in the United States between 2001 and 2010. The show also aired throughout the world, including in Europe, Latin America, Africa, Australia, and the Middle East. See Peter Morey and Amina Yaqin, *Framing Muslims: Stereotyping and Representation after 9/11* (Cambridge, MA: Harvard University Press, 2011), 145.
29. Alsultany, *Arabs and Muslims in the Media*, 2.

to foil each terrorist plot. Muslim characters are prominent throughout the series, though they are not always portrayed as the antagonists. In some instances, they are sympathetic characters, either cooperating with Bauer or falling victim to profiling and stereotyping.

In many instances, Muslims feature prominently as loathsome terrorists. In the second season, Bauer tracks down a Muslim terrorist, Syed Ali, after a prayer service at a Los Angeles mosque. Bauer subsequently tortures Ali in order to get him to confess the whereabouts of a nuclear bomb. Ali proves resistant to torture, and when Bauer insists that he is able to inflict even more pain, Ali responds with great fervor: "Then I will have much more pleasure in paradise."[30] In the fourth season, the main terrorist group is called the Turkish Crimson Jihad. A Turkish family living in the United States is a part of this organization, working as a sleeper cell in the hopes of killing Americans. The family's father in particular is portrayed as a zealous, extremist Muslim bent on jihad and willing to kill his own family to carry out his mission against America. In the eighth season, Muslim terrorists from the fictional country of Kamistan, fueled in part by anti-American sentiment, must be stopped from assassinating that country's president as he signs a treaty with the United States.

Homeland focuses on a US Marine sergeant, Nick Brody, who returns home after being held captive in Iraq for eight years. Carrie Mathison, a CIA officer, becomes suspicious of Brody and seeks to discover whether he has become an al-Qaeda sleeper agent with the mission of carrying out a terrorist plot on American soil. The main twist to the story is that Brody converted to Islam while a prisoner in Iraq, though he keeps this hidden from his family and friends. Given that he is not a stereotypical Muslim character—he is the poster

---

30. Quoted in Morey and Yaqin, *Framing Muslims*, 148.

child of a white, all-American boy scout—his Muslim faith keeps the audience guessing throughout the first season whether he is "one of us" or "one of them."

Of course, *Homeland* has its share of Muslim villains. The terrorist mastermind in the first two seasons is Abu Nazir. We learn that Brody fell under Nazir's influence while in Iraq. Nazir wants to use Brody to carry out a suicide attack against the US government, aimed in particular at killing the vice president, who, while serving as the CIA director, ordered a drone strike that killed Nazir's young son. Nazir epitomizes the anti-American, Muslim terrorist who shows no regard for innocent lives in order to enact revenge in the name of his religion. Other Muslim terrorist accomplices include Afsal Hamid, one of Brody's prison guards from Iraq who is shown in one flashback urinating on Brody, and Roya Hammad, a Palestinian journalist working in the United States who serves as a liaison between Nazir and Brody. By the end of the second season, Abu Nazir and his network have succeeded in killing the vice president and planting a car bomb at CIA headquarters in Langley that results in hundreds of deaths, including those of top government officials.

The portrayal of Muslims as terrorists in shows such as *24* and *Homeland* has led to some highly publicized criticisms. The Council on American-Islamic Relations (CAIR) accused *24* of stereotyping Muslims and Arabs as terrorists, insisting that "repeated association of acts of terrorism with Islam will only serve to increase anti-Muslim prejudice." The producers and writers of *24* responded by noting that the show had "not singled out any ethnic or religious group for blame in creating the characters." They added that "the villains have included shadowy Anglo businessmen, Baltic Europeans, Germans, Russians, Islamic fundamentalists, and even the (Anglo-American) president of the United States."[31] At one point during the show's run, the Fox television network aired a public service announcement during a commercial break for one of the episodes. It featured the lead actor, Kiefer Sutherland, warning viewers about the dangers of stereotyping Muslims as terrorists.

The network's response to CAIR's complaints represents a deliberate strategy to deflect criticism by pointing out that Muslim characters are not always the villains. In some instances, they are even the "good guys." Scholar Evelyn Alsultany refers to these strategies as "simplified complex representations": "Simplified complex representations are strategies used by television producers, writers, and directors to give the impression that the representations they are producing are complex. . . . These representations appear to challenge or complicate former stereotypes and contribute to a multicultural or post-race illusion."[32] Some of the strategies employed include reversing the enemy, creating patriotic or otherwise "positive" Muslim and Arab characters, and humanizing the terrorist.[33]

24's producers and writers provide an example of reversing the enemy, or what Alsutany refers to as "flipping the enemy," in their response to CAIR. They pointed to the range of non-Muslim "bad guys" in the show as proof that *24* did not engage in Muslim stereotyping. In *Homeland*, this strategy is evident in the depiction of US government and intelligence officials, including the vice president and the CIA director, as engaged in war crimes that include a deliberate drone strike on Iraqi children. Patriotic Muslims, or Muslims on "our side," include Nadia Yassir, a member of the CTU in *24*, and Danny Galvez, a CIA officer in *Homeland*. Both are

---

31. Quoted in "24 under Fire from Muslim Groups," *BBC News* (UK), January 19, 2007, http://news.bbc.co.uk/2/hi/entertainment/6280315.stm.

32. Alsultany, *Arabs and Muslims in the Media*, 21.

33. Alsultany identifies seven strategies often employed by television writers, producers, and directors. For the sake of space, I am focusing on only three of the strategies. For a discussion of all seven, see ibid., 21–26.

Muslims who fight Muslim terrorists on behalf of US intelligence agencies.

The Turkish family in *24*, discussed earlier, is an example of the strategy of humanizing terrorists, as we learn much about their backstories and interpersonal relations that presumably add complexity to their motives.[34] *Homeland* goes to great lengths to humanize Brody. Even though Brody, a convert to Islam, is contemplating carrying out a terrorist attack, the show focuses considerable attention on the experiences he endured while in Iraq, the psychological trauma of readjusting to life in the United States, and the strained relations he has with his wife and children in light of his prolonged absence from them.

Alsultany reminds us that these strategies, even when well-intentioned, reinforce stereotypes and narrow views of Muslims. They reinscribe a "good Muslim" versus "bad Muslim" dichotomy that simplifies more than it complexifies. "Bad Muslims" are typically terrorists, and "good Muslims" are the ones who support the US government in its battle against terrorism.[35] But *all* Muslim characters in these dramas are defined primarily in relation to violence and terrorism (whether they are for or against these things). Non-Muslim characters, by contrast, have more diverse or nuanced storylines. For example, *Homeland*'s main protagonist, Carrie Mathison, not only fights terrorism but also battles bipolar disorder. Her struggles with mental illness constitute an important part of her storyline. We rarely encounter Muslim characters struggling with any psychological disorder other than religious fanaticism. Moreover, white, non-Muslim characters can be found in a wide variety of television shows that have nothing to do with terrorism. This is not the case with Muslim or Arab characters. In short, simplified complex

34. Ibid., 24–25.
35. Ibid., 26–31.

representational strategies contribute to the illusion that Muslims are not victims of stereotyping, but, unfortunately, these strategies fail to present the true diversity and complexity of Muslims and Muslim Americans.

Even when shows not focused on terrorism attempt to include Muslim characters, the old stereotypes are rarely far away. For example, consider the popular program *Lost* (2004–2010). *Lost* follows the survivors of a commercial airplane that crashes on a mysterious island with supernatural forces. One of the survivors is Sayid Jarrah. Sayid's character hails from Iraq, and we learn from various episodes that he is both a Muslim and a former soldier in the Iraqi Republican Guard during the Persian Gulf War (1990–1991). Because terrorism is not the show's focus, Sayid is not portrayed primarily in relation to terrorism.[36] Yet his character is portrayed in relation to violence. While all of the characters on *Lost* are wrestling with demons from their past, Sayid's particular demon is violence. Sayid struggles throughout the series with whether or not he is violent by nature. We learn from flashbacks that he was a torturer in the Iraqi army, a skill he occasionally uses on some of the other survivors or island inhabitants, though usually for some greater good.

When Sayid is temporarily off the island in the fourth and fifth seasons, he is employed as an assassin. After a brief reprieve from this work, his former employer, Ben Linus, seeks to hire Sayid for another assignment, to which he responds, "What makes you think I want to [kill again]?" Ben explains, "Because, Sayid, to put it simply, you're capable of things that most other men aren't. Every choice you've made in life, whether it was to murder or torture, it hasn't really been

36. We do learn, however, that Sayid was arrested on trumped-up terrorism charges and forced to work as an informant for the CIA and Australia's intelligence service. He infiltrates a terrorist cell in Sydney, and his work there sets off a chain of events leading him to take the flight to Los Angeles that crashes on the mysterious island. See *Lost*, "The Greater Good," ABC, May 4, 2005, written by Leonard Dick, directed by David Grossman.

a choice at all, has it? It's in your nature. It's what you are. You're a killer, Sayid." Sayid disagrees, saying, "I'm not what you think I am. I don't like killing." Later in the episode, Sayid comes around and confesses his true nature to Ben: "You were right about me. I am a killer."[37]

Sayid is a character that the audience is intended to like. He often shows a softer, more romantic side, and he heroically and frequently comes to the rescue of his fellow survivors. Here again we have an example of simplified complex representation. But it is telling that the Muslim character is the only prominent character on the show to struggle with the question of whether he (or she) is inherently prone to violence.

Positive Television Portrayals of Muslims

Television programs challenging simplified complex representations of Muslims are few and far between, but they do exist. In the United States, shows such as *All-American Muslim* (2011–2012) and *Community* (2009–2014) push beyond common stereotypes and narrow characterizations. *All-American Muslim* is a reality show that follows five Muslim families living in Dearborn, Michigan, known for its sizable Muslim community. Viewers have an opportunity to observe the daily lives of these families and how their faith informs who they are. The general manager of TLC, the cable network airing the program, stated: "We wanted to show there was diversity even within the Muslim community. These are families that might have beliefs that are different than yours, but we are all living similar daily lives and hopefully we will bring that to light."[38] Unfortunately, the network canceled the show after one season. The show suffered

---

37. *Lost*, "He's Our You," ABC, March 25, 2009, written by Edward Kitsis and Adam Horowitz, directed by Greg Yaitanes.

from low ratings and from a controversy in which some sponsors pulled their ads after the Florida Family Association, a conservative Christian organization, launched a campaign against the program on the basis that it promoted "propaganda that riskily hides the Islamic agenda's clear and present danger to American liberties and traditional values."[39] Because the show did not include extremist Muslims, insisted the organization, it provided the public with an inaccurate view of Islam's true nature.

The sitcom *Community* faired much better. The show focuses on community college students in Colorado. One of the students is Abed Nadir, a Palestinian American. Abed's social awkwardness and fixation with popular culture are central to his character, but, notably, his Muslim faith is not. He is an excellent example of a character that pushes beyond simplified complex representations and the practice of defining Muslim characters in relation to violence or terrorism.

In Canada, the critically acclaimed sitcom *Little Mosque on the Prairie* (2007–2012) details the lives of Muslims who open a mosque and community center in a small Canadian town. The show gives viewers a glimpse into Islamic rituals and the tensions between liberal and conservative Muslims, but with a comic take. The storylines, moreover, focus on mundane topics. Terrorism is neither central to the plot nor to understanding the characters.[40]

Finally, shows such as *EastEnders* (1985–present) in Britain and *Türkisch für Anfänger* (*Turkish for Beginners*, 2006–2009) in Germany are notable for their efforts in defying Muslim stereotypes. In *EastEnders*, a Muslim character has a gay love affair and grapples with

---

38. "TLC Filming New Reality Show 'All American Muslim' in Dearborn," *Arab American News*, July 29, 2011, http://www.arabamericannews.com/news/news/id_4546.

39. Paul Farhi, "Reality TV Catches up to Reality with Muslim Show," *Washington Post*, December 12, 2011, http://www.washingtonpost.com/lifestyle/style/reality-tv-catches-up-to-reality-with-muslim-show/2011/12/12/gIQAB3geqO_story.html.

40. Alsultany, *Arabs and Muslims in the Media*, 174–76.

the subsequent tension between his religious and sexual identities.[41] *Türkisch für Anfänger* focuses on the challenges facing the merging of two families after a German woman marries a man of Turkish background. Each parent brings two children into the marriage. On the husband's side, there is a daughter, Yagmur, who wears a headscarf and seeks to be a devout Muslim. The show contains storylines in which Yagmur wrestles with the challenges of reconciling her Muslim and German identities, yet the show avoids a simplistic resolution. Room is left for Yagmur to be both German and Muslim.[42]

These shows represent the emergence of new television programming containing Muslim characters and storylines that are not confined to terrorism, violence, or the dichotomy between "good Muslim" and "bad Muslim." Television shows that traffic in Muslim stereotypes are still the norm, but these alternative representations are promising signs that popular television can play a more constructive role in how the West imagines and understands Muslims.

At the Movies

Muslim and Arab characters have been a part of the film industry from the beginning. Jack Shaheen, the foremost expert on Hollywood's portrayal of Muslims and Arabs, argues that the history of these groups in film is not pretty: "From 1896 until today, filmmakers have collectively indicted Arabs as Public Enemy #1—brutal, heartless, uncivilized religious fanatics and money-mad

41. Leigh Holmwood and Gareth McLean, "EastEnders: Muslim Character to Have Gay Love Affair," *Guardian* (UK), May 28, 2009, http://www.theguardian.com/media/2009/may/28/eastenders-gay-love-affair.

42. Brent Peterson, "Turkish for Beginners: Teaching Cosmopolitanism to Germans," in *Turkish German Cinema in the New Millennium*, ed. Sabine Hake and Barbara Caroline Mennel (New York: Berghahn Books, 2012), 99–101.

cultural 'others' bent on terrorizing civilized Westerners, especially Christians and Jews."[43] Shaheen adds that Islam in particular gets hit hard in movies, increasingly so in recent decades: "Today's imagemakers regularly link the Islamic faith with male supremacy, holy war, and acts of terror, depicting Arabs and Muslims as hostile alien intruders, and as lecherous, oily sheikhs intent on using nuclear weapons."[44] Shaheen estimates that, as of 2008, the number of films maligning Muslims and Arabs in one way or another exceeds 1,150.[45]

Hollywood's Muslim Villains

Even though it may seem likely that films portraying Muslims and Arabs as prone to anti-American violence or terrorism would be primarily a post-9/11 phenomenon, all evidence points to the contrary. From *Old Ironsides* (1926) and *Golden Hands of Kurigal* (1949) to *True Lies* (1994) and *The Siege* (1998), Hollywood has an extensive history of presenting Muslims as terrorists and enemies bent on the destruction of the United States and Americans. Muslim violence directed at both Arab and Western women is also found in many pre-9/11 movies, from *Captured by Bedouins* (1912) and *The Corsair* (1914) to *Bulletproof* (1988) and *The Pelican Brief* (1993).[46] The stereotype of the violent, vengeful Muslim is deeply embedded in Hollywood's psyche.

One of the most egregious depictions of violent Muslims just prior to 9/11 is found in *Rules of Engagement* (2000), a movie produced in cooperation with the US Marine Corps and the US Department of Defense (DOD). Early in the film, we see a horde of Muslims

43. Shaheen, *Reel Bad Arabs*, 8.
44. Ibid., 15.
45. Shaheen, *Guilty*, xiv.
46. Shaheen, *Reel Bad Arabs*, 22–23, 129–30, 158, 381.

demonstrating outside the US embassy in Yemen. Veiled women, bearded men, and children chant, wave anti-American banners, and hurl rocks and firebombs. Helicopters deliver marines to the embassy to protect it. Under attack from a few snipers, a colonel orders his soldiers to open fire on the crowd. The soldiers succeed in killing eighty-three protestors. The attack initially seems unjustified. An investigation ensues, revealing that the protestors were in fact armed with weapons and fired first on the marines. What seemed like a brutal slaughter of civilians was actually an act of self-defense. The investigator even uncovers an audio recording of a Muslim prior to the attack proclaiming: "[This is a] declaration of Islamic Jihad against the United States. . . . We call on every Muslim who believes in God . . . to kill Americans and their allies, both civilian and military. It is the duty of every Muslim, everywhere . . . to kill Americans."[47] The movie portrays all Muslims in the crowd, even the children, as ruthless, anti-American terrorists driven by religious extremism. We are meant to cheer for the Marines as they are vindicated in their killing of the Yemeni men, women, and children. The film's director, William Friedkin, affirmed as much: "I've seen audiences stand up and applaud the film throughout the United States."[48]

Rules of Engagement reveals the enduring strength and persistence of the stereotype of violent, hateful Muslims dedicated to destroying the United States and the West. The movie "works" even without the 9/11 worldview. But after 9/11, the damage inflicted by such stereotypes is much greater. Shaheen notes that during times of war and armed conflict, this sort of stereotyping meets little resistance.[49] Western audiences see these disparaging characterizations as confirming the reasons for real-world events such as the destruction

47. Ibid., 435.
48. Ibid., 21.
49. Shaheen, *Guilty*, xi–xii.

of the World Trade Center or the Pentagon. Put simply, movies with Muslim and Arab villains seem even more realistic after 9/11 because of the assumption that Muslims are our real-world enemies who attacked us on 9/11 and with whom we are at war in Afghanistan and Iraq.

Plenty of post-9/11 films pick up where *Rules of Engagement* left off—with US military or government forces battling Muslim enemies and terrorists. In *Black Hawk Down* (2002), also filmed in cooperation with the DOD, US Rangers and Delta Force soldiers attempting to capture a Somali warlord's top lieutenants find themselves outnumbered in a bloody battle with the warlord's troops. The film, based on the Battle of Mogadishu in 1993, routinely depicts the US soldiers as brave and heroic, while, according to author Michael Massing, the Somali Muslims are portrayed "as uniformly grasping, creepy and savage."[50]

In *The Kingdom* (2007), agents from the FBI fly to Saudi Arabia to investigate the deaths of American oil workers and their families after a terrorist attack in Riyadh. Much of the action revolves around the agents killing scores of Saudi Muslims, too many to count. Shaheen describes the movie as "Hollywood's most anti-Arab post-9/11 film."[51] Film critic A. O. Scott of the *New York Times* argues that the film is a fantasy war on terror: "Just as *Rambo* offered the fantasy of do-over on Vietnam, *The Kingdom* can be seen as a wishful revisionist scenario for the American response to Islamic fundamentalist terrorism."[52]

The "real" War on Terror is central to a number of post-9/11 movies, including *Zero Dark Thirty* (2012) and *American Sniper*

---

50. Quoted in ibid., 100.
51. Ibid., 127.
52. A. O. Scott, "F.B.I. Agents Solve the Terrorist Problem," *New York Times*, September 28, 2007, http://www.nytimes.com/2007/09/28/movies/28king.html.

(2014), two Oscar-nominated films based on real-life events. *Zero Dark Thirty* traces the CIA's efforts to hunt down Osama bin Laden after 9/11. The central character is Maya, a CIA operative who becomes obsessed in her pursuit of bin Laden. Her tenacity pays off when a US Navy SEAL team, relying on Maya's lead, locates and assassinates bin Laden in a Pakistani compound in 2011. While the film courted controversy for portraying torture as a reliable tool for gathering the information needed to track down bin Laden, the larger problem with *Zero Dark Thirty* is the recycled plot of good Americans fighting evil Muslims. Any brown character in the movie, be they Arab or South Asian, is automatically assumed to be a Muslim "bad guy" plotting to destroy all Americans, though here and there we get a glimpse of a Muslim "good guy." Even in these cases, what we really have are simplified complex representations.[53]

Similar observations apply to *American Sniper*, a film that follows the story of Chris Kyle, the most lethal sniper in US military history. Kyle is a Navy SEAL sharpshooter who is tasked with protecting his fellow soldiers during four tours of duty in Iraq by killing anyone who appears to pose a threat to them. Like *Zero Dark Thirty*, almost every Muslim who appears on screen is the enemy. In fact, Kyle opens fire not only on menacing Muslim men but on women and children too, and he does so with little remorse. He repeatedly refers to the people of Iraq as "savages" and sees himself as a Christian crusader (with a crusader's cross tattoo on one of his arms to prove it).

---

53. As Deepa Kumar points out in her critique of *Zero Dark Thirty*: "The only way to be brown and not to be a villain in [director Kathryn Bigelow's] narrative is to be unflinchingly loyal to the Americans, as the translator working for the CIA is. The 'good Muslim' does not question, he simply acts to pave the way for American interests." Kumar adds that the movie is little more than government propaganda supporting the Obama administration's view that extrajudicial killing is necessary and that the CIA is a trusted agency whose techniques for identifying and destroying terroirsts are the best means of defeating the Muslim enemy. See Kumar, "Rebranding the War on Terror for the Age of Obama: 'Zero Dark Thirty' and the Promotion of Extra Judicial Killing," *Mondoweiss*, January 15, 2013, http://mondoweiss.net/2013/01/rebranding-promotion-judicial.

While Clint Eastwood, the film's director, is willing to probe some of the complexities of Kyle's character, such as the toll that sustained participation in violence takes on Kyle's marriage and psyche, Eastwood never challenges Kyle's Manichean worldview of "evil Muslims" versus "righteous Americans."

The film that beat out *Zero Dark Thirty* for the Best Picture Oscar in 2013, *Argo* (2012), is based on the historical event that marked a turning point in the United States' relationship with political Islam: the Iranian hostage crisis of 1979. After Iranian revolutionaries storm the US embassy and take sixty-six Americans hostage, six employees manage to escape the embassy and make their way to the home of Iran's Canadian ambassador. The CIA relies on an exfiltration expert, Tony Mendez, to devise a scheme for rescuing the employees by entering Iran under the guise of a Canadian film crew and smuggling the employees out of the country.

The plot is not a conventional shoot-'em-up narrative as with *Black Hawk Down*, *The Kingdom*, or *Zero Dark Thirty*, but it is yet another variation on a common theme: the US government versus violent, hostile, anti-American Muslims. The Muslims in question are technically not Arab but Persian, but would many Western audiences know or care about the difference? After all, they behave like the Muslims in many of the other movies discussed. They are angry, vengeful, irrational, and completely unsympathetic characters. They protest, riot, harass Westerners, and burn the American flag, but they have no sympathetic qualities that humanize them. The embassy workers, by contrast, are portrayed as innocent victims who live in constant fear of torture and execution if they are caught, a fear that Mendez encourages.

It should be mentioned that these portrayals did attract criticism. Ken Taylor, the Canadian ambassador in Iran who helped orchestrate the embassy workers' escape, complained that the movie ignored the

Iranians' "more hospitable side and an intent that they were looking for some degree of justice and hope and that it all wasn't just a violent demonstration for nothing."[54]

The movie contains a prologue that attempts to circumvent charges that the Iranians are being portrayed unfairly at the expense of the Americans. It contains a brief narration of the United States' involvement in the overthrow of the democratically elected prime minister, Mohammad Mosaddegh, in 1953, and American support for the Shah and his autocratic and at times brutal rule. The prologue's message: the United States has not always been the "good guy," and the Iranians may have some justification for their animosity. But the prologue has no impact on the characterization of the Iranians or the Americans that follow. Juan Cole describes the prologue as "emotionally flat" and little more than an "info-dump." The prologue "tells, it doesn't show." He adds: "The film tells but doesn't show some of the US atrocities in Iran. It shows the plight of the hapless US diplomats. In making that key dramatic decision, and then in Orientalizing the Iranian protagonists as angry and irrational, the film betrays its subject matter and becomes propaganda, lacking true moral or emotional ambiguity."[55] What we have is yet another movie in which courageous Americans thwart the unsavory intentions of hostile Muslims.

While Muslim terrorists and enemies bent on destroying American lives and freedoms is a prominent theme in post-9/11 films, at least one other stereotype tends to surface: menacing Muslim men who threaten to harm Western women physically or sexually (or both).

54. Quoted in Nima Shirazi, "Argo Fact Check: Best Picture Is Full of Inaccuracies," *PolicyMic*, February 26, 2013, http://mic.com/articles/28131/argo-fact-check-best-picture-is-full-of-inaccuracies.

55. Juan Cole, "'Argo' as Orientalism and Why It Upsets Iranians," *Informed Comment: Thoughts on the Middle East, History and Religion*, February 26, 2013, http://www.juancole.com/2013/02/orientalism-upsets-iranians.html.

A clear illustration of this stereotype is found in the *Taken* movies. *Taken* (2008) follows Bryan Mills, a former CIA agent who flies to Paris in order to find his seventeen-year-old daughter, Kim, after she has been kidnapped during a visit to the city with a friend. He quickly finds out that she has been abducted by an Albanian gang specializing in sex trafficking and prostitution. The movie ends with Mills discovering that Kim has been sold to an Arab sheikh who intends to add her to his harem. Mills tracks down the sheikh and kills him along with his henchmen.

Taken 2 (2012) opens with the family of one of Mills's Albanian victims (from the first movie) mourning at a Muslim funeral. The father of the victim vows to avenge his son's death by killing Mills. The rest of the movie involves the abduction of Mills's ex-wife in Turkey and another pursuit by Mills that ends with a high Muslim body count and the rescue of yet another damsel in distress.

The *Taken* movies portray Muslim men as cruel and lustful. Muslims are connected with rape, child slavery, violence, and vengeance. They exploit Western women for profit, sexual pleasure, and retribution. Women are never safe from Muslim men in these films, and the fact that the first film takes place in France reveals that these men have infiltrated the West and now pose an internal threat. These two movies serve as stark reminders of the persistence of the stereotype of Muslim misogyny and of the threat posed by Muslim men to "our" women.

Positive Movie Portrayals of Muslims

As in television, so in the movies we encounter examples that challenge the negative stereotypes of Muslims and Islam. We saw this already before 9/11 in movies ranging from *The Thief of Bagdad*

(1924) to *The Black Tent* (1956) to *Robin Hood: Prince of Thieves* (1991), but the list is much shorter than the one of films vilifying Muslims. The same holds true for the post-9/11 era, but films portraying Muslims and Islam favorably and with greater nuance do exist.

Kingdom of Heaven (2005) tells the story of Saladin's conquering of the Christian Kingdom of Jerusalem during the Crusades. Saladin is depicted as a virtuous and respectful leader. When the king of Jerusalem falls ill, Saladin sends his own doctors to attend to the king. And when Saladin finally takes Jerusalem, he finds a large cross on the floor in the king's palace. He picks up the cross and carefully places it back on the altar. During a screening of the movie in Beirut, journalist Robert Fisk observed the following reaction from the audience in response to this scene: "And at this point, the audience rose to their feet and clapped and shouted their appreciation. They loved that gesture of honour. They wanted Islam to be merciful as well as strong."[56] The movie definitely acknowledges the violence and brutality committed by both Christians and Muslims during the Crusades, but *Kingdom of Heaven* goes to great lengths not to make Muslims or Islam the scapegoat.

Other films with sympathetic portrayals of Muslims include *Babel* (2006), *Paris, je t'aime* (2006), and *Mooz-Lum* (2010). *Babel* traces the events following an accidental shooting of an American tourist on a bus in Morocco. Many of the Moroccan characters—including a fellow bus passenger, doctors, and local villagers—come to the aid of the American. In the French film, *Paris, je t'aime* (*Paris, I Love You*), an Arab Muslim teenager named Zarka teaches a young French admirer, François, that her hijab does not hide her beauty but represents what real beauty is—her identification with Islam.[57] In *Mooz-Lum*, a young

---

56. Robert Fisk, "Screening Kingdom of Heaven in Beirut," *Counterpunch*, June 10–12, 2005, http://www.counterpunch.org/2005/06/10/screening-kingdom-of-heaven-in-beirut/.

African American Muslim, Tariq, wrestles with his religious identity in light of both a strict and traumatic upbringing and the events of 9/11. The film adopts Tariq's point of view and demonstrates the challenges and complexities of Muslim American identity in the post-9/11 era.[58] All three films provide Muslim characters that are relatable and sympathetic. They represent a slow but growing trend in movies challenging the violent, misogynist Muslim stereotype that has plagued Western cinema for much of its history.

◆ ◆ ◆ ◆ ◆

A common defense of films containing blatant anti-Muslim stereotypes or brutality against Muslim "enemies" is the claim, "it's just a movie." The director Kathryn Bigelow used this line of defense for *Zero Dark Thirty* when it met with protests concerning its portrayal of torture.[59] Yes, these are "just" movies, but movies, like newspapers and television programs, construct the realities in which we live. Film historian Annette Insdorf observes that, of all forms of art, "film is the one that gives the greatest illusion of authenticity, of truth."[60] Indeed, all forms of media in one way or another provide an "illusion of authenticity" by framing events and people in such a way that we confuse a constructed reality, built on stereotypes and caricatures, with pure, untainted reality. When the media frames or depicts Muslims as prone to violence, terrorism, and oppressive behavior, audiences take these depictions as "truth" and act (or react) accordingly. The hostility and discrimination Muslims face in Western societies, discussed in detail in the next chapter, cannot be

57. Shaheen, *Guilty*, 97–98, 149–50.
58. Andy Webster, "For One Young Muslim the Path to Faith Is Rocky," *New York Times*, February 27, 2001, http://www.nytimes.com/2011/02/28/movies/28mooz.html.
59. Kevin Cirilli, "Protestors at 'Zero Dark Thirty' D.C. Premiere," *Politico*, January 9, 2013, http://www.politico.com/story/2013/01/zero-dark-thirty-torture-cloud-follows-film-premiere-85939.html.
60. Quoted in Shaheen, *Guilty*, xx.

divorced from the mischaracterizations and stereotypes that dominate the media.

8

Islamophobia and Its Casualties

We recall from chapter 1 that the Runnymede Report defines Islamophobia as "an unfounded hostility toward Islam" or a "fear or dislike of all or most Muslims" that has practical implications, particularly discrimination and the exclusion of Muslims from mainstream social and political life.[1] Islamophobia, in other words, includes both what people feel toward Muslims (hostility, fear) and how those feelings are translated into concrete actions against Muslims (discrimination, exclusion).

Much of the book has surveyed Western fears and anxieties toward Muslims. We have explored the historical, political, economic, social, and religious roots of anti-Muslim prejudice, focusing on how theologians, philosophers, colonizers, politicians, scholars, native informants, journalists, and filmmakers have constructed Muslims as the violent, backward, misogynist, and uncivilized "Other."

---

1. Commission on British Muslims and Islamophobia, *Islamophobia: A Challenge for Us All* (London: Runnymede Trust, 1997), 1, 4.

We now turn our attention to the consequences and casualties of Islamophobia—the discrimination, exclusion, and violence experienced by Muslims as a result of decades and indeed centuries of animosity. We discussed some of these consequences for Muslims outside the West already in chapter 4—for example, the death toll and destruction resulting from the War on Terror in Afghanistan and Iraq. In this chapter, I survey the impact of Islamophobia on Muslims living in the West, noting the restrictions on civil liberties and the harsh treatment Muslims have received at the hands of governments, law enforcement officials, and non-Muslim citizens. Facing detentions and deportations, hate crimes and headscarf bans, Muslims have emerged as the most overtly targeted and besieged minority community in the West in the post-9/11 era.

Surveillance and Profiling

While antiterrorism laws existed long before 9/11, the 9/11 attacks generated an unprecedented wave of new legislation and counterterrorism measures that greatly expanded the power of Western governments and law enforcement agencies to identify and eliminate the "internal threat" posed by suspected domestic terrorists. In 2001, the US attorney general, John Ashcroft, tapped into this fear to defend the use of extraordinary measures to battle this enemy: "The attacks of September 11 were acts of terrorism against America orchestrated and carried out by individuals living within our borders. Today's terrorists enjoy the benefits of our free society even as they commit themselves to our destruction. They live in our communities—plotting, planning and waiting to kill Americans again."[2] Given the religious identities of the 9/11 perpetrators, it is

2. John Ashcroft, "Prepared Remarks for the US Mayors Conference," Yale Law School, Avalon Project, October 25, 2001, http://avalon.law.yale.edu/sept11/doj_brief020.asp.

clear that the "they" to whom Ashcroft refers are the Muslims in our midst. Ashcroft implies that measures must be taken to ensure that Muslims do not exploit "the benefits of our free society" to attack the United States again.

Initial US Counterterrorism Measures after 9/11

The most prominent measure adopted in the United States after 9/11 to battle domestic terrorism was the USA PATRIOT Act.[3] Passed overwhelmingly by Congress in October 2001 and renewed or extended several times since then, the act expanded the US government's power to wiretap and conduct surveillance without prior cause, to access private records without oversight, and to detain indefinitely immigrants suspected of supporting terrorism, among other provisions. It accompanied

The USA PATRIOT Act (2001) was enacted by the US Congress soon after 9/11. The act expanded the government's power to conduct surveillance programs and to detain immigrants suspected of supporting terrorism.

additional measures that enabled the government to freeze the financial assets of any individual or organization alleged to have terrorist ties and to restrict nonimmigrant visas for individuals coming from countries believed to sponsor terrorism.

Much of this legislation paved the way for surveillance programs, racial and religious profiling, detentions, deportations, and renditions carried out by agents of the US government and directed

---

3. The title of the USA PATRIOT Act is an acronym. It means Uniting and Strengthening America by Providing Appropriate Tools Required to Intercept and Obstruct Terrorism.

overwhelmingly at Muslims and Arabs. It also reflected the continuation of a historical trend whereby those deemed to be representative of current "foreign enemies" are singled out as threats to national security. During World War II, for example, over one hundred thousand people of Japanese descent in the United States, many of whom were citizens, were placed in internment camps following Japan's bombing of Pearl Harbor. The Japanese at home came to symbolize the Japanese enemy abroad. In much the same way, Muslims residing in the United States after 9/11 came to function as stand-ins for the Muslim enemy in the global War on Terror. Domestic counterterrorism measures targeting Arabs and Muslims thereby became linked with efforts to shore up public support for US military and political intervention in the Muslim world.[4]

One of the most extensive counterterrorism measures after 9/11 was the religious and racial profiling of Arabs and Muslims via the National Security Entry-Exit Registration System (NSEERS). Introduced in 2002, the program required men from twenty-three Muslim-majority countries, as well as from North Korea, to register with the US government. The men were interviewed, fingerprinted, and photographed by federal officials. According to data provided by the Department of Homeland Security (DHS), between September 11, 2002, and June 1, 2003, almost 128,000 Arab and Muslim men were registered at their US port of entry, while approximately 83,000 Arabs and Muslims already residing in the United States were registered.[5] While the DHS initially indicated that targeting men from these nationalities was necessary for national security, in 2011

---

4. Deepa Kumar makes a strong case that counterterrorism measures in the United States after 9/11 serve the larger goals of the War on Terror. See Kumar, *Islamophobia and the Politics or Empire* (Chicago: Haymarket, 2012), 139–58.

5. Louise Cainkar, *Homeland Insecurity: The Arab American and Muslim Experience after 9/11* (New York: Russell Sage Foundation, 2009), 128.

the department reversed course and suspended the program, noting that collecting such data "no longer provides any increase in security."[6] A grand total of zero terrorism convictions resulted from the program.[7]

FBI and NYPD Surveillance and Profiling Programs

Initial profiling measures, such as the registration program, were highly visible. But as the 9/11 dust settled, government and law enforcement agencies turned to profiling methods that were practically invisible to the general public. These included surveillance programs operated by two of the nation's most prestigious law enforcement organizations: the Federal Bureau of Investigation (FBI) and the New York Police Department (NYPD).

After 9/11, the FBI adopted a preemptive strategy in its counterterrorism measures. It relied increasingly on informants and agents provocateurs, individuals tasked with inciting others to engage in terrorism so that they could be identified and arrested. In other words, the FBI secretly infiltrated Muslim communities, targeting individuals who were not engaged in criminal activity in an effort to transform them into terrorism suspects. The idea was to stop terrorism at its roots, before it had a chance to materialize and do damage, but it was based on the assumption that Muslims were already guilty of terrorism. On this model, the job of law enforcement was to induce Muslims to actualize their latent terrorist tendencies.

6. Office of the Secretary, Department of Homeland Security, "Removing Designated Countries from the National Security Entry-Exit Registration System (NSEERS)," Federal Register 76, no. 82 (April 28, 2011): 23830–31, http://www.gpo.gov/fdsys/pkg/FR-2011-04-28/html/2011-10305.htm.

7. Chris Rickerd, "Homeland Security Suspends Ineffective, Discriminatory Immigration Program," American Civil Liberties Union, May 6, 2011, https://www.aclu.org/blog/immigrants-rights-racial-justice/homeland-security-suspends-ineffective-discriminatory.

These tactics were employed in the case of the Newburgh Four.[8] An FBI informant named Shahed Hussain, posing as a wealthy Pakistani businessman, lured four men from Newburgh, New York, into a plot to bomb two synagogues. Hussain was responsible for creating the plot, for overseeing the surveillance of the synagogues, and for providing fake weapons to the men. All four men were African Americans from impoverished backgrounds. One had a mental illness. Another had a brother in desperate need of a liver transplant. Hussain preyed on their vulnerabilities and used financial incentives to convince the four to join his plot.

The case raises many troubling issues concerning the government's surveillance and profiling of Muslims. First, the case, and many others like it, crosses the line into what is legally known as entrapment. Entrapment involves the government inducing individuals to commit a crime they would not otherwise commit. But entrapment defenses are difficult to pull off in court. The government only has to prove that the accused were predisposed to carry out the acts, even if the defendants demonstrate that the government induced them to do so.[9] Predisposition operates on the assumption that Muslims are prone to terrorism. Juries readily embrace the notion of predisposition, and, as a result, the entrapment defense usually does not work. It did not work in the trial of the Newburgh Four. All four were found guilty, and each was sentenced to twenty-five years in prison.

Second, many FBI informants are not trained as law enforcement officers and have ulterior motives for the assistance they provide. They often receive enticements, such as money or a reduction in a pending criminal sentence, in exchange for collaborating with the FBI. Hussain received $100,000, among other perks, for his work as

8. A summary of this case can be found in Center for Human Rights and Global Justice, *Targeted and Entrapped: Manufacturing the "Homegrown Threat" in the United States* (New York: NYU School of Law, 2011), 21–24.
9. Ibid., 15.

an FBI informant in the Newburgh case.[10] And Hussain is not alone. The FBI maintains some fifteen thousand informants, in addition to tens of thousands of unofficial informants.[11]

Finally, the FBI's use of informants to generate terrorism arrests and convictions gives the impression that the government is succeeding in its battle against domestic terrorism. In fact, cases such as the Newburgh Four involve concocted terrorist plots that would not exist if the FBI did not work so hard to create them. The US district judge in the Newburgh trial, Colleen McMahon, indicated as much during the sentencing as she rebuked the government: "The government did not act to infiltrate and foil some nefarious plot; there was no plot to foil."[12] These are instances in which the FBI creates a disease—a terrorist plot—only to turn around and offer the cure—arresting and convicting individuals lured into the plot by informants. The FBI is manufacturing the very threat that it is fighting.

The FBI is not alone in implementing clandestine surveillance and profiling programs targeting Muslims. After 9/11, the NYPD, with some assistance from the CIA, began extensive surveillance of Muslim communities in the New York City metropolitan area as well as the surrounding states of New Jersey, Connecticut, and Pennsylvania. A secret unit within the NYPD, the Demographics Unit, mapped, monitored, and spied on Muslims with ancestry from every conceivable Muslim-majority country in addition to African American Muslims.[13]

10. Phil Hirschkorn, "The Newburgh Sting," *Huffington Post*, April 29, 2014, http://www.huffingtonpost.com/phil-hirschkorn/the-newburgh-sting_b_5234822.html.
11. Diala Shamas, "Where's the Outrage When the FBI Targets Muslims?," *Nation*, October 31, 2013, http://www.thenation.com/article/176911/wheres-outrage-when-fbi-targets-muslims#.
12. Quoted in Hirschkorn, "Newburgh Sting."
13. Muslim American Civil Liberties Coalition (MACLC), Creating Law Enforcement Accountability and Responsibility (CLEAR), and the Asian American Legal Defense and

The NYPD's program depended on a theory of radicalization elaborated in its 2007 report, *Radicalization in the West: The Homegrown Threat*. The report spells out four stages of radicalization: preradicalization, self-identification, indoctrination, and jihadization. Descriptions of these stages are telling. For example, Muslims in the preradicalization stage are young (under the age of thirty-five), middle-class men. They are recent converts with little or no criminal history. Oftentimes, they are not particularly devout, at least at this stage.[14] As these men move through the other stages, they become more devout and politically active. They may stop smoking or drinking and grow a beard.[15] At this point, the document assumes, Muslims are clearly on the path toward radicalization. If they continue on this path, they start to withdraw from their mosques and adopt jihadist ideologies bent on killing innocent people.

The report also points to "Radicalization Incubators" that set Muslim men on a path to radicalization. These are places such as mosques, cafés, student associations, nongovernmental organizations, and bookstores.[16] We now know that these are exactly the places that the NYPD sent spies and "mosque-crawlers" to monitor Muslims.

The NYPD is not the only law enforcement agency to rely on so-called radicalization theories; the FBI has its own version, as do some intelligence services in Europe. Such theories automatically suspect practicing Muslim men of harboring terrorist tendencies. The more Muslim they become (becoming politically active, growing facial hair), the more likely they will turn into radical jihadists.

Education Fund (AALDEF), *Mapping Muslims: NYPD Spying and Its Impact on American Muslims* (Long Island, NY: MACLC, CLEAR, and AALDEF, 2013), 7.

14. Mitchell D. Silber and Arvin Bhatt, *Radicalization in the West: The Homegrown Threat* (New York: New York City Police Department, 2007), 24–25.

15. Ibid., 33.

16. Ibid., 22.

Driven by its radicalization theory, the NYPD engaged in scrupulous monitoring of the activities and habits of Muslim men. For example, undercover agents documented how many times Muslim students prayed during a rafting excursion, which Egyptian businesses closed during daily prayers, and which restaurants played the Middle East–based news network Al-Jazeera.[17] They infiltrated mosques and recorded what attendees and imams said. And they participated in "create and capture" schemes in which an agent or informant initiated conversations with Muslims about terrorism and recorded the responses.[18]

Journalists brought details of the NYPD's secret surveillance program to light in 2011. The news generated considerable criticism from Muslims and civil rights organizations, particularly regarding the program's overt reliance on racial and religious profiling. In the midst of the controversy, the chief of the NYPD intelligence division admitted that the program had not produced one criminal lead since its inception.[19] Although the NYPD disbanded the program in 2014, it has not yet disavowed some of its questionable surveillance tactics, including the use of informants, the designation of some mosques as "terrorism enterprises," and the theory of Islamic radicalization.[20]

In recent years, details of surveillance programs conducted by other law enforcement and intelligence agencies have also surfaced. To take just one example, in July 2014, an investigation by one news publication revealed that between 2002 and 2008 the National Security Agency (NSA), in collaboration with the FBI, monitored the e-mail communications of five prominent Muslim Americans,

---

17. MACLC, CLEAR, and AALDEF, *Mapping Muslims*, 8.
18. Ibid., 10–11.
19. Ibid., 4.
20. Noa Yachot, "NYPD Shutters Muslim Mapping Unit—But What About Other Tactics?," *American Civil Liberties Union*, April 15, 2014, https://www.aclu.org/blog/national-security-religion-belief/nypd-shutters-muslim-spying-unit-what-about-its-tactics.

including Nihad Awad, the executive director of the Council on American-Islamic Relations (CAIR), and Hooshang Amirahmadi, a professor at Rutgers University and president of the American Iranian Council. The NSA and FBI found nothing incriminating in the communications and did not offer any explanation for their surveillance of these individuals.[21]

European Surveillance and Profiling Programs

In Europe, the 9/11 attacks, and later the Madrid and London bombings of 2004 and 2005, resulted in a wave of counterterrorism measures rivaling those in the United States. Britain, France, Germany, and other nations passed laws that expanded government and law enforcement powers to investigate suspected terrorist activity. Though the powers varied from country to country, they included the authority to detain foreign nationals indefinitely, to search vehicles and unoccupied premises for evidence of terrorism, and to freeze and confiscate funds of individuals or organizations suspected of being tied to terrorism. In Europe, as in the United States, these powers enabled government and law enforcement officials to operate extensive profiling and surveillance programs focused on Muslims.

Stop-and-search practices by police departments became increasingly common in countries such as Britain, Denmark, France, Greece, Italy, and Sweden. The purpose of such programs included preventing crime, deporting "illegal immigrants," and fighting domestic terrorism. These practices targeted certain racial or ethnic groups containing high percentages of Muslims. In Britain, for

21. Glenn Greenwald and Murtaza Hussain, "Meet the Muslim-American Leaders the FBI and NSA Have Been Spying On," *Intercept*, July 9, 2014, https://firstlook.org/theintercept/article/2014/07/09/under-surveillance/.

example, according to data from 2008, blacks were 7.4 times more likely to be stopped and searched by police than whites, while Asians were 2.3 times more likely than whites to undergo these procedures.[22] Both Asian and black Muslims have complained that the practice is discriminatory and symptomatic of legalized Islamophobia.

Greece inaugurated a massive ethnic profiling program in 2012 called Operation Xenios Zeus, which used nationwide stop-and-search operations in an effort to detain and deport asylum seekers and undocumented immigrants. Reports surfaced of police targeting people who "looked" Muslim, leading organizations such as Human Rights Watch (HRW) to challenge the program as illegal and unethical because it relied on religious and racial profiling.[23]

Some profiling programs targeted Muslims who engaged in political activity, particularly public demonstrations. After Israel's invasion of Gaza late in 2008, Muslims participated in demonstrations across Britain. A large protest was held in London in January 2009, with hundreds of thousands of participants. As a result of some scuffles and property damage at the demonstration, the Metropolitan Police of London initiated Operation Ute, designed to identify and arrest Muslim protestors, mostly young men, in some cases months after the demonstration. Almost 120 people were arrested. Many were served with immigration notices threatening deportation and were asked to surrender their passports, despite the fact that most were British citizens.[24] In July 2014, after Israel launched another invasion of Gaza, French authorities in some cities, including Paris, banned pro-Palestinian protests after a few small groups participated

---

22. European Network Against Racism (ENAR), *Ethnic Profiling*, ENAR Fact Sheet 40 (Brussels: ENAR, 2009), 8–9.
23. Human Rights Watch, *Unwelcome Guests: Greek Police Abuses of Migrants in Athens* (New York: Human Rights Watch, 2013).
24. Harmit Athwal, "Gaza Protestors Defence Campaign Launched," Institute of Race Relations, March 12, 2010, http://www.irr.org.uk/news/gaza-protesters-defence-campaign-launched/.

in vandalism and violence against synagogues. The ban did not apply to pro-Israel protests, even though it was clear that militants from the Jewish Defense League engaged in violence against pro-Palestinian demonstrators.[25] These restrictions raise an important question, one articulated by scholar Liz Fekete: "Are we seeing a new form of religious profiling? A new offence: 'Demonstrating for Palestine while Muslim'?"[26]

Muslims in Europe have also endured other forms of intrusive surveillance and profiling. After the 2005 London bombings, the leader of Germany's Christian Democratic Union Party called for the video surveillance of mosques and for more intense monitoring of Muslims. Some communities implemented such schemes. In the cities of Osnabrück and Braunschweig, neighborhoods were locked down, mosques were searched, and the identities of those attending Friday prayers were checked.[27] In Birmingham, England, a secret police operation known as Project Champion led to the installation of cameras in neighborhoods to monitor thousands of Muslims.[28]

All of these surveillance and profiling programs in Europe and the United States thrive on assumptions about Islam and Muslims that reflect some of the "closed views" of Islamophobia as identified by the Runnymede Report: Islam as monolithic and unvarying, Islam as the enemy, and racial discrimination against Muslims as justified, among others. As we will see, such assumptions extend beyond these

25. Angela Charlton, "Paris Bans Pro-Palestinian Protest as Gaza Conflict Escalates," *The Huffington Post*, July 18, 2014, http://www.huffingtonpost.com/2014/07/18/paris-ban-palestine-protest-gaza_n_5599351.html.

26. Liz Fekete, "Which Way Forward on Racial Profiling?," Institute of Race Relations, December 6, 2012, http://www.irr.org.uk/news/which-way-forward-on-racial-profiling/.

27. Sam Cherribi, "An Obsession Renewed: Islamophobia in the Netherlands, Austria, and Germany," in *Islmaophobia: The Challenge of Pluralism in the 21st Century*, ed. John L. Esposito and Ibrahim Kalin (New York: Oxford University Press, 2011), 56.

28. Paul Lewis, "Police Surveillance of Muslims Set Up with 'No Regard for Law,'" *Guardian* (UK), September 30, 2010, http://www.theguardian.com/uk/2010/sep/30/police-surveillance-muslims-no-regard-law.

programs and factor into more troubling treatment of Muslims: detentions, deportations, and hate crimes.

Detentions and Deportations

The heightened fear and anxiety after 9/11 over the internal Muslim threat in the United States resulted in the arrest and detention of scores of Arabs and Muslims. Shortly after the attacks, the Department of Justice (DOJ) oversaw the arrest of some twelve hundred Arab and Muslim men. Citing national security concerns, the government refused to release the names of those arrested and in many cases searched for violations with which to charge the men *after* they were arrested. The government also refused to give many detainees access to a lawyer or to allow them to speak with their families. All of this was done while government officials investigated whether or not the detainees had ties to terrorism. Such actions were illegal. While it is permissible to arrest individuals who have violated US immigration laws, it is clear that the DOJ targeted Muslim and Arab men in a discriminatory manner. US criminal law also demands probable cause for arrest, the right of court-appointed counsel, and the right to be brought before a judge within forty-eight hours after arrest. Under the cover of immigration law, the DOJ bypassed the criminal justice system in many of these arrests.[29]

The secretive and illegal nature of the arrests, combined with overt racial and religious profiling, led HRW, the American Civil Liberties Union (ACLU), the DOJ inspector general, and even members of Congress to denounce the arrests and to call for government accountability. According to an HRW report, the real "crime" committed by those arrested was their connection to Islam: "Being a

---

29. Human Rights Watch, "Presumption of Guilt: Human Rights Abuses of Post–September 11 Detainees," *Human Rights Watch* 14 (2002): 4.

male Muslim non-citizen from certain countries became a proxy for suspicious behavior."[30]

A later HRW report, coauthored with the ACLU and relying on interviews with some of the detainees, revealed other constitutional and human rights violations. Those arrested were subjected to verbal and physical abuse, solitary confinement, the use of leg chains, and repeated strip searches.[31] All of this happened in US custody and without any of the detainees being charged with terrorism. In fact, none of the detainees were ever charged with supporting or engaging in terrorism. The gravest crime in many instances was a visa violation. Many of those charged with such a violation were deported after months and in some cases years of detention.[32]

The hundreds of Muslim and Arab men deported from this initial round of arrests represent a fraction of the deportations and deportation attempts that took place after 9/11. Of the nearly 83,000 Muslim and Arab men who registered under the NSEERS program in 2003, deportation orders were issued for over 13,000 of them.[33] Another deportation program, launched by the DOJ in 2002 and called Operation Absconder, sought to deport 6,000 young men, mostly from Middle Eastern countries, out of a list of about 314,000 individuals still present in the country despite receiving deportation orders. The focus on Middle Eastern immigrants is all the more telling given the fact that the majority of the 314,000 came from Latin America and not the Middle East.[34] The deportation of

---

30. Ibid., 12.

31. Human Rights Watch, "Witness to Abuse: Human Rights Abuses under the Material Witness Law since September 11," *Human Rights Watch* 17 (2005): 1–101.

32. Elaine Cassel, *The War on Civil Liberties: How Bush and Ashcroft Have Dismantled the Bill of Rights* (Chicago: Lawrence Hill Books, 2004), 108; Lori A. Peek, *Behind the Backlash: Muslim Americans after 9/11* (Philadelphia: Temple University Press, 2010), 33.

33. Cainkar, *Homeland Insecurity*, 128.

34. John Tehranian, *Whitewashed: America's Invisible Middle Eastern Minority* (New York: New York University Press, 2009), 125.

thousands of Muslim and Arab men constituted an integral part of the government's counterterrorism strategies in the months and years following 9/11.

European security and police forces often aided and abetted the United States in using secret and indefinite detentions to battle terrorism. We have evidence of law enforcement agents throughout Europe arresting and detaining suspects, often Muslim men, and then turning them over to US custody without judicial process. Some suspects became victims of extraordinary rendition, the process by which they were transferred from US custody to countries or locations where they encountered the possibility of torture.[35] In fact, the CIA sustained its rendition program in part by making use of Europe's airports to transport suspects to secret interrogation and detention centers around the world. Some of these CIA detention centers, referred to by the US government as "black sites," were located in European countries such as Poland and Romania.

This type of rendition can be seen in Sweden in the case of two Egyptian asylum seekers, Ahmed Agiza and Mohammed al-Zery. The Swedish Security Police suspected the men of participating in terrorism and, with permission from the Swedish government, secretly apprehended the two men in December 2001. The police drove them to an airport outside Stockholm and handed them over to masked CIA agents. The agents stripped the men of their clothing, inserted suppositories into their anuses, dressed them in disposable underpants and overalls, chained their hands and feet, and put hoods over their heads. The two men were then put on a plane for Cairo, Egypt, where they were imprisoned, interrogated, and tortured.[36] Al-Zery was released in 2003 and Agiza in 2011. This rendition,

35. Amnesty International, *State of Denial: Europe's Role in Rendition and Secret Detention* (London: Amnesty International, 2008), 1.
36. Ibid., 10.

like many others, constituted a violation of international law and the United Nations Convention against Torture.[37] It also reflected the experiences awaiting a number of other Muslims in the West suspected of having terrorist ties.

Hate Crimes

The cruel and repressive treatment of Muslims after 9/11 did not come only from Western governments and their agencies. Ordinary non-Muslim citizens also exhibited hostile behavior toward Muslims that at times reached the level of hate crimes. Hate crimes involve violence or other criminal behavior motivated by bias against gender, race, ethnicity, sexual orientation, or religion. These crimes include actions against one's property (theft, vandalism, arson) and actions against persons (intimidation, aggravated assault, sexual assault, murder).

Anti-Muslim Hate Crimes in the United States

Anti-Muslim hate crimes in the United States rose dramatically in the immediate aftermath of 9/11. The FBI recorded 481 incidents of hate crimes against Muslims and Muslim "look-alikes" (that is, non-Muslim Arabs, Sikhs, and others mistaken as Muslims by the perpetrator) in 2001 (Figure 8.1). This number reflected a 1,600 percent increase from 2000. More than half of the incidents in 2001 took place in the three-and-a-half months after the attacks.[38] The trend decreased in the course of the decade, though it never returned to pre-9/11 levels. Moreover, by 2010 and 2011, anti-Muslim hate crimes were on the rise again, probably as a result of the growing

37. Ibid., 13–15.
38. Peek, *Behind the Backlash*, 28.

power of the professional Islamophobia industry and the media attention given to its campaigns in 2010 to prevent the construction of an Islamic center in New York City and to ban Sharia law in various states.

Figure 8.1. Anti-Muslim Hate Crimes in the US, 2000–2012

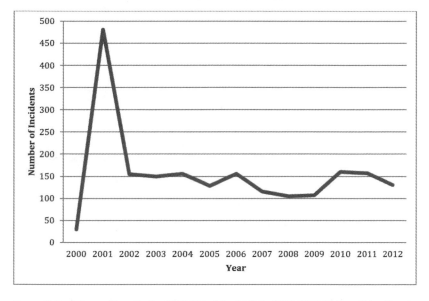

Source: Federal Bureau of Investigation (FBI), Hate Crime Statistics (2000–2012), Uniform Crime Reports, http://www.fbi.gov/about-us/cjis/ucr/ucr-publications#Hate.

The numbers provided by the FBI do not tell the whole story about anti-Muslim hate crimes. Among other problems, the FBI statistics only include incidents reported to the authorities by victims or incidents reported to the FBI by local law enforcement agencies, so underreporting and misreporting are significant issues. This is true of all hate crimes. One report by the Bureau of Justice Statistics indicates that the actual number of hate crimes in the United States is anywhere from nineteen to thirty-one times higher than the FBI's numbers. Approximately 56 percent of hate crimes are not reported to the police, and more than half that are reported are mislabeled as other types of crimes.[39] This means that the FBI statistics represent the most conservative estimate of anti-Muslim hate crimes. The importance of the statistics lies not in their accuracy but in the larger trends toward which they point.

Anti-Muslim Hate Crimes in Europe

Hate crimes against Muslims in Europe also became a significant problem after 9/11. While many European countries do not collect data on such crimes, some studies offer at least a glimpse of what Muslims experience.[40] The European Union Minorities and Discrimination Survey reported that one in ten Muslims in EU states was a victim of an "in-person" hate crime (physical assault, verbal intimidation, and so forth) in the previous year. The survey, however, stressed that anti-Muslim hate crimes throughout Europe were undercounted, estimating that anywhere from 53 percent to 98 percent of victims do not report the crimes to the police.[41]

We also have data from individual European countries and cities that points to periodic upswings in anti-Muslim hate crimes in response to particular controversies, similar to what is found in the United States. The Collective against Islamophobia in France recorded a significant increase in anti-Muslim incidents from 2010 to 2013. In 2010, there were 188 incidents. This number rose to 298

---

39. "Report: FBI Hate Crime Statistics Vastly Understate Problem," *Southern Poverty Law Center: Intelligence Report*, no. 120 (Winter 2005), http://www.splcenter.org/get-informed/intelligence-report/browse-all-issues/2005/winter/hate-crime.

40. Katya Andrusz from the European Union Agency for Fundamental Rights (FRA) observes that most EU states do not collect data about anti-Muslim hate crimes. Only six of the twenty-eight EU member states keep records on such crimes, and not all of the six separate anti-Muslim incidents from hate crimes against other minority groups. See Bernd Riegert, "EU Collects 'Too Little' Data on Anti-Muslim Attacks," *Deutsche Welle*, August 17, 2013, http://www.dw.de/eu-collects-too-little-data-on-anti-muslim-attacks/a-17026919.

41. European Union Agency for Fundamental Rights (FRA), *European Union Minorities and Discrimination Survey (EU-MIDIS), Data in Focus Report 2: Muslims* (FRA, 2009), 12, http://fra.europa.eu/en/publication/2010/eu-midis-data-focus-report-2-muslims.

in 2011, 469 in 2012, and 691 in 2013.[42] What explains the upsurge? The increase was likely due to the intense political campaign against face veils that led the French Parliament to approve a ban on them in 2010. The campaign, which will be discussed in more detail later in the chapter, exacerbated perceptions of Islam as foreign and misogynist. It also painted some Muslim women as defying French standards of femininity. Given that women constituted the majority of victims of anti-Muslim aggression and discrimination (78 percent in 2013) and that many of these women wore headscarves, it is reasonable to conclude that the campaign for the ban, and its subsequent implementation, drove much of the increase.

In chapter 5, we discussed the upsurge of anti-Muslim hate crimes immediately after the bombings of July 7, 2005. The London Metropolitan Police Service reported massive increases in "faith-hate" incidents, many involving Muslims, in the weeks following the attacks. The number of anti-Muslim incidents also soared in 2013. Tell MAMA, a project tracking anti-Muslim attacks in the UK, recorded 840 cases between April 2013 and December 2013. By contrast, the project documented 582 cases from March 2012 to March 2013. The incident triggering this increase was the murder of Lee Rigby in May 2013.[43] Rigby was a British soldier killed in broad daylight by two Muslim extremists in southeast London. The intense media coverage of the murder, including video footage of the perpetrators with blood-soaked hands defending their actions to shocked onlookers, led to the proliferation of anti-Muslim attacks, particularly in the week following the event. Tell MAMA recorded

---

42. Collectif Contre l'Islamophobie en France, *Rapport Annuel 2013*, http://www.islamophobie.net/sites/default/files/file_attach/RAPPORT-ANNUEL-CCIF-2013.pdf; Collectif Contre l'Islamophobie en France, *Rapport Annuel 2014*, http://www.islamophobie.net/sites/default/files/CCIF-RAPPORT-2014.pdf.

43. "UK Anti-Muslim Hate Crime Soars, Police Figures Show," *Guardian* (UK), December 26, 2013, http://www.theguardian.com/society/2013/dec/27/uk-anti-muslim-hate-crime-soars.

a 400 percent increase in anti-Muslim attacks from the week prior to the week following the Rigby murder.[44] These instances from Britain and France reinforce the view that anti-Muslim hate crimes spike whenever there are highly publicized episodes casting Muslims in a negative light.

Hate Crimes against Sikhs and Muslim "Look-Alikes"

What is not always clear in the data on anti-Muslim hate crimes is the extent to which non-Muslims become victims of such crimes. Organizations that keep track of this data often put Muslim "look-alikes," or those the perpetrator mistakes as Muslim, into the same category as Muslims. As a result, it is easy to overlook the other victims of Islamophobic hate and violence.

Sikhs, practitioners of a religion with roots in the Punjab region of India, are an obvious example. Sikh men in particular are sometimes victims of crimes motivated by anti-Muslim bias, largely due to race and to the turbans they wear that perpetrators mistake for Islamic dress. In fact, the first victim of a retaliatory murder in the United States after 9/11 was not a Muslim but a Sikh. Balbir Singh Sodhi was shot five times just days after the 9/11 attacks while planting flowers outside of his gas station in Mesa, Arizona. His killer, Frank Roque, boasted to patrons at a bar just prior to the murder that he was going to "kill the ragheads" responsible for the attacks.[45] Sikhs and Muslims were one and the same in Roque's mind. This same observation may hold true for Wade Michael Page, a US Army veteran and white

44. Matthew Feldman and Mark Littler, *Tell MAMA Reporting 2013/14: Anti-Muslim Overview, Analysis and 'Cumulative Extremism'* (Middlesbrough, UK: Teesside University, Center for Fascist, Anti-Fascist and Post-Fascist Studies, 2014), http://tellmamauk.org/wp-content/uploads/2014/07/finalreport.pdf.
45. Stephan Salisbury, *Mohamed's Ghosts: An American Love Story and Fear in the Homeland* (New York: Perseus Books, 2010), 73.

supremacist who opened fire at a Sikh temple near Milwaukee in August 2012. Page killed six Sikhs before turning the gun on himself, possibly because he mistook Sikhs for Muslims.[46]

The European Union Monitoring Centre on Racism and Xenophobia reported that hate crimes against Sikhs increased after 9/11 in countries such as Austria, Britain, Germany, Portugal, and Spain. In most cases, crimes against Sikhs in Europe were prompted by mistaken identity, as in the United States.[47] The fact that ignorance was a major factor in these incidents should not belittle the hostility that Sikhs experience. Hate crimes against Sikhs, as against Muslims, reflect a larger pattern in the West, dating back centuries, of constructing and responding to racial and religious minorities as the foreign, threatening "Other." Nevertheless, hostility toward Sikhs, not to mention other groups such as non-Muslim Arabs, reminds us that victims of Islamophobic hate crimes can be found outside the Muslim community.

The Norway Attacks

At first glance, it may be tempting to conclude that deliberate attacks on non-Muslims—that is, attacks in which the perpetrator knows that his or her targets are not Muslim—have no place in the current discussion. Yet there are instances of hate crimes motivated by anti-Muslim bias that intentionally target people who are not Muslim. The most prominent example involves Anders Behring Breivik, a far

---

46. Moustafa Bayoumi, "Did Islamophobia Fuel the Oak Creek Massacre?," *Nation*, August 10, 2012, http://www.thenation.com/article/169322/did-islamophobia-fuel-oak-creek-massacre#.

47. Christopher Allen and Jørgen S. Nielsen, *Summary Report on Islamophobia in the EU after 11 September 2001* (Vienna: European Monitoring Centre on Racism and Xenophobia, 2002), 36–37, http://fra.europa.eu/sites/default/files/fra_uploads/199-Synthesis-report_en.pdf

right extremist who killed seventy-seven people in Norway on a Friday afternoon in July 2011.[48]

Anders Behring Breivik (1979–) was the perpetrator of the deadliest mass murder in Norway's history. On July 22, 2011, Breivik detonated a bomb in the government quarter of Oslo before traveling to the island of Utøya and opening fire on unsuspecting participants at a youth summer camp affiliated with Norway's Labor Party. Breivik, who killed seventy-seven people that day, was motivated in part by a fear that Muslims were taking over Europe and that European governments, including the Norwegian government, were complicit in this takeover.

Breivik unleashed a two-pronged attack. The first involved a car bomb that was detonated in Oslo's government quarter, a section containing various ministry offices, including the Office of the Prime Minister (see image 8). The bomb killed eight people. The second involved a shooting spree on the island of Utøya outside of Oslo. The island was hosting a summer camp for the Worker's Youth League, a youth organization affiliated with Norway's Labor Party. Breivik took a boat to the island after the first bomb detonated. Outfitted in full police regalia, Breivik gathered unsuspecting campers and counselors around him, under the pretense of securing their safety, and then opened fire. Sixty-nine people died in the Utøya attacks before Breivik surrendered to police.

Bad media habits in reporting on terrorist attacks die hard, if at all. The Norway murders were no exception. In the absence of a positive identification of the suspect the morning after the attacks, major newspapers, including the *New York Times,* the *Washington Post*, and the *Wall Street Journal*, ran stories and columns pointing the finger at Muslims.[49] As it turned out, the perpetrator was a thirty-two-year-old native Norwegian with Viking heritage who claimed a Christian identity. Media analysis of what was initially labeled a "terrorist attack" quickly morphed into debates over right-wing "extremism." The word *terrorism* no longer seemed applicable when the culprit self-identified as Christian.[50]

In the aftermath of the attacks, it surfaced that Breivik was the author of a fifteen-hundred-page online manifesto that revealed his hatred of Marxism, multiculturalism, and Muslims.[51] The title of the manifesto, "2083—A European Declaration of Independence," reflects Breivik's convictions that Europe is at war with Muslims. The year 2083 refers to the forthcoming four-hundredth anniversary of the Battle of Vienna. This battle witnessed the defeat of the Ottoman Turks at the hands of European Christians. For Breivik, the battle is significant because it marked the end of the Muslim empire's attempt to take over the lands of Christendom. Unfortunately, argues Breivik, Muslims are once again on the march, attempting to colonize Europe as part of a "demographic jihad." Through immigration and breeding, Muslims are determined to create a "Eurabia." Breivik sees himself as a participant in a crusade to seize military and political

---

48. For an overview of how the Anders Breivik attacks unfolded, see Nathan Lean, *The Islamophobia Industry: How the Right Manufactures Fear of Muslims* (London: Pluto, 2012), 156–61.

49. Glenn Greenwald, "The Omnipotence of Al Qaeda and Meaninglessness of 'Terrorism,'" *Salon,* July 23, 2011, http://www.salon.com/2011/07/23/nyt_17/.

50. Todd Green, "The Face of Christian Terrorism?," *Huffington Post,* July 25, 2011, http://www.huffingtonpost.com/todd-green-phd/anders-behring-breivik-christian-terrorism_b_908163.html.

51. A link to the full text of Anders Breivik's "2083—A European Declaration of Independence" (2011) can be found at http://unitednations.ispnw.org/archives/breivik-manifesto-2011.pdf. The quotations in this discussion of Breivik come from this document.

control of Western Europe in order to "save millions of European lives from the war that most certainly awaits us when the Muslims in any given country become the dominating force." Islam, after all, is not really a religion but "a political ideology that exists in a fundamental and permanent state of war with non-Islamic civilizations, cultures, and individuals."

Breivik blames European governments for the dire predicament the continent faces in light of growing Muslim populations. He takes particular aim at policies of multiculturalism, insisting that political correctness and ignorance of Islam's true nature lead governments to encourage Muslim immigration in the name of tolerance and diversity. His arguments reflect the positions articulated by the US professional Islamophobia industry. In fact, many of the key figures discussed in chapter 6, including Daniel Pipes, Pamela Geller, and Robert Spencer, feature prominently in Breivik's manifesto.[52] Spencer is a particular favorite—Breivik cites him 162 times.[53] But Breivik also finds inspiration in Europe's far right, from the English Defence League to the Dutch populist Geert Wilders. Breivik's estimation of these figures is so high that he deems Wilders, Spencer, and a few other anti-Muslim activists, including Ayaan Hirsi Ali, as worthy of the Nobel Peace Prize.

Despite Breivik's fear of a Muslim takeover of Europe, he targeted non-Muslims, particularly people he identified as symbols of the political establishment. Since the government was to blame for the Muslim threat, an assault on the government was necessary to save European civilization. But without a doubt, Islamophobia fueled Breivik's killing rampage. Bias against Muslims was translated into a hate crime deliberately carried out against non-Muslims. After the

52. For a discussion of the influence of the US Islamophobia industry on Breivik, see Arun Kundnani, *The Muslims Are Coming! Islamophobia, Extremism, and the Domestic War on Terror* (London: Verso, 2014), 261–62; and Lean, *Islamophphobia Industry*, 163–71.
53. Lean, *The Islamophobia Industry*, 167.

Norway shootings, no one seemed safe from the threat of anti-Muslim hate crimes.

Hijabs and Burqas

Breivik may represent the extreme fringe of Europe's far right, but his manifesto's themes resonate with larger political debates taking place across the continent. It is not difficult to find examples of politicians questioning multiculturalism or expressing doubts about whether Muslims can successfully integrate into Western societies. These misgivings have arisen against the backdrop of a growing Muslim population and the perception that Islam's increasing presence and visibility in public space represents a threat to what it means to be European, not to mention Belgian, British, Danish, French, or German.

In the past two decades, laws have been proposed throughout Europe to reduce the public presence of what is deemed a foreign and even threatening religion at odds with Western values. In some countries, considerable restrictions on the free exercise of religion have been imposed on Muslim minority communities. The restrictions primarily target Muslim clothing and worship structures, the two most visible symbols of Islamic identity in public space. But even in countries that have not enacted restrictive laws, controversies over what Muslims can wear and build are not difficult to find.

In no other country is the debate over what Muslim women can and cannot wear more intense than France. The initial controversy dates back to the late 1980s, when a debate erupted over whether Muslim girls in public schools should be allowed to wear the *hijab*—what the French often refer to as "the veil" (*le voile*) and what more broadly in Europe is translated as "headscarf." The hijab is a garment that covers the hair but leaves the face exposed. It symbolizes modesty for many Muslim girls and women who choose to wear it. In the original controversy, a middle school expelled three Muslim girls after they refused to remove their headscarves. The principal insisted that wearing the headscarf violated *laïcité*, a word that loosely translates as "secularism" and that reflects a firm French commitment to keep religion out of public, secular space. This conflict was resolved in part because of the intervention of the king of Morocco, who publicly requested that two of the three girls, both of whom were sisters with Moroccan heritage, remove their headscarves when entering the classroom. The girls complied, and the issue faded for a time.

Significant conflict over the hijab surfaced two more times: in 1994 and 2003. In 1994, teachers went on strike at one school after several girls refused to remove their headscarves during gym class. In 2003, two sisters were removed from gym class for refusing to remove their headscarves. Their case was notable in part because they wore the headscarves against their family's wishes. Their father, in fact, described himself as a Jewish atheist who personally did not agree with his daughters' choice to wear headscarves but supported their right to choose. During this same year, France's minister of the interior, Nicolas Sarkozy, generated debate when he insisted that Muslim women remove their headscarves when taking pictures for official identification. He argued that such action was needed to maintain national security in light of the dangers of terrorism after 9/11.

In many ways, 9/11 exacerbated anxieties over the threat of Muslim terrorism within the West and concerns that Muslim minorities were not integrated enough into Western societies. The headscarf controversies of 2003 contributed to these anxieties, leading to a political environment ripe for creating legislation against headscarves. In July 2003, President Jacques Chirac established a commission to explore the possibility of a law to deal with the hijab "problem" in public schools. The commission issued its report in December, recommending a prohibition on prominent religious symbols. The commission's report coincided with a sharp rise in public opinion that favored a new law. A poll conducted in early December revealed that 72 percent of those surveyed supported a ban on visible symbols of religious affiliation in public schools.[54]

The French Parliament passed a law in March 2004 that banned "the wearing of signs or clothing [in public schools] which conspicuously manifest students' religious affiliation." The law explicitly banned "conspicuous signs such as a large cross, a veil, or a skullcap."[55] The inclusion of clothing or symbols from other religions was an effort to circumvent charges that the law was discriminatory by singling out Muslims alone. However, the public controversies

The French hijab ban (2004) refers to a law passed by the French Parliament in 2004 that banned "conspicuous signs" of religious affiliation in public schools. The ban included not only Muslim hijabs and headscarves but also large crosses, skullcaps, and symbols from other religious traditions and communities. Nevertheless, the context of the ban was an ongoing debate over clothing worn by Muslim schoolgirls dating to the late 1980s.

54. John Bowen, *Why the French Don't Like Headscarves* (Princeton: Princeton University Press, 2007), 124.
55. Quoted in Joan Wallach Scott, *The Politics of the Veil* (Princeton: Princeton University Press, 2007), 1.

preceding the law and the government commission's deliberations make clear that headscarves worn by some Muslim girls were the concern that led to the law. The law was commonly justified by arguing that such religious clothing symbolized oppression and submission, in contrast to the French commitment to equality of the sexes and presumed openness toward expressions of sexuality. Politicians across the spectrum assumed that Muslim girls would never freely choose to wear headscarves. The law would protect them from having this clothing imposed on them by male family members.

The factors that led to the law are more complex and cannot be reduced only to prejudice against Muslims. The French principle of *laïcité* is deeply embedded in modern French identity and reflects an overall tendency to privatize all forms of religious expression. Moreover, there is a longer history of the government fighting to exclude religious expression and symbols from public schools, dating back to the late nineteenth century and the Third Republic's campaign to rid schools of significant Roman Catholic influence.

But, without a doubt, anxiety over Muslims and their ability to embrace a French identity and French values drove much of the support for the law. The fact that neither the government commission nor members of the French Parliament paid much attention to arguments made by Muslim girls and women about why they wore headscarves was indicative of the hostile political climate for French Muslims. The prevailing assumption was that Muslim girls were coerced into wearing a garment that symbolized women's inferiority. Evidence that complicated this picture made little difference. Remember that the two sisters in 2003 removed from gym class came from a family that discouraged them from wearing headscarves. Moreover, some girls wore the hijab because they did not want to be treated as sex objects. They saw tight clothing, short skirts, and exposed skin as evidence of sexual exploitation, not liberation. But the idea that a law was needed to liberate oppressed Muslim girls, irrespective of their own views, was persuasive, and it received broad support across the political spectrum.

France is not the only country with restrictions on headscarves, though it is the only one with a national law. In Belgium, each school and municipality determines whether or not headscarves are allowed in public schools. Many schools prohibit students and teachers from wearing headscarves.[56] The city of Ghent imposed a ban on civil servants wearing headscarves or other religious symbols in 2007, though the ban was removed in 2013.[57] In Germany, teachers, not students, are the ones prohibited from wearing headscarves in some regions. Eight German states currently have regulations that prevent teachers from wearing headscarves. In one state, Hesse, the ban extends to all women who work as public officers.[58] Most other European countries, along with the United States, have witnessed less conflict over headscarves, largely because public expressions of religiosity are less regulated and, particularly in the United States, considered more acceptable. Indeed, few Western countries rival France in its discomfort over religious expression in the public sphere.

In more recent years, attention has shifted to the *burqa*. The term is often used to refer to clothing that covers the entire body, including the face.[59] For this reason, a common English translation is "face

56. Ismail Guven, "Globalisation, Political Islam and the Headscarf in Education, with Special Reference to the Turkish Educational System," in *Education and Religion: Global Pressures, Local Responses*, ed. Keith Watson and William I. Ozanne (New York: Routledge, 2012), 116.

57. Philip Blenkinsop, "Belgian City Scraps Headscarf Ban Imposed by Center-Right in 2007," *Reuters*, May 28, 2013, http://www.reuters.com/article/2013/05/28/us-belgium-headscarf-idUSBRE94R06L20130528.

58. Jörn Thielmann and Kathrin Vorholzer, "Burqa in Germany—Not Really an Issue: A Short Note," in *The Burqa Affair across Europe: Between Public and Private Space*, ed. Alessandro Ferrari and Sabrina Pastorelli (Burlington, VT: Ashgate, 2013), 193.

59. The burqa is sometimes confused with the *niqab*. A niqab is similar to a burqa but covers the face below the eyes and usually comes in black or white. A burqa is usually a more colorful garment with eyeholes or a grid covering the eyes. Niqabs are more common in Europe than burqas, but neither form of clothing is widespread among Muslim women in Europe.

veil." The hostility toward face veils increased significantly from 2005 onward, resulting in national legislation in two countries in 2010. Compared to the prior headscarf controversies, conflict over face veils has been even more intense, and political campaigns opposing them have received even broader political support.

Several factors have driven the increasing anxiety over face veils. First, apprehensions about the internal threat posed by Muslims in the West, a fixture of the post-9/11 world, picked up steam after the Madrid and London bombings of 2004 and 2005. Media coverage of these events focused heavily on the fact that many of the perpetrators were raised in Europe. This coverage fortified the impression that Muslims, even when they were born and raised in Europe, were not integrating into their "host" countries. Second, multiculturalism continued to face significant political challenges, in part because of terrorist attacks and fears that Muslims were not integrating, in part as a result of the growing popularity of far right political parties, most of which played up the notion that Islam and the West were engaged in a clash of civilizations. Finally, the earlier controversies over headscarves, particularly in France, reinforced the narrative of oppressed Muslim women in need of liberation from enlightened European states. This narrative became embedded in the broader European discourse on Muslim women's rights as the focus shifted to face veils.

France once again led the way. In 2010, a law banning face veils passed both chambers of the French Parliament almost unanimously. The law, which took effect the following year, prohibited all forms

See Ralph Grillo and Prakash Shah, "The Anti-Burqa Movement in Western Europe," in *The Burqa Affair across Europe: Between Public and Private Space*, ed. Alessandro Ferrari and Sabrina Pastorelli (Burlington, VT: Ashgate, 2013), 198; and Sara Silvestri, "Comparing Burqa Debates in Europe: Satorial Styles, Religious Prescriptions, and Political Ideologies," in *Religion in Public Spaces: A European Perspective*, ed. Silvio Ferrari and Sabrina Pastorelli (Farnham: Ashgate, 2012), 275–76.

of dress concealing the face in public space. Face veils could be worn in the private sphere—homes, houses of worship, personal automobiles—but wearing them most anywhere else would result in a fine and mandatory citizenship training. This law, like the one banning headscarves in 2004, had strong public support. According to a poll conducted in April 2010, approximately two-thirds of the French population approved of a ban on face veils.[60]

The irony in this massive opposition to face veils is that they are rarely worn in France. Best estimates are that around 1,900 women wore face veils in 2010 when the law was passed, a mere fraction of the 1.5 million adult Muslim women in France.[61] It seems that the French government and even the broader public went through a great deal of trouble to ban a symbol that is rarely encountered.

The reasons offered for the "burqa ban" were similar to the ones that emerged during the previous debate over headscarves: (1) the face veil impeded security measures, (2) it represented what President Nicolas Sarkozy called "a sign of the subjugation, of the submission, of women,"[62] and (3) women wore it only because male family members coerced them into doing so.[63] Moreover, the face veil posed some problems not present with headscarves. In particular, according to the French government, the face veil hindered healthy relations between citizens because it prevented others from being able to see the face of the veiled woman. The European Court of Human Rights upheld the law in 2014 on this basis, agreeing with the French government that the veil represented a barrier that breached "the

60. Silvestri, "Comparing Burqa Debates in Europe," 281.
61. "European Court Ruling on Full-Face Veils Punishes Women for Expressing Their Beliefs," Amnesty International, July 1, 2014, http://www.amnesty.org/en/news/european-court-ruling-full-face-veils-punishes-women-expressing-their-religion-2014-07-01.
62. Quoted in Doreen Carvajal, "Sarkozy Backs Drive to Eliminate the Burqa," New York Times, June 22, 2009, http://www.nytimes.com/2009/06/23/world/europe/23france.html.
63. For an outstanding critique of these reasons, see Martha Nussbaum, "Veiled Threats," New York Times, July 11, 2010, http://opinionator.blogs.nytimes.com/2010/07/11/veiled-threats/.

right of others to live in a space of socialization which made living together easier."[64]

Belgium quickly followed in France's footsteps, enacting a law banning face veils in public space that also took effect in 2011. In the Belgian vote, not one representative voted against the measure in the lower house of parliament.[65] While no other European state has enacted a ban—the Netherlands came close but failed in 2012—bans have surfaced at the regional and local levels. The Italian-speaking Swiss canton of Ticino imposed a ban in 2013, the result of a popular referendum in which 65 percent of the voters approved of prohibiting face veils in public space.[66] In Barcelona, Spain, the city council voted in 2010 to bar face veils from municipal offices and public markets, though not in city streets. The council acknowledged, however, that the measure was symbolic, given that very few women actually wear face veils in the city. Two other towns in the same region of Spain also enacted bans in 2010.[67] In Novara, Italy, the town council, controlled by the far right Northern League, passed an ordinance in January 2010 prohibiting face veils in public space.[68]

The burqa debate across Europe is not likely to go away anytime soon. Politicians in many European countries have taken up the debate, oftentimes encouraged by favorable opinion polls. According

64. Registrar of the Court, "French Ban on the Wearing in Public of Clothing Designed to Conceal One's Face Does Not Brach the Convention," *European Court of Human Rights* (ECHR), ECHR 191 (2014), http://hudoc.echr.coe.int/webservices/content/pdf/003-4809142-5861661.

65. Jocelyne Cesari, *Why the West Fears Islam: An Exploration of Muslims in Liberal Democracies* (New York: Palgrave Macmillan, 2013), 101.

66. Samuel Jaberg, "Ticino Burka Vote Could Spawn Others," *Swissinfo.ch*, September 25, 2013, http://www.swissinfo.ch/eng/ticino-burka-vote-could-spawn-others/36974276.

67. "Barcelona To Ban Islamic Veils in Some Public Spaces," *BBC News Europe*, June 15, 2010, http://www.bbc.com/news/10316696.

68. Nick Squires, "Muslim Woman Fined £430 for Wearing Burka in Italy," *Telegraph* (UK), May 4, 2010, http://www.telegraph.co.uk/news/worldnews/europe/italy/7676367/Muslim-woman-fined-430-for-wearing-burka-in-Italy.html.

to a poll from 2010, majorities in Britain, France, Italy, Spain, and Germany all favored a face veil ban in their respective countries. But, as in the headscarf controversy, the hysteria over burqas has not been imported by the United States. Only one-third of Americans indicated that they would favor a French-style "burqa ban."[69] Non-Muslim Americans are not always comfortable with face veils or even headscarves for that matter, but the United States has demonstrated a greater willingness to accommodate religious diversity in the public sphere than have countries such as France and Belgium.

Mosques and Minarets

While legal restrictions on the free exercise of religion for Muslims are less prominent in the United States, this does not mean an absence of conflict over the presence of Muslims in public space. Mosques, as opposed to hijabs and burqas, have been the focus of conflict since 9/11. The highest-profile controversy pertained to the proposed Islamic center in Lower Manhattan. As we discussed in chapter 6, Pamela Geller's media campaign against the center, also known as the Park51 project, played a significant role in generating the controversy in 2010.

A real estate company, led by Sharif El-Gamal, purchased property several blocks away from the site of the World Trade Center in 2009. The company, partnering initially with an interfaith activist named Imam Feisal Abdul Rauf, began developing plans to transform the space into a thirteen-story Islamic community center modeled on the Jewish Community Center and the Young Men's Christian

---

69. Harris Interactive, "Most Adults in Largest European Countries, U.S. and China Agree Full Body Scanners Should be Introduced in Airports," *Financial Times/Harris Poll*, March 3, 2010, http://www.harrisinteractive.com/vault/HI_FinancialTimes_HarrisPoll_March_2010_02.pdf.

The Park51 Controversy (2010) involved the proposed construction of an Islamic center in Lower Manhattan, blocks away from the World Trade Center site. The proximity to that site caught the attention of Pamela Geller, who led a campaign against the so-called Ground Zero Mosque. The media attention given to the proposal resulted in political debates about the appropriateness of building an Islamic center near the site that Muslim terrorists attacked on 9/11.

Association. The local community board approved the project in May 2010, but that did not prevent the Geller-led controversy from erupting over what became known as the "Ground Zero Mosque." Politicians weighed in on the project, many expressing concerns about the proximity of an Islamic center to the former World Trade Center towers. Newt Gingrich argued that building a mosque at the site would be like "putting a Nazi sign next to the Holocaust Museum."[70] Peter King called the project "particularly offensive" since "so many Muslim leaders have failed to speak out against radical Islam, against the [9/11] attacks."[71] Sarah Palin opined: "To build a mosque at Ground Zero is a stab in the heart of the families of the innocent victims of those horrific attacks."[72]

---

70. Quoted in Edward Wyatt, "3 Republicans Criticize Obama's Endorsement of Mosque," *New York Times*, August 14, 2010, http://www.nytimes.com/2010/08/15/us/politics/15reaction.html?_r=0.

71. Quoted in William Saletan, "Muslims, Keep Out: The Republican Campaign against a Ground Zero Mosque," *Slate*, August 2, 2010, http://www.slate.com/articles/news_and_politics/frame_game/2010/08/muslims_keep_out.html.

72. Ibid.

Not all politicians shared these sentiments. Mayor Michael Bloomberg, for one, warned against caving into popular sentiment, insisting that "we would betray our values if we were to treat Muslims differently than anyone else."[73] But the mood in the United States was decidedly against the project. A poll from July 2010 indicated that 54 percent of Americans were opposed to building the center on the proposed site, compared to 20 percent in favor.[74] The project did proceed, even though El-Gamal downsized the initial plans in light of public opinion. But the controversy revealed just how much larger anxieties over Islam's presence in public space were driven by assumptions concerning the presumed guilt of all Muslims for the 9/11 attacks.

The "Ground Zero Mosque" controversy was not the only one in the United States at this time. From Tennessee to Wisconsin to California, protests developed in response to plans by local Muslim communities to build mosques. Arguments against the mosques by local residents were often similar to those lodged against the Park51 project—namely, that Islam was a dangerous political ideology bent on violence and conquest. As Lou Ann Zelenik, a congressional candidate, stated in her opposition to a mosque in Murfreesboro, Tennessee: "Islam does not claim to be a religion, but a social and political system that intends to dominate every facet of our lives."[75] For this reason, argued Zelenik, the building of mosques should

---

73. Quoted in Michael Barbaro and Javier C. Hernandez, "Mosque Plan Clears Hurdle in New York," *New York Times*, August 3, 2010, http://www.nytimes.com/2010/08/04/nyregion/04mosque.html?pagewanted=all.

74. "20% Favor Mosque Near Ground Zero, 54% Oppose," *Rasmussen Reports*, July 22, 2010, http://www.rasmussenreports.com/public_content/politics/general_politics/july_2010/20_favor_mosque_near_ground_zero_54_oppose.

75. Quoted in Marie Kemph, "Murfreesboro Mosque Ruling Fuels More Questions," *Murfreesboro Post*, May 31, 2012, http://www.murfreesboropost.com/murfreesboro-mosque-ruling-fuels-more-questions-cms-31356.

not be protected by the First Amendment's guarantee of freedom of religion.

Mosque Conflicts in Europe

Europe has witnessed its own share of mosque conflicts in the past couple of decades. These conflicts have accompanied Islam's growth and increasing visibility in public space. Prior to the 1990s, one would be hard pressed to find many controversies involving mosques, largely because very few purpose-built mosques—worship structures built from scratch with the intention of serving as mosques—existed in the earliest waves of Muslim immigration. When Muslims worshipped, they did so in makeshift prayer rooms in apartment buildings and the back rooms of factories, out of sight and out of mind from the non-Muslim majority. As Muslims established more permanent roots by the 1970s and 1980s, they began to build visible mosques. Yet this transition from invisibility to visibility generated conflicts over mosques. Mosques became symbols of Islam's permanent status and residence in Europe; their public presence led to fears of the "Islamization" of public space.[76]

The highest-profile conflicts in recent decades have involved large purpose-built mosques. The Essalam Mosque in Rotterdam, the largest in the Netherlands, took eleven years to build. It encountered significant opposition from a right-of-center city council beginning in 2000, with far right groups focusing considerable energy on preventing its construction. It was eventually built, opening its doors in 2010, though this did not prevent Geert Wilders from quipping: "That horrible thing does not belong here but in Saudi Arabia."[77]

---

76. Todd H. Green, "The Resistance to Minarets in Europe," *Journal of Church and State* 52 (2010): 625–26.

In Britain, the proposed Abbey Mills Mosque in East London encountered resistance beginning in 2005.[78] The reasons for this resistance included the size of the mosque (intended to hold tens of thousands of worshippers), the timing of the construction in light of the 2012 London Olympics, and the controversial profile of Tablighi Jamaat, the group building the mosque. Some media stories raised questions about whether Tablighi Jamaat had ties to radical Islam or even terrorism, though no evidence was presented to substantiate such speculation. The group tried to alleviate the controversy by downsizing the scale of the proposed mosque, referred to in the media as the "Mega Mosque," but in December 2012 a city council rejected the group's plans, citing the size of the mosque as one of its main concerns.

In Germany, a local far right group began campaigning in 2007 against the construction in Cologne of what would be the largest mosque in the country. The group, Pro Cologne, feared that the mosque would encourage the development of a parallel Islamic society in Germany. It also raised concerns about the height of the minarets, fearing that they would rival the spires of the famous Cologne Cathedral. The group was unsuccessful in its efforts, and the construction of the mosque proceeded.

Minaret Conflicts in Europe

The conflict over the height of the minarets in Cologne points toward a possible shift in the debate over the place of Islam in public

77. Ferry Biedermann, "Essalam, a Symbol of Pride, Opens Its Doors in Holland," *National* (Abu Dhabi), December 23, 2010, http://www.thenational.ae/news/world/europe/essalam-a-symbol-of-pride-opens-its-doors-in-holland.
78. For a helpful overview of this controversy, see Daniel Nilsson DeHanas and Zacharias P. Pieri, "Olympic Proportions: The Expanding Scalar Politics of the London 'Olympics Mega-Mosque' Controversy," *Sociology* 45 (2011): 798–814.

minaret: tower attached or located next to a mosque from which Muslims are called to prayer.

space. There are plenty of instances in which minarets attract more controversy than mosques. This may seem odd, given that both are permanent, immovable structures that symbolize Islam's presence in public space. Both are also associated with a religion often deemed foreign and hostile to European and Western values. So why would minarets be considered *more* threatening than mosques in some instances? The answer lies in the ability of minarets to occupy and define public space more expansively than mosques. Minarets can reach soaring heights and dominate surrounding structures. They can also be seen at greater distances as they rival other towers and buildings in the skyline. Minarets can also have, at least in theory, an acoustical presence. If the Islamic call to prayer, or the *adhan*, is issued from a minaret, it conveys an Islamic presence just as powerfully as

adhan: **the Islamic call to prayer.**

the physical structure. The possible sound of the adhan in Arabic being broadcast from minarets taps into anxieties that Muslims are taking over public space and imposing a foreign religion (and language!) on other Europeans.[79]

In Cologne, the minarets generated just as much controversy as the mosque itself. The local Muslim community and the architect responded by lowering the two proposed minarets to allay fears that they would compete with the spires of Cologne Cathedral. In fact, a pamphlet published by the Turkish organization behind the mosque provides a scale drawing of the mosque and its minarets, placing them

---

79. Green, "The Resistance to Minarets in Europe," 631.

alongside other prominent buildings in Cologne. The minarets reach a height of 55 meters, much shorter than the almost 160-meter height of the cathedral's spires, and nowhere near the height of Cologne's tallest structure, the Colonius, which measures almost 270 meters.[80] But such a campaign to allay fears over the minarets' height reveals just how much anxiety accompanies the prominent presence of an Islamic structure. We see examples of this anxiety in other locations, such as Pforzheim, Germany, where a minaret was allowed only if it were lower than the steeple of a local church.[81]

In other minaret controversies, the fear of the call to prayer is more central. Normally, such a fear would be irrelevant since, in many localities in Europe, noise ordinances prevent the call to prayer. But, in recent years, we are seeing more allowances for it. In 2010, local authorities in Rendsburg, Germany, gave the mosque permission to issue the call to prayer on Fridays.[82] In 2013, the Fittja Mosque in Stockholm became the first one in Sweden to receive permission to broadcast the adhan from the minaret.[83] But there are also notable instances of resistance to such efforts. For example, when the Central Oxford Mosque proposed to broadcast the daily call to prayer from its minaret in 2007, local residents mounted a fierce opposition. Mosque leaders eventually backed off the proposal.

To alleviate concerns over the adhan or to comply with noise ordinances, some Muslim communities have found creative ways to issue the call to prayer. The Grand Mosque in Marseille, France, uses a flashing light to issue the call. Other communities make use of text messaging or shortwave transmitters.[84]

80. DITIB, "Der Moscheebau in Köln-Ehrenfeld: Gemeindezentrum mit Moschee," http://www.zentralmoschee-koeln.de/media/File/info_flyer_2008.pdf.
81. Green, "The Resistance to Minarets in Europe," 632.
82. Ibid., 633.
83. Ann Törnkvist, "Historic Prayer Call Heard at Stockholm Mosque," *Local* (Stockholm), April 26, 2013, http://www.thelocal.se/20130426/47576.
84. Green, "The Resistance to Minarets in Europe," 633–34.

The flexibility demonstrated by Muslim communities concerning minarets has not been matched by the far right. Far right parties have increasingly targeted minarets and campaigned to have them banned. Their efforts have borne fruit. In 2008, two far right parties succeeded in banning the construction of minarets and even mosques in the Austrian provinces of Carinthia and Vorarlberg. This marked the first instance of an outright ban on Islamic worship structures in Europe.

The most notorious ban on minarets, and the only nationwide ban in Europe, is in Switzerland.[85] The controversy over minarets dates back to 2005, when a Turkish association requested permission from the local authorities to build a small minaret on the building that functioned as its mosque in the town of Wangen bei Olten. A local member of the Swiss People's Party collected several hundred signatures from residents to block the construction. The petition failed, but it paved the way for the party to wage a nationwide campaign to ban minarets throughout the country. The party launched a federal initiative in 2007 titled "Against the Building of Minarets." The party collected enough signatures from citizens to place

The Swiss minaret ban (2009) was the result of a campaign led by the far right Swiss People's Party. The party succeeded in placing an amendment to the Swiss constitution on a nationwide referendum that called for a ban on the construction of minarets. Approximately 58 percent of voters approved the amendment, making Switzerland the first and only Western nation to prohibit the building of minarets.

a proposed amendment to the federal constitution on a nationwide referendum. The amendment would prevent the future construction of minarets, even though the country had only four minarets, and none of them were used for the adhan.

The Swiss People's Party campaigned fiercely in favor of the amendment. One of the party's major spokespersons, Oskar Freysinger, invoked the specter of an Islamic conquest taking the form of minarets, referring to them as "the flags that generals place on strategic military maps to identify a conquered territory."[86] This militant image found expression in the campaign's most infamous poster, depicting a Swiss flag populated with minarets in the form of missiles. The party warned that minarets would open the door to Sharia law and to the oppression of women. In fact, the same poster also contained the image of a veiled woman in the foreground. Minarets and the loss of freedom for women became intertwined in the campaign.

One party member summed up the campaign against minarets by invoking the problem of an Islamic presence: "Minarets mark presence and communicate in public space the message visible for all to see: Islam has arrived here and wants to play a role in public life."[87] The campaign to ban minarets was ultimately about rendering Islam invisible and preventing it from defining or "Islamizing" public space. In response to concerns about violating Muslims' freedom of religion, the party assured prospective voters that this was not an issue for two reasons: First, minarets do not serve a religious function since their absence does not prevent Muslims from gathering for prayer. And,

---

85. For an overview of the Swiss minaret ban, including the Swiss People's Party campaign against minarets, see ibid., 635–42.

86. Oskar Freysinger, "Des Jihads Leuchttürme," May 3, 2007, http://www.minarett-verbot.ch/referate/archiv-2007/des-jihads-leuchttuerme.html.

87. Barbara Steinemann, "Kein Minarett ohne Muezzin," October 2009, http://www.minarett-verbot.ch/downloads/kein_minarett_ohne_muezzin.pdf

second, minarets represent political power, and, as political symbols, they are not protected by Switzerland's commitment to freedom of religion. The latter argument is reminiscent of the case against the Murfreesboro mosque by Lou Ann Zelenik. Casting Islam as a political ideology and not a religion is one way to circumvent charges of violating Muslims' right to freedom of religion.

Despite opposition to the initiative from the Swiss government and several prominent Christian religious organizations, the campaign to ban minarets succeeded in the referendum held in November 2009. A double majority was needed for the referendum to pass—a majority of voters and a majority of cantons had to approve the ban. In the end, 57.5 percent of the voters approved, as did twenty-two of twenty-six cantons.

The ban met with strong criticism outside of Switzerland. The Vatican, the UN high commissioner for human rights, and the Organisation of the Islamic Conference condemned the ban, as did many political leaders. Far right parties throughout Europe, by contrast, welcomed the ban and expressed hope that similar bans in the future would take effect in their countries. Their optimism was not misplaced. Polling in the weeks following the ban indicated that support for similar bans across Europe was gaining traction. Approximately 59 percent of those polled in Belgium favored a minaret ban, as did 46 percent in France and 37 percent in Britain. The Swiss ban galvanized far right politicians throughout Europe, providing them with a possible blueprint for minimizing Islam's presence in the public sphere.

◆◆◆◆◆

Our discussion of the surveillance, religious profiling, detentions, deportations, hate crimes, and impediments to the free exercise of religion touches on the most prominent instances of the discrimination, exclusion, and even violence experienced by Muslims. While this is not an exhaustive list, it is a reminder of some of the overwhelming challenges facing Muslims who seek to live as productive members of Western societies. It is also a reminder that racism and bigotry are not confined to individual attitudes and actions but are systemic and take institutionalized form. The perpetuation of Islamophobia by government agencies and non-Muslim citizens reveals the magnitude of the problem. But is the problem insurmountable, or are there effective ways to combat Islamophobia? That is the question that concerns us in the final chapter.

9

—————

Combating Islamophobia

Islamophobia constitutes one of the most acceptable forms of bigotry in the West today. This book has surveyed both the origins and the contemporary manifestations of this bigotry. By now, the problem of Islamophobia is clear. But how do we address this problem? What are some effective strategies for reducing or eliminating Islamophobia?

In this concluding chapter, I invite readers to think through these questions by engaging the viewpoints of eight prominent individuals I interviewed on the topic of combating Islamophobia.[1] These eight do not constitute a representative sample of all public figures devoted to fighting Islamophobia. However, there are good reasons for featuring and analyzing their perspectives. First, all are frequently referenced in either local or national debates over how to counter Islamophobia. In other words, they occupy a prominent place in the public discourse on challenging Islamophobia. Second, they represent

1. The interviews that I conducted with all eight individuals form the basis for the direct quotes and paraphrased material in this chapter. Brief bios of all eight individuals can be found in the appendix. Full transcripts of some of the interviews can be found at http://www.thefearofislam.com/.

a number of occupations; among them are journalists, politicians, and academics. Readers will gain a sense of how a person's vocation shapes the way she or he interprets and responds to Islamophobia. Third, they live and work in different parts of the West—Europe, Canada, and the United States. Readers will therefore acquire some insight into the different challenges involved in combating Islamophobia in Europe versus North America. Other considerations factoring into my interview selections include gender diversity and the desire to incorporate Muslim and non-Muslim perspectives. Because Islamophobia is anything but simple, I wanted to view it from a range of viewpoints.

In all eight interviews, I asked the same set of questions. These questions provide the organizational basis for this chapter. While space constraints do not allow me to provide a full account of every individual response to every question, I make an effort to include enough material to offer readers a larger sense of both the common themes and the diversity of perspectives that emerged from the interviews.

The responses of these eight individuals provide a beginning template for developing effective responses to Islamophobia. Taken together, their insights suggest that any successful effort to combat Islamophobia must involve the following strategies: (1) speaking out whenever and wherever Islamophobia occurs, (2) targeting and discrediting the individuals and institutions that benefit financially and politically from spreading misinformation about Islam, (3) cultivating interpersonal and interfaith relationships between Muslims and non-Muslims, and (4) educating the public about Islam, particularly its diversity and the common ground it shares with the West and other religious traditions.

Why do many non-Muslims in the West
have such strong feelings about Islam
even though they know very little about Islam?

The first question invites interviewees to reflect on the sources of anti-Muslim sentiment in the West. A common theme in the responses is the dominant role played by the Islamophobia industry, the focus of chapter 6, in manufacturing anti-Muslim bigotry for political and financial profit.

Keith Ellison, a congressional representative from Minnesota and the first Muslim elected to the US Congress, places the blame with the likes of Pamela Geller and Robert Spencer, people who market themselves as terrorism experts but who in fact get paid to promote hate.[2] Tariq Ramadan, professor of contemporary Islamic studies at Oxford University, makes a similar point for Europe, noting that far right parties and populists generate and instrumentalize Islamophobia for political gain.[3]

Dalia Mogahed, director of research at the Institute for Social Policy and Understanding and the former executive director of the Gallup Center for Muslim Studies, agrees with Ellison and Ramadan on the impact of the deliberate campaign to misinform Western publics about Islam.[4] She adds that hatred of others is not a natural response to the unknown; it is a learned response. "I reject the idea that people fear what they don't know," Mogahed insists. "They don't fear what they don't know. They fear what they have been *taught* to fear."

The success of professional Islamophobia in teaching non-Muslims to fear Muslims depends to a large degree on the fact that many non-Muslims lack either personal relationships with Muslims or a broader

2. Interview with Keith Ellison in his office on Capitol Hill in Washington, DC, on May 30, 2014.
3. Interview with Tariq Ramadan via Skype on May 28, 2014.
4. Interview with Dalia Mogahed via Skype on June 5, 2014.

base of knowledge concerning Islam. John Esposito, professor of religion and international affairs and Islamic studies at Georgetown University, points out how these realities become obstacles to combating the misinformation of the Islamophobia industry, particularly as it relates to how the industry characterizes all Muslims as extremists.[5] "Most people in the West do not have a context to understand religious extremism," Esposito explains, "and the fact that they don't know a Muslim or much about Islam means they cannot get a clearer perspective on religious extremism and what drives it."

Given the power and financial resources of the Islamophobia industry, what is needed to counteract the messaging of this network? Ellison points to the significance of political leadership. Political leaders must signal the importance of including and embracing Muslims. On this issue, he has been disappointed with President Obama's leadership. While Ellison is a huge Obama supporter, he feels let down by Obama's past failures to speak out strongly against anti-Muslim prejudice, particularly during his two presidential campaigns. For example, when opponents accused Obama of being a Muslim during the 2008 presidential campaign, he failed to point out that there is no shame in being a Muslim. It took Colin Powell, the former secretary of state, to go on television and make that point.

Ellison contrasts Obama with President Bush, who immediately after 9/11 went to a mosque and declared Islam to be a religion of peace. The Islamophobia industry has gained power under Obama in part because Obama's public messaging on Islam has been weaker. Nevertheless, Ellison sees signs of hope with Obama, expressing appreciation for his willingness to associate publicly at an *iftar* dinner with Huma Abedin, aide to Secretary of State Hillary Clinton, during a 2012 controversy in which some falsely accused Abedin of acting as

5. Interview with John Esposito via Skype on May 8, 2014.

a Muslim Brotherhood infiltrator in the US government. Ellison thinks we need more of this kind of leadership from Obama.

Even with strong leadership, the power of professional Islamophobia is not easily broken, mostly because anti-Muslim stereotypes are difficult

iftar: **the evening meal during the holy month of Ramadan that marks the end of the day's fasting.**

to dislodge from the population at large. This is a point that Ingrid Mattson makes by referencing Islamic law. Mattson, professor of Islamic studies at the University of Western Ontario and former president of the Islamic Society of North America, notes the distinction in Islamic law between "simple ignorance" and "complex ignorance."[6] The former refers to inadequate knowledge on a matter resulting from a lack of information. The latter refers to assumed knowledge on a matter even though one is mistaken or has faulty information. With complex ignorance, one has cognitive frames that will not allow correct information to enter the mind and to transform one's thinking. This means that an entire deconstruction process must take place before one can be open to receiving correct knowledge.

Mattson argues that complex ignorance explains why simply providing the larger public with correct information about Islam is ineffective. She refers to her own experience of public speaking engagements after 9/11 in which many people would sit through her lectures on Islamic teachings and practices, only to respond at the end with incredulity. They were convinced they knew more about Islam than she did, even though her education in and experience of Islam far exceeded theirs. Mattson's observations on complex ignorance of Islam shed some light on why responding to the Islamophobia

6. Interview with Ingrid Mattson via Skype on May 28, 2014.

industry by presenting straightforward facts and data will have a limited impact. We must deconstruct the very narrative and assumptions at work in the industry and even in larger segments of Western societies if we are to counter the hate speech employed by this industry.

What is the best way to address the media's negative portrayal of Islam?

Many of the responses to the first question make implicit references to the role played by the media in constructing negative images of Muslims. This is understandable, given that the Islamophobia industry's influence depends on widespread media coverage. This second question attempts to tease out the interviewees' understandings of the media's role in Islamophobia and how best to counteract it. All interviewees accept that media framing, a concept discussed in some detail in chapter 7, shapes what we know about Islam, usually for the worse. Eboo Patel, founder of the Interfaith Youth Core in Chicago, recalls a story that illustrates this point:[7]

> I gave a talk in Kansas City some years ago, and somebody stood up and said, "What the heck is wrong with you Muslims?" My response was if the only thing I knew about Kansas City was the first minute of the local news every night, I would say to you, "What the heck is wrong with you people in Kansas City?" If the only thing I know is the murders and rapes I hear about on the evening news, then I have a very skewed view of who you are.

Patel adds that since most Americans see only the bad stuff that some Muslims are doing on the evening news, it makes sense that they have a fear of Muslims and Islam.

---

7. Interview with Eboo Patel at DePaul University in Chicago on August 7, 2014.

The media's framing of Islam is powerful and pervasive, but it is not an insurmountable obstacle in the fight against Islamophobia. Ellison reminds Americans that they live in a country that provides ample opportunity for freedom of speech. People who want to challenge media portrayals of Muslims must take advantage of this freedom and make their voices heard. "You have to inject yourself into the marketplace of ideas," insists Ellison. "As you do this, it means putting in your own ideas, but it also means confronting people who are putting out negative media and messaging."

Myriam Francois-Cerrah, a freelance journalist and Islamic studies scholar in Britain, makes a similar point.[8] Readers and viewers have an obligation to make their voices heard in response to negative portrayals of Muslims or of anyone else for that matter. Drawing on her own experience as a journalist, Francois-Cerrah feels that most journalists are fairly receptive to feedback from the public. If they encounter significant criticism for their coverage of Muslims or any other topic, they are likely to take this criticism into account in the future.

It is one thing to embrace the philosophy of making one's voice heard, but it is quite another to determine *how* to go about doing this, particularly when the average person seeking to combat Islamophobia lacks the resources of many journalists. For Esposito, social media provide venues for presenting alternative representations of Islam and for counteracting the negative stereotypes found in the mainstream media. He encourages anti-Islamophobia activists to use platforms such as Facebook and Twitter to discredit negative messaging about Muslims and Islam. But Esposito has no illusions about the difficulty of this approach, if for no other reason than the fact that social media is a two-edged sword. The Islamophobia

8. Interview with Myriam Francois-Cerrah via Skype on July 15, 2014.

network is quite savvy in its use of social media, and it has far greater financial resources to make use of such platforms. It will take more financial resources, more networking, and more sophisticated coordination among anti-Islamophobia activists to challenge the persistent anti-Muslim rhetoric coming from the Islamophobia industry.

But there are success stories when it comes to concerned individuals joining forces to create alternative representations of Muslims. Francois-Cerrah points to a video created by British Muslims in 2014 that went viral. The video shows British Muslims from all walks of life lip-syncing and dancing along to Pharrell Williams's popular hit song "Happy." Francois-Cerrah, who also participated in the project, explains her reasons for doing so: "I agreed to be a part of the project because I like the idea of Muslims defining themselves outside of the usual debates. Many of us who participated in the video relished the opportunity to just be. To just be ourselves. To just reflect a few seconds or minutes of a person having a laugh, a person who just *happens* to be Muslim. It's a window into a community that doesn't often get public airtime on such neutral ground." She adds that, in the age of technology and the Internet, anyone can create alternative narratives that enable a broader public to glimpse a slice of Muslim life and identity rarely presented in the mainstream media.

Mattson's approach focuses less on correcting the media through social media networks and more on educating the public about the psychological effects that negative media coverage has on us. Her own research into the psychology of knowledge and its relationship to the media was prompted by her frustration over so many people after 9/11 continuing to ask why Muslims do not condemn terrorism, even though she felt there were enough media stories addressing such condemnations. Why did this information not stick?

In her research, she discovered that negative, threatening images and stories remain with us in ways that positive news stories do not because our brains are set up to prioritize information that is existentially vital: "There's nothing more important than a threat to your life and to your security and safety. Even if there are one hundred stories about Muslims doing good things (denouncing terrorism, engaging in humanitarian work, etc.), this information will not stick with people." For Mattson, this explains why most Americans know the name Osama bin Laden but have no idea who Tawakkol Karman is. Karman, winner of the Nobel Peace Prize in 2011, is a Muslim making positive contributions. But her story is not threatening, nor does it fit into the cognitive frames many in the West have developed about Islam (that is, Islam is violent, Islam is opposed to Muslim women having prominent public roles, and so on). Her story does not stick.

Mattson feels that we as consumers of the mass media need to be educated about how media coverage both impacts our brains and contributes to our own psychological distress by generating anxiety toward Muslims and Islam. We need to take a step back and recognize that the media is not a neutral source of information. We should approach the media with the same caution with which we would approach any drug that has the potential to do great harm to our minds or to alter our perceptions of reality.

What is the one thing you wish more people in the West knew about Islam?

Negative media coverage of Islam often prevents many in the West from recognizing the common ground they share with Muslims. For this reason, it is perhaps no surprise that the answers to this third question reflect a desire to raise awareness of our commonalities.

For Ramadan, the common ground is the complexity and diversity within Islam. "Islam is as complex as Judaism, Christianity, or Buddhism," he insists. "There is one Islam but many Muslims, one Islam and many interpretations. All of this is part of what we need to understand about Islam." Otherwise, we reduce Islam to the good and the bad in a way that we would not for many other religions. We force Islam into an Orientalist model that fails to do justice to the complexity and diversity of the tradition.

Marjorie Dove Kent, the executive director of Jews for Racial and Economic Justice in New York City, also lifts up the connection between Islam and other religions, particularly the Abrahamic faiths.[9] She notes that many common themes in Islamic teachings—such as peace and worship of the one God—are part of Judaism and Christianity as well. Islam's relationship to the People of the Book inspires Muslims to show great respect for Jewish and Christian prophetic figures. The similarities among the Abrahamic traditions also extend to less pleasant aspects, such as violence. While the Qur'an has its share of violent passages, she notes that the same is true for Jewish and Christian scriptures. None of the Abrahamic traditions have a monopoly on violent texts.

Ellison wishes more non-Muslims knew the role that love plays as "an important animating concept in Islam," analogous to its role in Christianity. "There's only one sura in the Qur'an that does not begin with the phrase, 'In the Name of the Most Compassionate, the Most Merciful,'" Ellison observes.[10] At the same time, he acknowledges that Muslims are largely to blame for not talking enough about the centrality of love in Islam:

I think it's fair for people of other faiths to ask Muslims to reflect on where love fits into Islam. In Christianity, love is a highly prominent

9. Interview with Marjorie Dove Kent in her office in New York City on May 27, 2014.
10. The sura or chapter from the Qur'an to which Ellison refers is Sura al-Tawba, or Sura 9.

concept. But in Islam, we talk about obligation, duty, and ritual a lot. We've reduced our faith in some instances to a set of dos and don'ts, but there's more to Islam than not drinking, not gambling, and not eating pork. There's got to be. There's more to Islam than praying at a specific time of day five times a day. There's way more to it than that. And yet we've got to begin to acknowledge that the context of these rituals is love, compassion, and mercy.

Love, for Ellison, is what connects Islam to the values that many Westerners embrace in their own religious or ethical traditions.

Patel is also invested in connecting Islam to qualities that many people outside the tradition can admire, but he prefers to personalize this connection: "I want people to know that Muhammad Ali is a Muslim." He notes that we struggle to have a relationship with abstract ideas, but we long to have a relationship with people we admire:

> To take people that are broadly admired for athletic prowess or personal integrity, and to lift up a dimension of their being that is central to who they are but is not often thought about—this changes people's perspectives. There's lots of examples of this, such as Sandy Koufax and Judaism. A group is viewed very negatively, then there is somebody on the pantheon—in athletics, in the arts, in politics—who becomes broadly admired, and it comes out that this person is a part of a group that is viewed negatively.

If more Americans knew that some of the people they look up to are Muslim, people such as Muhammad Ali, Dave Chappelle, and Mos Def, this knowledge would change their perception of Islam and how it positively contributes to a person's identity.

While Patel focuses on creating awareness of high-profile and broadly admired Muslim Americans, Esposito and Mogahed concentrate on the common ground that exists between many ordinary Muslims and other Westerners. Both wish that more people knew the sociological data that confirm just how much Muslims and non-Muslims share in common. Esposito notes that data from the Pew Research Center and Gallup reveal the degree to which Muslim Americans are economically, educationally, and politically integrated into society. Muslim youth have high rates of college education and are economically equal to if not better off than many non-Muslims. Muslim Americans, in other words, are not operating as alienated outsiders in the United States, despite the bigotry and discrimination they experience. Polls indicate that they are full participants in American political and social life.

Mogahed wants more Westerners to know that Islam does not motivate extremist or violent behavior any more than other religions do. Her work at Gallup gave her the opportunity to oversee numerous public opinion polls among Muslims. The findings confirmed that Muslim religiosity did *not* correlate with the tendency to sympathize with terrorism. If anything, higher levels of religiosity were linked to a propensity among Muslims to reject terrorism. "Islam as a net influence is the reason there is so little terrorism," Mogahed argues. "Islam as a net influence is the reason we don't have more hate and animosity between Muslims and the West." Mogahed feels that if more people knew this and considered the implications, perceptions of Islam might start to change.

What can Muslims do to help combat Islamophobia?

In light of how deeply ingrained anti-Muslim stereotypes are, what strategies can Muslims adopt to improve how non-Muslims perceive them? For many of the interviewees, the most basic strategy involves developing personal relationships with non-Muslims. The personal, human element is missing from many of the stereotypes and caricatures of Muslims dominating the media and public discourse. "We've got to start talking to our neighbors a little bit more about what we go through," Ellison maintains. "Interpersonal interactions are a very strong antidote for the anti-Muslim hate that we see messaged in our society."

Mattson agrees. "There really can't be any significant improvement without personal connections and interactions. It is the humanization and personalization of Muslims that tips the situation for people." She suggests facilitating interpersonal interactions through local mosques. Mosques must play a more central role in combating Islamophobia: "Mosques are certainly supposed to be places where Muslims gather to pray, but in today's age, they have to be something more. Muslim communities should give at least 50 percent of their time and attention to developing outreach programs and sponsoring activities where people in the community gather and engage Muslims." She adds that Muslims should think more about how they design and make use of mosques. Mosques should be attractive, with lots of open and inviting spaces. They should be staffed with volunteers or employees to greet visitors and take them on tours. "Mosques need to be welcoming, transparent places where people in the community know they can drop in and experience hospitality and neighborliness."

Other interviewees also lift up the importance of interpersonal interactions but focus more on the need for Muslims to do so through civic engagement. For Mogahed, this is an area in which Muslims in both Europe and the United States must improve. "Many Muslims see themselves as grateful guests rather than engaged members and citizens," Mogahed argues. "But the problem with grateful guests is that while they are quiet and don't demand too much from their gracious host, they also don't build. And they don't sacrifice." Greater civic engagement leads Muslims to form ties with other citizens and to work together for the greater good of their community and society.

Ramadan strikes a similar note, observing that Islamophobia tempts Muslim Europeans into isolating themselves when in fact they need to do the opposite and become more engaged citizens. Muslims cannot combat Islamophobia by becoming invisible and isolated:

> We as Muslims have to normalize our *visible* presence. This means we have to be visible, but not only when we are speaking about Islam. We must be visible and involved in anything that has to do with society—in education, in the economy, in the environment. We must be at home; we must contribute and be a part of the social fabric. We must make it clear that we do not become visible only when Islam is attacked and then disappear when human dignity is at stake. Civic belonging is essential.

Ramadan adds that it is time to leave behind the concept of integration. "The time of integration is past," he insists. "Now is the time of contribution, to be of added value." Ramadan believes that once Muslims fully invest in civic engagement, the non–Muslim majority will stop looking at Muslims as a problem to be solved and start looking to Muslims as partners in building a healthy society.

Patel's message for Muslim Americans is similar. Muslims must contribute to society, and they must forge relationships and partnerships with other citizens: "It is a part of American citizenship and Islam that you are positively disposed to basic community affairs, and that means everything from smiling at your neighbor to being involved in the PTA to coaching Little League. If you are going to be a beneficiary of American society, from its good roads to its civil rights laws, you ought to contribute." Patel acknowledges that some Muslim Americans isolate themselves and even find justification in a certain interpretation of Islam for doing so. But there are more constructive ways of understanding Islam. "One is contributing to a community that is diverse. And to the extent that you are a part of a diverse society, you have a responsibility to participate in it."

Francois-Cerrah encourages Muslims to avoid an us–versus–them narrative. Any successful effort by Muslims to combat Islamophobia will recognize that Islamophobia is not a sectarian issue. It is a form of injustice, "something that anybody with a conscience would oppose." Francois-Cerrah believes that Muslims should make it clear that they are against *all* forms of bigotry and injustice, not just Islamophobia. "I would hate for Muslims to become a narrow interest group, only focused on combating Islamophobia." Forging alliances with other citizens in the battle to eliminate prejudice and intolerance of all kinds is vital if Muslims hope to loosen Islamophobia's grip on the West.

There are limits to how much Muslims should accommodate to the expectations of the non-Muslim majority for the sake of forging harmonious relationships, particularly when Islamophobia informs those expectations. This is a point that Mogahed makes quite strongly. There are instances, such as terrorism, when Muslims need to go on the offensive and challenge the demands being made of them:

> I will never condemn terrorism again. In fact, not only will I not condemn it again, but from now on, I will call out the person who asks me to condemn it. It is implicitly and in many cases explicitly a racist statement to ask Muslims to prove to their fellow citizens that they think that the murder of innocent people is wrong. The fact that this is not already assumed in the way it would be with other groups means that what we are dealing with is a racist assumption.

It is understandable that Muslims might feel tempted to accommodate requests or demands from the non-Muslim majority to denounce terrorism, but Mogahed feels this is counterproductive. If anything, it exacerbates Islamophobia by giving credit to the idea that Muslims should be singled out and required to answer for crimes committed by others.

Esposito and Kent do not offer any particular advice to Muslims for combating Islamophobia. For Esposito, Muslims in the United States and Europe are already doing plenty in this area. The media does not always pick up on the positive contributions that Muslims are making in society or the many ways that Muslims challenge extremism or terrorism. But Muslims are quite active in the fight to combat Islamophobia and to provide alternative narratives to what one finds in the mainstream media. They are also becoming more organized and are developing better networks for responding to terrorism and other negative media stories.

Kent, like Esposito, appreciates the efforts Muslims are already making in the battle against Islamophobia. She offers no advice on what they can do differently, in part because, as someone who is not a Muslim, she feels this is not her place. In fact, the very question of what Muslims can do to combat Islamophobia makes her uncomfortable. To explain her discomfort, she draws a parallel with anti-Semitism: "If a Christian were to stand up in front of an audience of Jews and say, 'Here's what you guys can do to combat anti-Semitism,' honestly, I would say, 'Screw you! Here's what *you* need to do to combat anti-Semitism! Jews are not responsible for the misinformation.' For the same reason, I would *not* want to tell Muslims what they need to do to combat Islamophobia because Islamophobia is in us. It's *our* job to counter it." Islamophobia, in other words, involves a bigotry and hatred of Muslims for which Muslims are not responsible. Kent thinks it is inappropriate to give Muslims advice on how to combat a problem whose source lies outside the Muslim community. We would not ask this of Jews or African Americans. We should not ask it of Muslims.

What can non-Muslims do to help combat Islamophobia?

If we accept Kent's point that non-Muslims bear considerable responsibility in the battle against Islamophobia, then how should they go about fighting the good fight? Should non-Muslims adopt different tactics than Muslims? Most of the interviewees advise non-Muslims to employ an alternative set of strategies in combating Islamophobia.

For Kent and Mogahed, the starting point for non-Muslim action must be naming the reality in order to make it socially unacceptable. When Muslims complain about discrimination, their voices are not heard as much as when the non-Muslim majority speaks out. Kent feels that non-Muslims must be relentless in calling out Islamophobia "in a visible and vocal way." "Interrupting it wherever and whenever you encounter it," she advises, "is an extremely important way to combat it." Mogahed agrees, insisting that Islamophobia will thrive as long as those who are not its immediate victims are silent. To do nothing in the face of Islamophobia is to offer tacit acceptance of it.

There is a difference between calling out Islamophobia when it happens and throwing the label of "Islamophobe" at every person who holds prejudicial views of Muslims. Patel's advice to non-Muslims concerned with combating Islamophobia is to pay particular attention to how prejudices are formed and dismantled and to proceed strategically. "Do not castigate your run-of-the-mill Islamophobe," Patel says. "Castigate the Islamophobes who know what they are doing. Castigate Pam Geller, David Horowitz, and others who are playing Wizard of Oz and who are creating Islamophobia." Patel argues that most people who harbor prejudice against Muslims have a very limited knowledge base and are making judgments about Muslims based on that shallow pool of knowledge.

Their intent is not malicious, so it therefore serves no purpose to call them racist.

If non-Muslims want to dismantle anti-Muslim bigotry, they must articulate to a broader public what they find attractive about Islam. Patel asks non-Muslims to consider the following: "What are the things that you genuinely find beautiful in Islam? Don't just learn the Five Pillars. What is it about the Shahada that you find beautiful? What is it about *zakat* that you find beautiful? Learn things that you appreciate, and then be curious about Muslims. And don't be afraid of sounding naive when talking with Muslims about their faith. You are naive. So be positively curious." Patel maintains that the job of non-Muslims is "to sing a song that those who harbor anti-Muslim prejudice are going to find beautiful. Your job is *not* to scold them for being out of tune." Nobody changes after being scolded. "People change when they are introduced to beauty."

zakat: **charitable giving according to Islamic law.**

Patel's advice to non-Muslims relies on the strategies of interfaith dialogue and interpersonal engagement. Variations of these strategies are found in some of the other answers as well. Mogahed does not think that we can leave it to the victims alone to fight this prejudice. No prejudice in American history has ever been overcome without "a critical mass of the broader society standing up and saying, 'Not in my name!'" She maintains that a broader coalition that includes Muslims and people of other traditions must materialize if the cancer of Islamophobia is to be eradicated. Ramadan agrees and suggests that non-Muslims can act as mediators by reaching out to Muslims "to create a new 'we.'"

Ellison focuses on interfaith dialogue and cooperation in his advice to non-Muslims. For those who are participants in the Abrahamic traditions, Ellison believes that more effort spent on discussing commonalities between Judaism, Christianity, and Islam will make a difference. This includes talking about the shared skeletons in the closet, such as the violent passages that can be found in the scriptures of all three traditions. But it also means discussing the shared love and common prophetic figures in the traditions. This type of interfaith dialogue will serve to strengthen relationships and reduce tensions between the religions.

But dialogue alone is not enough according to Ellison. Interfaith action is also essential: "Let's get a mosque, a synagogue, and a church together and go and feed the hungry. We're all motivated by our love for God and serving others for God. We all share that. Let's get busy. We've got a broken world that needs to be saved." For Ellison, focusing on mutual values and cooperative action between the three traditions is the most promising strategy to overcome anti-Muslim bigotry.

Francois-Cerrah shares Ellison's commitment to promoting relationships between Muslims and people of other faiths. She warns, however, that too much focus on agreement between religious traditions borders on cultural relativism and encourages only a shallow understanding: "I think it's really important in coexistence to recognize our disagreements rather than a wishy-washy interfaith engagement in which we don't really like to tread on areas of divergence at the risk of creating rifts. The healthiest relationships are those that recognize the areas of divergence and that learn to manage those areas." Combating Islamophobia successfully is not about pressuring non-Muslims into agreeing with Muslims on every controversial issue but about accepting legitimate differences between religious traditions and learning to live with these differences.

Ramadan agrees with Francois-Cerrah's point about recognizing differences. He encourages non-Muslims to ask Muslims difficult questions. Muslims should be asked about their positions on violence and their commitments to women's rights. Dare to question and to address the differences on key issues with Muslims if and when they exist. "These questions," Ramadan maintains, "signal that you are supportive of Muslims who are victims of discrimination but also that your support is not a blind support for everything." Both Ramadan and Francois-Cerrah take to heart one of the more common criticisms of the concept of Islamophobia discussed in chapter 1, that calling attention to Islamophobia has the potential to stifle legitimate criticisms of Muslims and Islam. Their response is that non-Muslims can fight Islamophobia without abandoning a critical engagement with Muslims.

Are you hopeful that Muslims will face less discrimination and hostility a generation from now?

The final question asks interviewees to look to the future. Are things getting better for Muslims in the West? Will Islamophobia be as much of a problem twenty-five years from now as it is today? The answers reflect a cautious optimism for the future tempered by the realization that things may remain the same or even become a little worse before they improve.

Both Mattson and Patel believe that geopolitical interests and developments will continue to feed Islamophobia in the West for the next generation. Mattson maintains that many global conflicts, including those between Muslim-majority regions and the West, pertain to energy and land. In light of these global conflicts, there are two things that can reduce Islamophobia: "The first is developing and refining more renewable energy. The second is some sort of peaceful resolution to the Israel-Palestine conflict. Those are the two big picture issues that will continue to fuel Islamophobia as long as they persist and as long as there are people who have political and economic interests in generating Islamophobia."

Patel also points to global conflict as a continuing source of Islamophobia, emphasizing the internal conflicts in Muslim-majority regions. "I do not think the news about the Muslim-majority world is going to get better," he warns. "I think that many parts of the Muslim-majority world are going to be in some version of a civil war for the next thirty years." Patel believes that news of these conflicts will continue to have a negative impact on Western perceptions of Muslims, though he is open to the possibility that improved relationships between Muslims and non-Muslims in the West will offset this impact.

For Francois-Cerrah, the ongoing debate over whether Muslim and European identities are reconcilable has the potential to exacerbate Islamophobia for some time to come. She notes that, in recent years, politicians and other public figures have been expanding their criticisms of Muslims beyond issues related to terrorism toward a larger critique of the illiberal views held by some Muslims:

> The question increasingly is this: can Muslims ever truly be European if they hold illiberal views? The question marks a dramatic shift in the discourse. It's also a very problematic question. If we define ourselves by what Prime Minister David Cameron refers to as "muscular liberalism," I fear that we are in danger of creating much more friction in the future. Are we going to move toward a Europe that can deal with its diversity through a liberalism that allows for a range of views to coexist, or are we moving toward a Europe that is increasingly committed to a narrow understanding of liberalism that seeks the eradication of illiberal views?

Francois-Cerrah fears that it is the latter, citing the murder of Lee Rigby by two Muslim extremists in May 2013 as a trigger event that is prompting many British politicians to argue that the country must do a better job of imposing liberal views on an intractable and dangerous Muslim minority. But she insists that an aggressive campaign to force Muslims to abandon illiberal views will only exacerbate tensions between Muslims and non-Muslims in the future.

While Muslims in the West will continue to face obstacles for the foreseeable future, there are reasons to hope that progress will be made in the battle against Islamophobia. For five of the interviewees, the basis for this hope, particularly in the United States, is history. History demonstrates that forces of inclusion and acceptance almost always triumph over forces of intolerance and bigotry.

Esposito and Patel point to the history of anti-Catholicism in the United States as a prime example of how significant prejudice against a religious minority eventually lost out to the forces of inclusion. Of course, the analogy is not perfect. As Esposito notes: "Since Catholics were Christians, there was always the possibility of finding some common ground with the Protestant majority. With Muslims, a shared religious heritage with the Protestant majority did not exist in the same way."

Patel agrees, adding that two other factors facilitated greater acceptance of Catholics by the late twentieth century. First, Catholics eventually grew to be the largest Christian community in the United States. Today, they comprise 25 percent of the population, which makes it more likely that non-Catholics will have opportunities to interact with them.[11] Muslims, by contrast, constitute only 1 to 2 percent of the population.[12] Second, Catholics have created massive institutions dedicated to serving the larger population, including

11. See Pew Research Religion and Public Life Project, *Religious Landscape Survey*, http://religions.pewforum.org/reports.

12. See Pew Research Religion and Public Life Project, *The Future of the Global Muslim Population*, "Region: Americas," January 27, 2011, http://www.pewforum.org/2011/01/27/future-of-the-global-muslim-population-regional-americas/.

hospitals, universities, and charities. "The chances of you benefiting from a Catholic civic institution that has helped you or your family are pretty high," Patel says. Comparable Muslim institutions, at least on the scale of Catholic ones, are lacking in the United States. There are simply far fewer opportunities for Muslim civic organizations to forge positive relationships with the non-Muslim majority. Even so, Patel, like Esposito, points to the reduction of anti-Catholic sentiment in American history as evidence that major prejudice against a maligned religious community can be overcome.

Kent and Ellison draw parallels to anti-Semitism in Western history. Kent observes that some racial, ethnic, or religious minority group has always been the "targeted Other," but, as history unfolds, another group ends up replacing the previous one as the primary target. Jews served as one of the main outgroups for much of Western history, whereas today Muslims are the most ostracized and feared group. But just as anti-Semitism eventually declined, Kent is optimistic that Islamophobia will diminish in time. Ellison shares her hope: "If we can push back and push down anti-Semitism, we can push down anti-Muslim hate as well." History can repeat itself.

Mogahed draws an analogy to interracial marriage. She explains that when the Gallup Poll first started measuring Americans' attitudes toward interracial marriage back in the 1950s, only 4 percent of Americans approved of the practice. This disapproval characterized the attitudes of both whites and African Americans. Today, 86 percent of Americans approve of interracial marriage.[13] Moreover, in 2008, the United States elected a president who is the product of an interracial marriage. "What all of these things tell me," Mogahed says, "is that we are a country that is capable of renewal." History is replete

---

13. See Jeffrey M. Jones, "Record High 86% Approve of Black-White Marriages," Gallup, September 12, 2011, http://www.gallup.com/poll/149390/record-high-approve-black-white-marriages.aspx.

with examples of long-held prejudices gradually eroding. There is every reason to hope that the same will occur with Islamophobia.

The belief that Muslims are becoming more integral parts of Western societies is another basis for hope that emerged from the interviews. As Muslims continue to put down roots and invest in their communities and in civic institutions, positive relationships between Muslim minorities and the non-Muslim majority will increase. This will likely take place at different rates in Europe than in the United States. Ramadan observes that Muslim Europeans are gradually settling down and engaging their neighbors and local governments. This constitutes a paradox for Muslims. In the near future, it means greater tension. "It's *because* Muslims are getting out of the social and geographical ghettoes and are becoming more visible," Ramadan argues, "that there is this impression that Muslims in Europe are not integrating." More visibility and activity from Muslims in the public sphere means that anxiety over Muslims will continue to rise to the surface. As the majority becomes more accustomed to the visibility of immigrant and religious minorities, and as there is more personal interaction with Muslim minorities, conditions will improve. For this reason, Ramadan estimates that, in two generations, Europe will see a significant reduction in Islamophobia.

Patel also thinks that Europe, more so than the United States, faces difficult times ahead when it comes to Islamophobia. This is primarily due to added tensions around issues of class and education. Muslims in Europe occupy lower rungs on the socioeconomic ladder and possess lower education levels than Muslims in the United States, and this complicates their relationship with non-Muslims in Europe. It will take more time for matters to improve in Europe, though Muslims in America also have a difficult road before them. Even so, Patel strikes a hopeful chord, predicting that non-Muslims will increasingly and more regularly come into contact with Muslims they know and admire. This contact, and the relationships that result, will contribute to a healthier, more robust pluralism in the West, one that is more inclusive of Muslims.

♦ ♦ ♦ ♦ ♦

Islamophobia is a massive problem that permeates many elements of Western societies. We have a long way to go before Islamophobia becomes as unacceptable in Western societies as other prejudices. But there is reason to hope for a better future. The growing list of books, websites, think tanks, religious leaders, civil rights activists, scholars, and politicians committed to fighting Islamophoia is a promising sign. Add to this the powerful witness provided by the eight individuals interviewed in this chapter, and there is every reason to believe that we are moving in the right direction.

Hostility toward the racial and religious "Other," while a formidable and dangerous force in Western history, rarely has the final word. As Dr. Martin Luther King Jr. reminds us: "The arc of the moral universe is long, but it bends toward justice."

Appendix: Interviewee Profiles

Keith Ellison represents the Fifth Congressional District of Minnesota in the US House of Representatives. He is the first Muslim ever to be elected to Congress and one of only two Muslims currently serving in Congress. He co-chairs the Congressional Progressive Caucus in the Democratic Party and serves as the party's chief deputy whip. He is the author of *My Country 'Tis of Thee: My Faith, My Family, Our Future* (Gallery Books/Karen Hunter Publishing, 2014).

John L. Esposito is university professor and professor of religion and international affairs and Islamic studies at Georgetown University. He is also founding director of the Prince Alwaleed bin Talal Center for Muslim-Christian Understanding in the Walsh School of Foreign Service at Georgetown University. He is the author of numerous books, including *The Future of Islam* (Oxford University Press, 2010) and *What Everyone Needs to Know about Islam* (Oxford University Press, 2011). He is one of the most recognized scholars of Islam in the United States.

Myriam Francois-Cerrah is an author, journalist, and scholar in Britain. She contributes articles to major publications such as the

Guardian, the *Independent*, the *New Statesman*, and the *Huffington Post*. She participates regularly in public debates pertaining to Islam on television networks and programs such as Sky News, *BBC Newsnight*, *BBC Big Questions*, and Channel 4 news. She is currently conducting postgraduate research at Oxford University, focusing on Islamic movements in Morocco.

Marjorie Dove Kent is the executive director of Jews for Racial & Economic Justice (JFREJ), an organization that mobilizes Jews to combat racism and economic inequity in New York City. The organization participates in a larger coalition called the Jews Against Islamophobia Coalition that arose in response to the Park51 controversy in lower Manhattan in 2010.

Ingrid Mattson is the London and Windsor Community Chair in Islamic Studies at Huron University College at the University of Western Ontario in Canada. She is the author of *The Story of the Qur'an: Its History and Place in Muslim Life* (Blackwell Publishing, 2013). She served as the first female president of the Islamic Society of North America from 2006 to 2010. She was also a member of both the Faith-Based Advisory Council for the US Department of Homeland Security and the Interfaith Task Force for the White House Office of Faith-Based and Neighborhood Partnerships. In 2007, *Time* magazine named her one of the hundred most influential people in the world.

Dalia Mogahed is director of research at the Institute for Social Policy and Understanding in Washington, DC. Along with John Esposito, she is the coauthor of *Who Speaks for Islam? What a Billion*

Muslims Really Think (Gallup, 2007). She is the former executive director of the Gallup Center for Muslim Studies, where she oversaw the analysis of surveys of Muslims globally from 2006 to 2012. She also served on President Obama's Advisory Council for the White House Office of Faith-Based and Neighborhood Partnerships.

Eboo Patel is the founder and executive director of the Interfaith Youth Core (IFYC), a Chicago-based organization devoted to interfaith work and partnerships among young adults. He is the author of two books: *Acts of Faith: The Story of an American Muslim, the Struggle for the Soul of a Generation* (Beacon, 2007), which won the Louisville Grawemeyer Award in Religion in 2010, and *Sacred Ground: Pluralism, Prejudice, and the Promise of America* (Beacon, 2012). He has served on the Faith-Based Advisory Council for the US Department of Homeland Security and on President Obama's Advisory Council for the White House Office of Faith-Based and Neighborhood Partnerships. *US News & World Report* named him one of America's Best Leaders in 2009.

Tariq Ramadan is professor of contemporary Islamic studies at Oxford University and president of European Muslim Network, a European think tank. He is the author of numerous books, including *Western Muslims and the Future of Islam* (Oxford University Press, 2004) and *Islam and the Arab Awakening* (Oxford University Press, 2012). He is one of Europe's most prominent Muslim intellectuals, writing and lecturing extensively on the place of Muslims in the West and on interfaith dialogue. In 2004, *Time* magazine named him one of the hundred most influential people in the world.

Glossary

adhan: the Islamic call to prayer

Allah: the Arabic word for God

anti-Semitism: prejudice and hatred toward Jews

Arab nationalism: a twentieth-century political movement focused on uniting Arab peoples based on their common linguistic, cultural, historical, and religious heritage; the movement was a response to the legacy of Western colonialism

Arab socialism: a twentieth-century political movement focused on state-sponsored economic development; made inroads in Egypt under General Nasser (r. 1956–1970) and in Iraq and Syria under the Ba'ath Party from the 1960s to the 1980s

burqa: a colorful garment worn by some Muslim women that covers most of the body and face but with eyeholes or a grid around the eyes

clash of civilizations: the belief that global conflict after the Cold War will result from cultural and civilizational differences, including religious ones, and not economic or ideological differences; the phrase is often invoked to reflect the belief that Islam and the West are bound to be in conflict because of irreconcilable cultural and religious values

colonialism: the conquest, occupation, and control of another country or land

Crusades: military campaigns sponsored by European rulers and church leaders to conquer or retake territory from Muslims in the Holy Land (Israel and Palestine) during the Middle Ages

cultural racism: hatred and hostility of others based on religious beliefs, cultural traditions, and ethnicity

decolonization: the process by which formerly colonized nations and peoples become independent from the colonial power

dhimmi: protected minorities, particularly Jews and Christians, under Islamic law

discourse: a system of meaning that fashions how we perceive, think about, and act in the world

Enlightenment: a cultural and intellectual movement of the seventeenth and eighteenth centuries in the West that emphasized reason

essentialism: the belief that a people, culture, or religious tradition possesses an unchanging set of characteristics or some inherent essence

fatwa: an unbinding legal opinion issued by a religious scholar (mufti)

fitna: trial or temptation

hadith: a collection of reports or accounts of Muhammad's words and deeds

halal: that which is permitted under Islamic law

haram: that which is forbidden under Islamic law

hijab: a headscarf worn by some Muslim women that covers the head but leaves the face exposed; more broadly, the term refers to modest dress and behavior for both Muslim women and men

hijra: the journey from Mecca to Medina by Muhammad and his followers in 622

iftar: the evening meal during the holy month of Ramadan that marks the end of the day's fasting

ijtihad: the use of independent reasoning and judgment in matters of Islamic law

imam: a prayer leader

Islamism: a movement that arose in the late twentieth century in an effort to create and implement a comprehensive social, economic, and political order rooted in Islam and in opposition to Western secularism

Islamophobia: hatred, hostility, and fear of Islam and Muslims, and the discriminatory and exclusionary practices that result

jahiliyah: the period of ignorance prior to Islam

jihad: literally "struggle," the term can refer either to outward action to defend Islam or to internal struggles against sinful inclinations

jizya: a special tax paid by dhimmis in return for protection by Muslim rulers

Ka'ba: a cubic structure in Mecca and one of Islam's most sacred sites; Muslims face toward the Ka'ba in daily prayers

masjid: the Arabic word for mosque

minaret: tower attached or located next to a mosque from which Muslims are called to prayer

mosque: a place of prayer and worship for Muslims

mufti: Muslim religious scholar who is qualified to issue a fatwa on matters of Islamic law

mujahideen: Islamist resistance fighters who battled the Soviets during the Soviet-Afghan War (1979–1989)

multiculturalism: the practice of acknowledging, accepting, and accommodating cultural and religious differences in the public sphere

native informants: Muslim and ex-Muslim "insiders" who draw on their personal knowledge and experience of Islam to promote the belief that Islam is at odds with Western values and to reassure Western audiences that their fear of Islam is justified

neocolonialism: the practice of a dominant nation controlling or influencing another country by economic or cultural means as opposed to direct political governance

niqab: a black-and-white garment worn by some Muslim women that is similar to a burqa but covers the face below the eyes

Orientalism: term originally coined to describe the scholarly study of the Middle East, North Africa, and Asia; in postcolonial thought, the term refers to a discourse of power that enables Western empires to rule and have authority over the Orient

People of the Book: a reference in the Qur'an primarily to Jews and Christians, both of whom possessed revealed texts and worshipped the God of Abraham

postcolonialism: the study of the economic, political, social, and psychological effects of Western colonialism

Qur'an: Islam's most sacred and authoritative text, revealed to Muhammad by God via the angel Gabriel; the word literally means "recitation"

Ramadan: the ninth month in the Islamic calendar, during which Muslims fast from dawn to sunset

Reconquista: the conquering of Muslim states in the Iberian Peninsula by Christian forces in the Middle Ages

Reformation: a theological movement that began under Martin Luther in 1517 that resulted in a permanent break in Western Christianity between Roman Catholicism and Protestantism

Renaissance: a cultural movement in Europe dating from the fourteenth century that drew inspiration from ancient Greek and Latin sources in the areas of art, literature, religion, and politics

Saracen: a term commonly used in medieval Europe to refer to Muslims

Shah: the historic title for a king or ruler in Iran

Shahada: the Islamic declaration of faith in which believers proclaim, "There is no god but God, and Muhammad is His messenger"

Sharia: Islamic law based on the Qur'an and the Sunna that provides a blueprint for proper conduct in accordance with God's revelations

Sufism: mystical orientation within Islam

Sunna: the example established by Muhammad's words and deeds that is recorded in the hadith

Umma: the global community of Muslims

zakat: charitable giving according to Islamic law

Zionism: a Jewish nationalist movement with the goal of creating and maintaining a Jewish state in Palestine

Further Reading

Chapter 1: What Is Islamophobia?

Allen, Christopher. *Islamophobia*. Burlington, VT: Ashgate, 2010.

Commission on British Muslims and Islamophobia. *Islamophobia: A Challenge for Us All*. London: Runnymede Trust, 1997.

Ernst, Carl W., ed. *Islamophobia in America: The Anatomy of Intolerance*. New York: Palgrave Macmillan, 2013.

Esposito, John L., and Ibrahim Kalin, eds. *Islamophobia: The Challenge of Pluralism in the 21st Century*. New York: Oxford University Press, 2011.

Chapter 2: The Historical Foundations of Islamophobia

Rodinson, Maxime. *Europe and the Mystique of Islam*. Seattle: University of Washington Press, 1987.

Sonn, Tamara. *Islam: A Brief History*. 2nd ed. Malden, MA: Wiley-Blackwell, 2010.

Southern, R. W. *Western Views of Islam in the Middle Ages*. Cambridge, MA: Harvard University Press, 1962.

Tolan, John, Gilles Veinstein, and Henry Laurens. *Europe and the Islamic World: A History*. Princeton: Princeton University Press, 2013.

Tolan, John. *Saracens: Islam in the Medieval European Imagination*. New York: Columbia University Press, 2002.

Chapter 3: Colonialism, Orientalism, and the Clash of Civilizations

Lockman, Zachary. *Contending Visions of the Middle East: The History and Politics of Orientalism*. Cambridge: Cambridge University Press, 2004.

Loomba, Ania. *Colonialism/Postcolonialism*. New York: Routledge, 2005.

Quinn, Frederick. *The Sum of All Heresies: The Image of Islam in Western Thought*. Oxford: Oxford University Press, 2008.

Said, Edward W. *Orientalism*. New York: Vintage, 1978.

Chapter 4: 9/11, the War on Terror, and the Rise of Political Islamophobia

Abu-Lughod, Lila. *Do Muslim Women Need Saving?* Cambridge, MA: Harvard University Press, 2013.

Cole, Juan. *Engaging the Muslim World*. New York: Palgrave Macmillan, 2009.

Coll, Steve. *Ghost Wars: The Secret History of the CIA, Afghanistan, and Bin Laden, from the Soviet Invasion to September 10, 2001*. New York: Penguin, 2004.

Esposito, John L., and Dalia Mogahed. *Who Speaks for Islam? What a Billion Muslims Really Think*. New York: Gallup, 2007.

Kumar, Deepa. *Islamophobia and the Politics of Empire*. Chicago: Haymarket, 2012.

Sheehi, Stephen. *Islamophobia: The Ideological Campaign against Muslims*. Atlanta: Clarity, 2011.

Chapter 5: The "Islamic Threat" in Contemporary Europe

Cesari, Jocelyne. *Why the West Fears Islam: An Exploration of Muslims in Liberal Democracies*. New York: Palgrave Macmillan, 2013.

Eyerman, Ron. *The Assassination of Theo van Gogh: From Social Drama to Cultural Trauma*. Durham, NC: Duke University Press, 2008.

Hussain, Yasmin, and Paul Bagguley. "Securitized Citzens: Islamophobia, Racism and the 7/7 London Bombings." *Sociological Review* 60 (2012): 715–34.

Klausen, Jytte. *The Cartoons That Shook the World*. New Haven, CT: Yale University Press, 2009.

Weller, Paul. *A Mirror for Our Times: "The Rushdie Affair" and the Future of Multiculturalism*. London: Continuum, 2009.

Chapter 6: Professional Islamophobia

Green, Todd H. "Who Speaks for Europe's Muslims? The Radical Right Obstacle to Dialogue." *CrossCurrents* 62 (2012): 337–49.

Lean, Nathan. *The Islamophobia Industry: How the Right Manufactures Fear of Muslims*. London. Pluto, 2012.

Wajahat, Ali, Eli Clifton, Matthew Duss, Lee Fang, Scott Keyes, and Faiz Shakir. *Fear, Inc.: The Roots of the Islamophobia Network in America*. Washington, DC: Center for American Progress, 2011.

Chapter 7: Menacing Muslims in the Media and at the Movies

Alsultany, Evelyn. *Arabs and Muslims in the Media: Race and Representation after 9/11*. New York: New York University Press, 2012.

Poole, Elizabeth, and John E. Richardson, eds. *Muslims and the News Media*. New York: I. B. Tauris, 2006.

Powell, Kimberly A. "Framing Islam: An Analysis of U.S. Media Coverage of Terrorism since 9/11." *Communication Studies* 62 (2011): 90–112.

Shaheen, Jack G. *Reel Bad Arabs: How Hollywood Villifies a People.* Northampton, MA: Olive Branch, 2009.

Chapter 8: Islamophobia and Its Casualties

Cainkar, Louise. *Homeland Insecurity: The Arab American and Muslim Experience after 9/11.* New York: Russell Sage Foundation, 2009.

Ferrari, Alessandro, and Sabrina Pastorelli, eds. *The Burqa Affair across Europe: Between Public and Private Space.* Burlington, VT: Ashgate, 2013.

Green, Todd H. "The Resistance to Minarets in Europe." *Journal of Church and State* 52 (2010): 619–43.

Kundnani, Arun. *The Muslims Are Coming! Islamophobia, Extremism, and the Domestic War on Terror.* London: Verso, 2014.

Peek, Lori A. *Behind the Backlash: Muslim Americans after 9/11.* Philadelphia: Temple University Press, 2010.

Scott, Joan Wallach. *The Politics of the Veil.* Princeton: Princeton University Press, 2007.

Index